FABRIC

OF

DREAMS

FABRIC OF DREAMS

DESIGNING MY OWN SUCCESS

ANTHONY MARK HANKINS
WITH DEBBIE MARKLEY

A DUTTON BOOK

DUTTON
Published by the Penguin Group
Penguin Putnam Inc., 375 Hudson Street,
New York, New York 10014, U.S.A.
Penguin Books Ltd, 27 Wrights Lane,
London W8 5TZ, England
Penguin Books Australia Ltd, Ringwood,
Victoria, Australia
Penguin Books Canada Ltd, 10 Alcorn Avenue,
Toronto, Ontario, Canada M4V 3B2
Penguin Books (N.Z.) Ltd, 182–190 Wairau Road,
Auckland 10, New Zealand

Penguin Books Ltd, Registered Offices:
Harmondsworth, Middlesex, England

First published by Dutton, an imprint of Dutton NAL,
a member of Penguin Putnam Inc.

First Printing, March, 1998
10 9 8 7 6 5 4 3 2 1

REGISTERED TRADEMARK—MARCA REGISTRADA

LIBRARY OF CONGRESS CATALOGING-IN-PUBLICATION DATA:

Hankins, Anthony Mark.
   Fabric of dreams : designing my own success / Anthony Mark
Hankins with Debbie Markley.
     p. cm.
   "A Dutton book."
   ISBN 0-525-94329-3 (alk. paper)
   1. Hankins, Anthony Mark. 2. Afro-American fashion designers—
Biography. 3. Costume design—United States. I. Markley, Debbie.
II. Title.
TT505.H265A3   1998
746.9'2'092—dc21
   [B]   97-37293
                                           CIP

Printed in the United States of America
Set in Meridien
Designed by Leonard Telesca

This book is printed on acid-free paper. ⊗

I dedicate this book to my mother, Mary, for all her love and support, and for always believing in my dreams. My mom has always given me the opportunity to be myself and to express my many art forms. For this, I am eternally grateful. I love you, Mom.

I can't believe we've finished this book! Lord knows it took a lot out of me to revisit all the struggles of my life. Debbie Markley, thank you for putting up with my many moods, girlfriend. You know there were days when I just could have passed out from sheer exhaustion. You're the best, so please never change. You made this journey worth the trip. I will always love you for your honesty and for sprinkling stardust on my words.

I also want to express my heartfelt thanks to my family, friends, colleagues, and mentors. Without your help, my dreams might not have become a reality. Success is always a collective effort, and you are all an integral part of that team.

For their unyielding support with this book project, my gratitude goes out to Bruce Ackerman, who has always supported my vision; my literary agent, Sam Hughes, for her expert guidance, along with her wonderful staff at the Dickens Group Literary Agency; and my editor at Dutton Signet, Audrey LaFehr, who has worked tirelessly to help me spread the word that our goals are never out of reach.

Contents

Introduction

Bruce Ackerman
President and CEO
Anthony Mark Hankins, Inc.

On April 21, 1997, *Newsweek* magazine listed Anthony Mark Hankins among the top "100 people to watch as America prepares to pass through the gate to the next millennium"—a heady distinction for a young twenty-eight-year-old fashion designer. In January, Anthony was honored as the Young Star recipient at the 1997 Trumpet Awards ceremony, which recognizes outstanding African-Americans. The Young Star award had been presented the previous year to golf sensation Tiger Woods.

Like Tiger Woods, Anthony Mark Hankins is a phenomenon. At twenty-three, Anthony became JCPenney's first in-house designer, and just two short years later he created his own company, which has been wildly successful, providing more than twelve hundred retailers from Target to Nordstrom with over $40 million in merchandise sales.

In 1992, when I first met Anthony Mark Hankins, I was manager of minority supplier development at JCPenney's corporate headquarters in Dallas. Anthony had flown in from California for a meeting with me and arrived in a chartreuse jacket, accented by an ascot, which screamed fashion and set him apart from all of us corporate "suits." This handsome young man shook my hand and greeted me with a strong, friendly voice and a great smile. Something about him told me even then that I was meeting a truly remarkable person.

During the presentation of his portfolio, which included his design concepts for the urban contemporary woman, Anthony struck me as wonderfully prepared and knowledgeable. I realized that this kid really knew what he was talking about and that his line was something that JCPenney really needed. The buyers are going to be impressed, I thought.

I had set aside the entire week for us to meet with more than twenty buyers, merchandise managers, and divisional vice presidents. After our first few meetings, I could see the buyers' enthusiasm building. You didn't have to be a genius to appreciate the talent that Anthony expressed through his designs and the knowledge that he had about fashion, color, and style. The marketing expertise he demonstrated was also impressive. The word about Anthony spread so fast that our buyers were soon buzzing with excitement. Less than eight weeks later, Anthony was hired as JCPenney's first and only in-house designer.

Unfortunately, not everyone at JCPenney embraced the design and fashion concepts of this talented young man. It was a rude awakening for Anthony to realize that certain executives had their own personal agendas and were determined to protect their turf. They simply could not believe that this young black man could have legitimately

achieved so much at his age. I was so thoroughly convinced of Anthony's talents and the need for his fashions
at JCPenney that I continued to mentor him, guiding
him through some of the tough political obstacles I saw
developing.

Anthony's true potential at JCPenney was still constantly thwarted by the powers that be, who told him to
"be patient. You have to walk before you can run." That
may be true for most, but Anthony is that exceptional person who always hits the ground running. After two years,
Anthony and I could see that the time had come for him to
leave JCPenney and form his own company. Anthony
asked me to join him in this new venture, and I didn't hesitate to say yes.

After thirty-seven years with JCPenney, I left the traditional corporate structure to become president and CEO of
Anthony's new company. For me, leaving JCPenney to
start a business with this dynamic young man, whose huge
future was still ahead of him, has been one of the most
exciting experiences I've ever had.

Since Anthony's design studio opened its doors in 1994,
the company has been on an exhilarating rocket ride, soaring to new heights of growth every day. There have been
over four hundred articles written about Anthony, and he
has become something of a celebrity, often appearing on
national and local television talk shows. He is also a well-
known personality who does monthly segments on the Home
Shopping Network, which has more than 40 million viewers.

I have always felt that Anthony's success, with every
step he takes forward, has enabled many other young people to take those same steps. Young people and minorities
are so often held back because they haven't "paid their
dues" according to corporate codes. There are some com-

panies, however, that don't adhere to these short-sighted principles, and they have willingly given Anthony, as well as others, a chance to prove themselves. These companies are the ones that are selling over $40 million worth of Anthony Mark Hankins fashions today and benefiting from his extraordinary talents.

One obstacle that Anthony still runs up against is that certain merchants want to pigeonhole him as strictly an African-American designer for African-American women. Yes, African-American women are great supporters of Anthony and his fashions, but I believe it is because they see in him someone they know—their son, nephew, or brother—and they want him to achieve the success to which everyone should be entitled in this country.

America is a melting pot of cultures, but it's important that we don't all end up looking and thinking alike. As Anthony often says, the world is more like a tossed salad, where all the ingredients are separate but just as important to the mix. Anthony Mark Hankins, you're the dressing on our salad, and who wants to eat just plain salad?

Anthony's meteoric rise in the fashion industry is an inspiration to everyone who dreams of breaking away from confining corporate structures to find his own path. Anyone who has felt like a maverick in his field will appreciate Anthony's struggles to climb his way to success.

Anthony blazed his own trail—a journey requiring courage and a strong heart. He has never forgotten the help his mentors provided, however, and is repaying that debt with his frequent visits to students, encouraging them to follow their own passions and never let obstacles stand in their way. Anthony refused to let anything block his path to success, and that is why his story is such an inspiration to us all.

Foreword

by the Honorable Ron Kirk, Mayor of the City of Dallas

Occasionally someone enters your life and leaves a mark so you may never forget them. Or they may open your eyes to new ideas and touch your heart. Sometimes they do both. Anthony Mark Hankins is such a person. He dared to dream big dreams and followed them. He set out to conquer the world, or more appropriately, clothe the world. This has been his mission in life since he was "knee-high to a sewing machine," one I have no doubt he will accomplish.

Anthony has appeared on local and national television and radio shows and has been the subject of more than four hundred articles. He has become a star of the fashion industry. Most of you are probably aware of his incredible success and sensational talent, but not of his tremendous character. Upon meeting Anthony, I quickly realized he is more than an outstanding designer. He is compassionate, personable, innovative, and visionary. He blazed his own trail to success.

Fabric of Dreams: Designing My Own Success illustrates the principle that when you control your own destiny, anything in life is possible. When you focus your mind on a goal and commit yourself completely, you have the power to make your dreams come true. As a young man, Anthony worked with what was available, which in the beginning meant accessorizing his sister's dolls. His first designs were sketched with crayons. His mother taught him to press the pattern and prepare the fabric as well as sew. He used the library to do research and checked out books on famous designers.

After becoming, I'm told, the second American and the first African-American to attend the École de la Chambre Syndicale de la Couture Parisienne, and later interning and working for his idol, Yves Saint Laurent, and other top designers, Anthony returned to America to share his magic. He showed us that talent and determination can triumph and that through love and faith all things can be accomplished.

Anthony was blessed to have a mother who was devoted to her children and knew the value of education. He made the most of the opportunities that came his way and took advantage of those he was able to create. His book is an inspiration for all. I anticipate even greater success for Anthony and look forward to reading the next installment of his life.

And, remember, follow your dream.

1

A Passion for Fashion

As a design intern for Yves Saint Laurent in Paris, I learned to craft buttonholes and stitch hems by hand on garments that sold for as much as $20,000. But, I thought, how many people can afford to buy a dress for $20,000? And how many people would see it? I wanted *everyone* to be able to wear and enjoy my creations, so I left behind the elite world of haute couture to develop my own line of affordable clothing. My goal was to dress all the women in America. It's been my mission in life since I was knee-high to a sewing machine.

I actually began training for my career as a fashion designer right after I was born. Even as a toddler, girlfriend, I was fascinated by color and anything shiny. I was already interested in fashion at the age of five, when my twin sister, Angie, gave me a book on it that she had found at a children's book fair. It was a Colorforms book that included cutout dolls with stick-on plastic clothes. I loved that book and put those dolls through so many fashion changes that finally the plastic clothes had to be taped on.

As a budding young designer, I had to work with what was available. I'd take Angie's dolls and fit them with a new "knit" dress made out of socks I'd cut up. My childhood fashions were accessorized with anything I could get my hands on—ribbons, buttons, bows. . . . The doll's new outfit didn't have to be simply a "day" ensemble. Oh, no, child. I could turn my creation into evening wear just by adding understated designs of glitter and sequins. I was flashy even then.

One time, though, when Angie discovered that her favorite doll, Wendy, had been molested with old socks, glue, and multicolored sequins, she went berserk. Before I could stop her, Angie ripped my creation off her doll—and I cried big buckets of salty tears. Girlfriend, I was a sensitive artiste and I couldn't tolerate anyone tampering with my designs. I started collecting my own dolls after that. I didn't want to have to deal with temperamental clients who didn't appreciate my passion for fashion.

I endlessly sketched fashions onto my childishly drawn stick figures of women. My Crayolas never stopped moving on my poster boards, and I constantly wore them down to nubs. Some of my neighborhood friends, though, just didn't understand my interests. My older sister Katie would hide my stuff when other kids were around so I wouldn't get teased, but even she didn't understand why I always wanted to draw and design women's clothes. Boys don't do that, Katie thought, so she tried to steer me toward other interests. I always went right back to fashion, though.

My four older brothers, especially, worried for a time about my masculinity. Was Anthony soft? Did he have a little sugar in him? My brothers teased me about my seeming lack of machismo, but, of course, they didn't give that right to anyone else. They didn't like it when other kids criticized my work. That was their job. My brothers were all trying to dominate one another, doing the macho bit, each trying to be the man of the house. And here *I* was, putting clothes on dolls—not the safest occupation for a young inner-city kid.

Being poor, you have to fight hard for what you have, and my brothers wanted me to be able to stand up for myself. They wanted to toughen me up and make a man out of me. When I was little, my older brothers would be outside playing and roughhousing while I would be inside the house crocheting and looking for material to create my latest dress design. No wonder they were worried about me.

I ignored them, though, and after a while my brothers began to understand that this was just something I had a talent for. James was my main tormentor, but even he couldn't belittle me too much because *I* knew his own unmanly weakness—comic books. James later admitted I had a viable skill when a friend of his admired my sketches one day and seriously asked me if I could make him a leather jacket. That was the first time James thought my strange preoccupation with sewing might actually pay off. I could be a tailor, he reasoned, which was a respectable male profession. Maybe there was hope for me yet.

Mom, too, couldn't figure out why a boy would be so fascinated by sewing—much less why I spent so much time making clothes for dolls and lusting after fabrics. She realized, though, that there was a bigger picture in life for everyone, including me. Mom had enough faith to allow me to be different, and she encouraged everyone else in the family to give me my space.

My career as a fashion designer was officially launched in 1976, when, at the tender age of seven, I made my mother a dress suit to wear to an important family wedding. It was a simple, buttercup-yellow satin suit with dime-store lace. When my busy little hands got through with it, the dress was a ghastly vision of crooked seams and uneven hems. My mother, however, actually wore it to the wedding, in spite of all its imperfections, proudly telling everyone there that I had made it.

"Little Anthony made that suit?" they asked incredulously.

The dress still hangs in one of our family closets, and looking at the childish workmanship on that suit today, I can see that it took a lot of courage for my mother to wear it to such an important social event. Her faith and support inspired me to continue with my childhood dreams of becoming a designer.

I had learned how to work a sewing machine a few months before from watching my sister Katie, who hated sewing, as she struggled in her attic bedroom to make Raggedy Ann and Andy aprons for her home ec class. She and the sewing machine were not getting along too well, so I started pestering her to let me try it. I was always nosy and into everyone's business. Katie taught me the basics on her sewing machine and I couldn't get enough of it. It fascinated me and I wanted to learn everything about sewing.

I bugged Katie to let me sew so often that she persuaded Mom to buy me some materials so I could make something on my own. I told Mom I wanted to make her a special dress to wear, so she took me to a fabric shop to buy the pattern and fabric. I think Mom was skeptical about a seven-year-old boy's ability to do this, but she probably went along with it just to humor me.

In the fabric shop, we picked out a simple Butterick See & Sew pattern and I searched the store with my neophyte-designer's eye to find just the right fabric that would make my first creation come alive! I was all over that store, girl-friend, pulling yards of fabric from the bolts and draping them over everything and everybody. I finally settled on a shiny charmeuse that Mom knew would be difficult to work with, but that's what I wanted.

Mom showed me how to press the pattern and cut it out, then how to prepare the fabric and lay it with the pattern. She sat with me at the machine to make sure I didn't sew my little fingers together. Even though I could hardly reach the pedals, I had that machine jammin', honey, whipping out crooked seam after crooked seam. When I had managed to piece the dress together, Mom taught me how to hem the skirt.

Although I made a lot of mistakes, it all still came together in the end. I held the dress up for Mom, and to me it looked like a dress fit for a queen—and my mother had the regal bearing to wear such a creation. Mom has always been a beautiful, elegant lady; back then, she was slender with long hair that she pinned up. To me, the dress looked spectacular on her.

I was triumphantly proud, just on top of the world, when Mom modeled it for everyone at home. I had met my first deadline—an Anthony Mark Hankins dress ready in time for its scheduled outing. Once I had made that first dress for my mom, there was no stopping me. Mom and Katie, impressed with this feat, continued to encourage me. By the time I was eight, I formally announced to my mother that I wanted to be a fashion designer when I grew up.

Mom's follow-through was incredible if she knew you really, really wanted something. She'd make sure you got it somehow. Meeting the bills for a large family must have been staggering enough, but Mom still managed to buy me my own sewing machine when I was eight. It was a used Singer that she had bought from the "Sewing Doctor"—a local guy who repaired sewing machines after years of working at a Singer plant. This old sewing machine didn't have backstitching, so you had to knot off each stitch, but I was thrilled.

I started sewing Albert Nipon patterns, which were available in the Butterick pattern book. My mom claims that I always had scissors in my hands and a project going on. I put the pedal to the metal on that machine and had it humming for hours at a time, making clothes, pillows, pot holders, Spiderman latch-rug sets, anything. I'm sure Mom has a "God Bless This House" picture somewhere which I made with one of my many needlepoint kits.

I picked up sewing techniques from friends and family. I used to tag along with my oldest brother Jeffrey to his friend Wade Fletcher's house. Wade's mother, Kim, was a magnificent seamstress, and I'd watch her sew with a mesmerized gaze. When it was time to go home, Jeffrey would often find me glued to Mrs. Fletcher's sewing machine, studying her every technique.

I also learned needlepoint and crochet, as well as other crafts, from various kits. My brothers were surprised that I could just open these kits up and start making things. They wondered how I knew what to do without someone teaching me, and I didn't know how to answer that. Any type of sewing craft just seemed to come very naturally to me.

As children, Angie and I hung out together all the time, even though our interests and personalities have always been quite different. We're typical of many twins, in that one is usually more outgoing than the other. I started out as a quiet kid, but as the years went by, I became pretty loud and boisterous. Angie, on the other hand, has always been the calm one.

When we were little, I knew how to push her buttons, though. I could get her revved up by remote control. As toddlers, I would tease Angie until she became mad enough to attack me in her baby stroller. "Sister," as Angie's known in the family, would throw down that baby rattler and come after me! Man, she was dangerous in that stroller.

As we got older, Angie was good in ballet but she also loved sports and anything mechanical. On the other hand, I loved anything that was handwork, like sewing or drawing. I remember that at one of the neighborhood kids' birthday parties, I had a great time helping the girls dress their dolls. Our neighbors the Petersons told my mother years later that they had noticed at this party how I was perfectly content to be dressing dolls. A strange interest for a boy, they thought.

"Oh, well," Mr. Peterson had sighed, "maybe he'll be a fashion designer someday." Twenty years later, once I had established my own design company, the Petersons remembered this conversation and related it to my mother.

But at the time, Angie was a tomboy who loved to climb trees and play baseball and basketball, while all I wanted to do was sew and make dresses. Mom couldn't help wondering what was wrong with this picture. She became quite concerned about our role reversals and consulted with Dr. Choi, one of our family doctors, about what to do. Luckily, he gave her good advice, which was to leave us alone to pursue our individual interests.

"Give Angie a baseball mitt and Anthony a sewing machine," he wisely suggested.

2

From Rector Street to Third Avenue

Except for the fact that my Grandmother Toy was a wonderful seamstress, no other fashion designers grew from the branches of our family tree. I was a complete anomaly within my family and the blue-collar neighborhood where my life began. Angie and I were born in St. Elizabeth's Hospital in Elizabeth, New Jersey, on November 10, 1968, just three blocks from where my mother, Mary, and father, Ramone Moya, lived on Rector Street in a two-story brick duplex house.

Rector Street was a short block with only about ten houses on it. It was a Tin Pan Alley kind of place with run-down country-looking cottages and people hanging wash on the line. There were warehouse loading docks right down the street. Just twenty miles from New York City, it was like a small Southern neighborhood with a rough

Brooklyn edge to it. There was an old factory close by called the Brewery, which had been converted from its original purpose into offices.

Angie and I were the youngest of seven children and we kept the house buzzing, girlfriend. Jeffrey, Katie, James, and Kevin were our half-siblings from my mom's first marriage. Raymond, my parents' first child together, was three years older than Angie and I. Before our birth, James remembered that the doctors were concerned that my mother might not make it during the delivery of the twins. Not only was there a medical concern about the birth, but there was a lot of friction between my parents over Angie's and my impending arrival. Having twins seemed to send my father over the edge, and his relationship with my mother became strained and volatile.

As a toddler, I wasn't aware of the anger that passed between my parents over our birth. I only saw my father, who worked as a security guard, as a charming man—an almost mythical figure to me. Out of his security-guard uniform, he seemed to me a very dapper person who smoked cigars and spoke English with a thick Cuban accent. In my eyes, he was tall, well-dressed, and handsome. I adored him.

Ramone Moya had fled Cuba during the revolution, when Castro came to power. He was an active part of the Cuban community in Elizabeth. We'd often visit my godfather, a Cuban named Hugo Acolea, who owned a pizza parlor on First Street, a barbershop, and several other buildings in town. My father and Hugo loved to play cards and smoke cigars together with other Cuban exiles.

To my mother, however, my father was a possessively jealous man who supported his children only occasionally. He was often in and out of our lives. When he and my mother separated, soon after Angie and I were born, he would come by on the weekends to pick up Raymond and spend time with him. Raymond told me later that my father would ask him every detail about what my mother had been doing while he'd been away. Even after my parents separated, he was jealous of her every move.

My father's sudden reappearances in our lives, however, kept my mother on an emotional roller-coaster. As a young child, I was blissfully unaware of these problems and only wished I could be with my father more. I missed him when he wasn't there.

Despite my father's volatile temperament, Mom took him back repeatedly. She had seven children to care for, and he did help out financially when he was around. I didn't blame him for always coming back to my mother. She's a wonderful woman—so how could he stay away?

As Jeffrey says even today, "Anthony's father loved beauty or he wouldn't have loved our mother."

My father's returns, however, never lasted for long, and Mom supplemented her job at a dry cleaner's with a night job cleaning bank offices. When Angie and I were babies, she managed to work mainly at night, so she could be there for us during the day. Our older brothers and sisters, mainly Katie and Jeffrey, looked after us when Mom was at work. Mom, determined not to be on welfare, worked hard to hold everything together. She was the glue that held our rambunctious family together.

Money was tight, but growing up, we didn't know it. Our house may have been full of used furniture, but it was always clean and comfortable. I remember a bright, airy house where the windows were always open, allowing the breeze to blow in. I spent most of my time in the kitchen— where my mother was most often when she was home. We always had an excuse to eat heartily at mealtime because Mom frequently reminded us to appreciate what we had. People over in Africa were starving, she said, and we weren't to forget that. I took that message to heart and made sure that not one crumb of food in our household was ever wasted.

A few years after Angie and I were born, the relative peace we experienced living on Rector Street was shattered when the street was designated as the future site of the new Elizabeth High School. All ten houses on Rector Street were to be taken by eminent domain. While most of our neighbors eventually gave up the ghost and moved to the projects, which were as dangerous then as they are now, my mother flatly refused to move her family there. No child of hers was going to be hanging around gang-bangers in the projects.

Although the odds of finding a new landlord who would accept seven children were stacked against her, Mom wouldn't give up. Through an acquaintance, she found out that a couple named the Glenns were looking for tenants for the other half of their large duplex house on Third Avenue in Roselle, a neighboring town. Mom met with the Glenns about renting the duplex, and miraculously, given the fact that Mom had so many active children, they agreed. That place to me, child, was like a castle—I felt wonderful in this huge five-bedroom house with its large yard.

In addition to the strong, positive influence of our mother, the Glenns turned out to be powerful role models for us kids. Mrs. Glenn was a black Martha Stewart who took great pride in her house and gardens. She didn't allow us kids to sit on her steps or play on her lawn. She didn't tolerate any noise from us, either. She especially put the fear of God into the older kids, lest they even think of getting into mischief or messing with her property.

Mrs. Glenn was picky, but that just helped to keep us all in line. I didn't mind her rules. After all, it was her house. She was a very religious person—and brave to rent to a family with seven very headstrong kids. The Glenns didn't have any children of their own, though, and I think that's why they enjoyed doting on Angie and me when we were little. They always had treats and little gifts for us.

In my five-year-old eyes, Mrs. Glenn was a beautiful grande dame; Mr. Glenn, one of the nicest men in the world, seemed like a lord of his manor. I always thought he dressed so neatly. He would arrive home from work each day in his big car, open the manual gate to his drive, then navigate that motored chariot up the long driveway to his castle. He had a compass in his car and we thought that was the coolest thing. We were always begging him, "Can we see it?" After he had shown us the mechanical wonders of his car, he'd walk proudly down the path from the garage to the house.

In our basement, there were connecting doors between our place and theirs. Angie and I would go down there, rap on the door, and yell, "Mrs. Glenn, are you in there?" Sometimes she'd happen to be in her basement doing her laundry and we'd be stunned to hear her actually answer us back. We'd scream and giggle as if we'd just heard a disembodied voice. I'm sure she finished her basement chores with an amused smile on her face, knowing she had startled the daylights out of us.

I was mesmerized by the items in the Glenns' house, which I associated with wealth at that tender age. When we knew they were home, Angie and I would race over and ring their doorbell, anticipating an invitation into Mrs. Glenn's kitchen, which always smelled of baking pies, cinnamon, and other heavenly aromas. Their doorbell, with its deep, melodic bong, sounded just like what Cinderella might have heard at the Prince's.

Mrs. Glenn would always invite us in for candy and refreshments. I loved her kitchen, girlfriend. She had brightly polished copper pots that hung from the ceiling, and she'd offer us our pick out of the large candy jar that was always filled with fabulous treats. And I loved to drink water out of her copper cups—the water would be so cold out of those cups! Her ice cubes even came out of "silver" metal trays! Not the plastic stuff like we had.

Her dining room and living room were wonderful, too, full of antique furniture and artwork, lace tablecloths, and fresh flowers. I loved looking at her exquisite china, elegantly displayed in her very own china cabinet. Even the house itself seemed opulent to me, with its molding and other detailing, including wallpaper instead of the cheap paneling I was accustomed to. I thought wallpaper was the classiest thing.

Moving to Third Avenue seemed like a cloud had lifted from our family. Life there was like a storybook—it was a magical part of my life. I always thought we'd live in this house forever. The neighborhood was racially mixed; white and black families respected one another and seemed to get along well. Most of the people on Third Avenue, many of them successful entrepreneurs, were homeowners who took pride in their houses. These people worked hard and had high standards and values. It was, and is, a beautiful tree-lined street with manicured lawns and large, neatly kept homes.

Our neighborhood was phenomenal—very loving and supportive. All the adults looked out for each other's children. We had lots of friends on this street, and everybody knew one another. When we'd walk home from school, one of the neighborhood ladies would often remind us, "Cross at the green, not in between."

For us kids, at least, the time we lived there seemed very carefree. Every day, there was a bicycle brigade of kids led by our friend Ramelle Massey, who was about five years older than Angie and I. She lived two houses down from us, and we had a great time playing with her. Her mother taught business education at that time, and Ramelle actually had a blackboard in her basement. We'd play "classroom" down in the basement, and I was always drawing and writing on that blackboard.

Angie and I did everything together, and I was very protective of her. Since Angie was a quiet person, I was usually the one to say, "Hey, this is what we're going to do. . . ." Child, I was a bundle of energy. "Let's get something going!" was my battle cry. Whatever our legion of kids decided to do, however, I always wanted to put a new slant on how we did it. I wanted to be innovative. Cutting-edge. If there was a traditional way of doing something, I wanted to try doing it another way.

Even then, I looked at our ragged childhood fashions with a critical eye. I already had definite opinions on what a woman should wear, what would accentuate the positive aspects of her figure, and what her clothes should be accessorized with. I was also a neat freak who wasn't caught too often playing in mud puddles. That wasn't my style, no way.

For a long time, on Third Avenue, Angie and Raymond and I shared a room. Angie and I had bunk beds. Down the hall, James and Kevin were roommates, although they didn't treat their habitat equally. James, a neat freak like myself, delineated himself from Kevin, whom he considered to be a slob, by literally putting a line across the floor up to a windowsill to mark his half of the room. James always knew, too, when Angie or I had been fooling around in his room. He could tell instantly if anything had been moved or borrowed.

While Mom was at work, Katie was the head honcho of our house. She was an extension of our mother and took the role seriously. Let me rephrase that: Katie was like a drill sergeant at boot camp. She made sure we all stayed in line. She took us where we needed to go, prepared our school lunches, and helped us with our homework. Katie was a tough bird, and nobody challenged her unless they wanted to tango with her iron-willed wrath.

Even as little kids, Angie and I had our chores around the house. We had to do them before Katie would let us go out to play. We waxed and dusted, straightened up the house, picked up our toys, cleaned our room. Once, when Angie had had enough of Katie's bossing, she bravely declared, "Katie, when you get to be an old woman, I'm going to take your cane and beat you with it!" I made sure I was out of harm's way when Angie said that!

Once our chores were done, though, girlfriend, Angie and I had fun. Our house had hardwood floors and we would often see how far we could glide across the floor in our socks. Before our eight o'clock bedtime, we loved to watch *Donny and Marie, The Brady Bunch,* and *The Bionic Woman* on television. We would often pretend to be famous singers and celebrities, raiding our mom's and brothers' closets for wigs and costumes. Angie and I had that whole Broadway thing happening right in our own house.

We kids weren't supposed to play in the living room because we had our own playroom and TV room designated for that. When Katie wasn't looking, however, I liked to take my crafts into the living room so I could spread out and have some privacy. Nobody ever bothered me.

One day, while Katie was upstairs and Mom at work, I took my projects into the forbidden living room. Using large diaper pins to help me pin up some thick fabric, I was working on my knees when an errant pin somehow went straight through my kneecap! I yelled for Kevin, who came running into the living room and then stopped short, gasping at the ghastly sight of that pin sticking deep into my knee.

I don't remember feeling pain—only panic, since I wasn't supposed to be in that room in the first place.

"Don't tell Katie!" I hissed. "Don't tell her or I'll kill you!"

Kevin carefully pulled the pin out of my kneecap as, stupidly, I continued to beg him to keep quiet about it. But we had to tell Katie, of course, and she insisted on taking me to the doctor, even though I swore to her that it was healing already.

I was prone to other odd injuries as well. When I was seven, I was invited to Angelique Hayes' house for a pool party. Angie and Angelique and I were always playing together. I was having a great time at the party until I got my finger caught in a folding chair and it literally pinched the tip of my finger off. Without telling anyone at the party what had happened, I quietly wrapped my bleeding hand in a towel and went home to get Band-Aids. I mean, why cause a scene just because you've just cut off your finger?

I hurried into the house, babbling something about Band-Aids, when Angie took the towel off my hand to see how bad my scratch could possibly be. She took one look and screamed—there was blood everywhere. I wasn't crying; I guess I was in shock. Mom was immediately called home from work and she rushed me to the hospital. The doctor took a skin graft from a bicep in my arm to replace the tip of my finger. The graft didn't heal correctly, though, and the tip of my finger is still discolored from the botched graft.

In spite of all these freak accidents, I always had my nose into everything. Nothing scared me. Raymond and I loved to catch bees and yellow jackets in our backyard and we often got stung. Once, we somehow caught a small snoozing bat in our ultrascientific bee-catching trap—an empty peanut butter jar. Excited, we ran full throttle into the house to show everyone. Tragically, the bottle fell out of my hands as we ran helter-skelter up the stairs. The glass broke and our bat, rudely awakened, flew hastily away.

One time, however, Raymond got a little too close to the bees. On Grandmother Toy's farm, my brothers were chasing each other in the woods along the banks of a small creek when Raymond decided to jump over the stream, landing right in a beehive. He was stung all over and looked like an ad for calamine lotion when my grandmother got through doctoring him up. Raymond sure found out who was the "bee's knees" that time.

3
On Our Own

As a single parent, Mom always worked several jobs at once while still managing to govern her children with an iron hand. She tried to work mainly at night so she could be with us during the day. Starting out as a counter person at a Dunkin' Donuts, Mom worked hard and was managing one of them within two years.

She also still cleaned a bank's offices in the evenings, and we'd sometimes wait for her out in the car. Angie and I always asked her to bring us lollipops because they were offered free in the bank's lobby. We'd fall asleep in the car but would miraculously wake up snuggled in our beds at home with lollipops waiting for us on our nightstands. Somehow, we had been magically transported safely under our bedcovers, and we never could figure out how she managed to do that without us waking up.

Mom even managed to earn extra money by selling Tupperware and jewelry lines, hosting sales parties at people's homes. Later, she worked at a candy store right down the street from us. Mom never complained about all her working. She's always been like the Energizer bunny: she keeps going and going and going. . . . Nothing could stop her, girlfriend.

We kids helped out all we could, too. We were raised to be independent and responsible; Mom depended on us to keep our family machine oiled and turning. No matter how hard our situation was, she always told us that we needed to stick together and that we were stronger as a unit than as separate individuals.

Some of us worked at the Dunkin' Donuts with her after school, and the older boys boxed groceries and earned pocket money shoveling snow, mowing lawns, and whatever else they could find. Even Christmas caroling turned out to be a good gig, as our neighbors tipped us for serenading them.

Jeffrey had a paper route before school and worked the night shift at the local A&P grocery store after school. He was determined to take some of the financial burden off Mom. He didn't want her having to depend on a man from outside the family. If she married again, he wanted it to be on her terms.

Some of the older kids later had an afternoon suburban paper route a couple of times a week, and Mom would go with them on the route. She was really a hands-on mother, despite her crushing work schedule. Our brothers and sisters would give her the money they made from their part-time jobs.

When Angie and I were little, we did what we could to help, too. We sold lemonade and Kool-Aid in front of our house on Third Avenue. We even had a traditional red-and-white-checkered tablecloth. We started out asking ten cents for a little Dixie cup–size serving but had to reduce the price to five cents because the cups were so small. Angie and I would buy Mom gifts from the proceeds of our lemonade sales.

Ghosts from the past were never far behind us, though. Everything came to a head on Third Avenue one day when my father suddenly showed up and tried to waltz back into Mom's life. Jeffrey, then sixteen, had been shouldering most of the responsibility as the man of the house. My father tried to resume his flawed position as head of the family, neglecting to realize that Jeffrey had grown quite a few inches and was now standing quite tall and proud. Tired of my father's absences, Jeffrey finally told him to leave our house and never come around again.

My father challenged him, but ultimately, Jeffrey won the showdown. My father left for good after that, much to my mother's mixed emotions. My father's presence made for tense situations, and although she wasn't at ease with his fiery disposition, she did, after all, welcome whatever financial help he gave.

Even though he hadn't been around all that much, realizing my father might never be there again left a huge void in my life. I always wondered what he was doing and what he would think of my progress in life. I was keenly aware of my friends' relationships with their fathers, good and bad, and I couldn't help wishing my own dad was home with us occasionally—even though he didn't deserve to be part of our lives again.

Our mother made it all work without my father's help after that. With seven mouths to feed, she was often forced to accept food donations to make sure we had enough. Our Thanksgiving turkey was usually donated. Mom always made sure she had something special, though, to give us on our birthdays and at Christmas. She worked longer hours at Christmastime so that she could provide a few extras for us then. Whatever we really needed or wanted, she found a way to provide it. Mom was determined that our family was going to be happy and as strong as a brick house.

"She was the architect of that piece," Jeffrey has said of our mother's role in our strong family structure.

Every year before Christmas, Angie and I would be on a mission to try to find where all the presents were stashed. We had been good enough kids that we were pretty sure we'd receive more than lumps of coal in our stockings. Mom and Katie were so good at squirreling presents away, though, that we only found them once. We were thrilled, but after we rifled through all the boxes, ruining Santa's surprises, our guilt got the best of us and we never searched for them again.

Opening presents on Christmas morning, we didn't always get the most popular brand-name toy we wanted; we'd get a close facsimile of the hotly-sought-after-but-expensive models that were blasted into our young brains by Saturday morning commercials. We would also get socks, along with other practical things we needed. I regarded socks as raw material for doll clothing, so I was a little more thrilled to receive them than my brothers were.

Every year, Mom created fun homemade gifts like her eclectic goodie bags that were made of brown paper bags with ribbon woven around the top of them. They were filled with walnuts, pecans, chocolates, peppermint canes, grapes, and little "dollar" toys. We may not have had much, but she always made the day special.

"What really matters is that we're all together—healthy, happy, and loved," she'd say, and we knew it was the gospel truth. We did indeed have a lot to be thankful for, and our Christmases were filled with good food, gifts, and laughter.

As I got older and my sewing became more proficient, I would try to make Mom a new dress, hat, or scarf so she could go to church on Sunday in style. I even made wrapping the present a designer event, with fresh flowers included with the ribbons and bows. Mom's love shone as she opened my designer-wrapped gift, and she'd always proudly wear my new creation, no matter how zany or outlandish it may have been.

Mom ran a tight ship and instilled in us boundaries that were so strong our conscience would bother us if we crossed them. All her kids were home after school, doing homework. And I mean HOME, with a capital "H." Even though Mom was often working in the evenings, she would call every few hours and you'd better be accountable to her. Mom ruled with an iron fist, and Jeffrey will tell you she could hit like a man. Mom wasn't about to let her kids run wild. Uh-uh. My mama didn't play that game.

Needless to say, we all had the deepest respect for her. None of us kids would curse in front of Mom. You just don't talk fresh to your mother, you know? She didn't put up with no flip lip. If Mom didn't like what you were saying to her, you'd hear her say, "Be real or be still." When she gave you a curfew, your feet better be coming through that door before the bell sounded. Ten o'clock, to her, meant ten o'clock. If Mom was at work, Katie was responsible for carrying out her orders.

Kevin, though, once slipped out of the house one night to go to a party at a friend's house, having put pillows in his bed to disguise the fact that he wasn't in it. Mom, after realizing his deception, sniffed him out like a bloodhound and actually went to the party to collect him. As she came in one door of the house, however, he bolted out another and beat it back home to pretend he'd never left his bed. There was no fooling Mom, though, and Kevin was in a pack of trouble for that stunt.

I managed to get into my own share of childhood mischief. Once, when I was five, I was playing over at my friend Janal Clay's house. We turned on the gas stove in the kitchen to play with the fire by feeding it newspaper strips. I think we were stomping out the charred remains of the paper on the floor when we got caught. We got our butts whipped good that time.

If we messed up, Mom would say, "Go get the switch from Mrs. Matthews' tree." Unfortunately for us, Mrs. Matthews had a willow tree that produced thin, pliable branches that made switches just perfect for tanning kids' behinds. We'd have to go pick our switch off the tree, trim the leaves off it, and hand it to Mom, who would then use it to the best of her ability on our backsides. When we knew a whipping was imminent, we would hide under our beds and try to wear her out before she could get us out! That tactic hardly ever worked, I'm sorry to say.

In spite of her heavy work hours, Mom somehow always made time for us and made sure that we all had activities after school and in the summers which corresponded to each child's interests. She was a den mother for my older brother's scout troop and for Katie's 4-H meetings. She also brought doughnuts and juice for Raymond's baseball games and helped him get involved with Sea Scouts, a program that allowed young boys to learn sailing and naval activities off Martha's Vineyard for a week in the summer.

For several years, when Angie and I were little, we attended a day camp for several weeks each summer. It was a religious camp affiliated with a Head Start program for inner-city kids. Man, it was a kicking camp. I remember it was integrated, the counselors were all laid-back and cool, and no kid there had anything more than any other kid. We learned crafts galore like macramé, embroidery, and needlepoint. I also loved acting in skits, too. We re-created scenes from the Bible and sang, sang, sang all the time.

Angie was a good swimmer at the camp, but I had a slight phobia about getting into pools or lakes. No matter how many times the swimming instructors tried to turn me into a fish, I resisted. No one was going to put funky water wings on this boy—forget that. I watched the swimmers from the shore, thankful that I wasn't being dragged, gasping and sputtering, back to safety by the lifeguards.

I think my fear of water stemmed from two things, one of which included the church baptisms I had witnessed as a young boy. There was a huge tank of water in the basement of our church which was used for baptismals. For baptisms, adults would emerge into a viewing area in white robes; after a few prayerful words from the pastor, I would watch in horror as he would totally submerge the baptismal candidates. As a child, I was always terrified these people were going to drown and I had nightmares of their bodies being fished out of the tank.

This horrible vision, coupled with the fact that a young boy had actually drowned in a backyard pool in our neighborhood, instilled in me a fear of being in water that I didn't conquer until I was an adult. I never learned to swim until I was twenty-four.

4

Circle of Love

Even with all of us kids to worry about, Mom was always willing to help a friend in need. When a beautiful young woman who worked with Mom confided in my mother about how she suffered from her abusive husband and wanted to leave him, Mom offered to let her young friend, who I'll call Iva, move in with us for a while until she could afford her own place. We all loved Iva; she quickly became one of the family and stayed in one of the attic bedrooms. She helped Mom out as well and they became good friends.

Iva gave us a green-and-blue parakeet named Phoebe. We loved this parakeet and let her fly all over the house. We had her for several years, and when she died, we wrapped her respectfully in a scarf, held a funeral service for her, then placed her delicate little body in a plastic bag and buried her in Mrs. Glenn's flower bed.

Mrs. Glenn was not too happy that we had had the burial by her prized roses, so she dug the bird up and brought it back to my mother. Phoebe had to be officially buried a second time.

Mom's main support system was the church, and you could often hear her saying around the house, "Lord, keep us safe today." She always prayed out loud and sang hymns. We went every Sunday to the Grace Temple Baptist Church in Newark, which was originally a storefront church. People walking by would hear all the singing and wander in to see what was going on.

I loved communion—child, I thought that grape juice was fine wine. I also envied the preacher's job. For a while I thought about becoming a preacher, but I think I was most attracted to all the drama and fine costuming associated with the job.

When I was eight, the ladies of our church put on a wonderful show called "The History of Fashion" to raise money for choir robes. Each lady wore elaborate costumes representing different eras and famous people like Jackie O, Eleanor Roosevelt, Billie Holliday, Diana Ross, and everyone else you could think of. I can still remember Sister Samson, a hot-dressing diva in her own right, sashaying down that church aisle brilliantly portraying Marie Antoinette.

With the money these ladies raised from their "History of Fashion" show, the church was able to buy gorgeous robes for its choir members. My favorite part of church was when the choir members would march down the aisle in those regal robes. I would watch them from my seat with the junior choir. All of us youngsters aspired to be in the older kids' choir, which was called the Heavenly Voices

Ensemble. The older church members were either in the Morning Stars choir or in the Gospel choir.

The Morning Stars' robes were black and midnight blue with angel sleeves, while the Gospel choir robes were lavender with bishop sleeves. Every Sunday, these two choirs battled it out, child, to see who could throw their audience into the most ecstasy. The Morning Stars would sing powerful hymns like "I'm Just a Soldier in the Army." And the fast, spiritual gospel songs would just put me out!

I just remember so much love being in that church. At the end of every service, we would stand up and form a Circle of Love. Everyone would hold hands and sing "Til We Meet Again." The church was such a strong backbone in our lives. It provided us with a support system that we could really rely on. Without it, I don't know how we ever would have made it.

I also found incredible fashion inspiration every Sunday in church. I loved to see what all the women were wearing. Those ladies were DRESSED, and I noticed everything about their outfits. The reverend's wife represented the highest level of dress in the congregation. Her clothing was fierce! The women all wore gloves and hats with everything then. My mother would be right there with them, dressed to the nines.

Every Sunday, Mom would get all gussied up for church and I would help her accessorize her look. Since she sold jewelry lines on the side, she had drawers full of costume pieces. One outfit she wore was a white starched organza blouse with an exaggerated-cut lapel, big French cuffs, and huge gold seventies cuff links. On the top, she wore this red cinching vest with gold double-breasted buttons all the way down and a floor-length plaid bias skirt. She looked like a glorified Diahann Carroll from the movie *Claudine*.

Mom, finally free of her relationship with my father, began to date again when her good friend, Sarah Davis, introduced her to Leon, a deacon in our church and a member of the Morning Stars choir. Leon was tall and athletic; his nickname was Champ. He took a real interest in our whole family and was a very positive role model for us. Leon would fix my shirt and straighten my tie. After church, he'd take us all to lunch. He was a genuinely nice man. On Mom's birthday, he'd throw her a party. They dated for several years, and I think he was the main reason my father never came around during this period.

Mom's friend Sarah Davis played piano for our church and for other local choirs, black gospel groups, and soloists. She has even accompanied Whitney Houston and Melba Moore, who are both from our area. Sarah needed a piano to practice on so when Mom saw an ad about a piano for sale in nearby Scotch Plains, she called and asked the owner if the piano was still available. Told it was, Mom immediately drove over to Scotch Plains to take a look at it. The white woman who answered the door, however, took one look at the black woman standing there and quickly told my mother the piano had just been sold.

Although I'm sure my mother was angered, she thanked the woman politely and left. Mom has always carried herself with dignity, even in the face of overt racism. She was raised in the South and was used to dealing with prejudice. She always tried, however, never to stoop to that low behavior. Mom always insisted that we treat everybody with the same amount of respect. She's a very positive person anyway, and I don't remember her ever being negative about anyone. She taught us our social skills, as well as how to get along and accept people for who they are.

* * *

My mother was a survivor, though. When your ancestors have survived slavery, you know you're from strong stock. She's from a large family herself and is the oldest of twelve children. She grew up on my grandparents' farm in Chatham, Virginia, where life was simple but good. After Grandfather Joe passed away, Grandmother Toy ran the farm with the help of my aunts and uncles.

It was a celebration when we were all together on the farm, and we enjoyed so much country cooking that the stove in my grandmother's kitchen never got a chance to cool down. My grandmother was a great cook, just like my mom and my Aunt Louella. Aunt Louella could really throw down a feast of pork chops, German sausage, or honey-cured hams, with candied yams, mashed potatoes, collard greens, fried okra, and, of course, corn bread.

We ate our fair share of chitlins and sweet potato pie, too. Yes, we did, girlfriend. And with my sweet tooth, I still couldn't wait for dessert, which was often coconut iced cake, punch-bowl cake, yogurt pie, or pineapple upside-down cake. We'd fill ourselves until we were weighted down to the dining room chairs, then sit back for hours, trading family stories over coffee.

Visiting the farm in the summers was like stepping into Jules Verne's time machine and traveling back a century. The farm was rustic, with none of the modern conveniences like air-conditioning and indoor plumbing. Grandmother Toy's house was a traditional white frame farmhouse with a large porch that had a rocking chair and swing. Out back was a chicken coop and an outhouse—yes, an outhouse. Katie and Angie, especially, hated the outhouse and would always use buckets and chamber pots instead.

Years ago, my grandparents were sharecroppers in the tobacco fields in back of the house. When I was growing up, however, they mainly raised vegetables. Grandma Toy canned a lot of fruits and vegetables. They also had chickens and cows, although Katie didn't eat chickens for a long time after she saw our farm relatives kill one for the evening meal. The water, pumped from a well outside the house, tasted great. At night, we city kids had to sleep in the DARK—country folks don't use no night-lights.

My grandmother told me many stories about her life, but the one I particularly remember was when she was growing up in the thirties and forties and could not afford to shop in certain department stores. Ready-made clothes were just too expensive, she said. Worse still, she was not allowed to even browse, much less try anything on, in most stores because she was African-American.

She and her sisters always wanted to be fashionable, though, so they would create their own garments from remnant material and patterns constructed from newspapers. I remember thinking to myself how horrible it must have been not to be able to buy or shop freely where you wanted. In those days, too, no one was designing the right colors or the latest styles for women who were on a budget.

My grandmother's stories have stayed with me and become part of my essence, spurring me on to design and create fashions that are not only stylish but affordable for women of every economic means.

5

School Days

Mom was always on us to get an education and do our best. She would show up at our schools unannounced to check on our work and talk with our teachers and principals. She would also make time to go to the school for Parents' Night. Mom wanted to make sure all her kids got their education.

She always taught us that the secret of power is believing in yourself. Once you have your education, she told us, you can do whatever you want to do. You just have to set your goals and go for it. When we were feeling the effects of her struggling so hard to make ends meet and despairing over the long hours Mom always had to work, she would say, "If you don't want to turn out like me, get an education. Just because my parents were sharecroppers doesn't mean my children have to be."

Of course, there was no cutting school under Mom's eagle eye. Fortunately for me, I always really enjoyed my classes, but for any of us who had a thought about cutting, we knew it wouldn't play well with Mom. After she left for work in the morning, Mom would often circle back by the house to make sure we were all en route to school. After school, we were expected to go straight home to do home-work. Mom would call us several times a night and we'd better be where she expected us to be.

In the second grade, at Washington Elementary School, I really got into fashion. "The Emperor's New Clothes" was my favorite story. We had a recording of it in class, and I was always asking the teacher to play it again. Even in the second grade, I was noticing how well people dressed, especially my teachers. Mrs. O'Connor, who taught second grade, wore beautiful clothes, and I was particularly partial to her tight cardigan sweaters and platform shoes. I studied what people were wearing and it always gave me ideas for my sketches.

I studied everything I could on fashion and designers. At the Roselle Public Library, I'd read all about Christian Dior, Norman Norell, and Yves Saint Laurent, as well as books on illustration, costume design, and the history of cos-tumes and fashion. A lot of these books were reference materials that weren't supposed to leave the library. They were full of rich paper and beautiful illustrations. I thought it was such a shame that these fabulous books were just sit-ting on the shelf, gathering dust and wasting away, so I would sneak them out to study them and then return them later.

I read one book on Oleg Cassini, who designed mostly men's suits, but found it boring because I was more inter-ested in designing for women. Later, though, I discovered he *had* designed a line for women. I also didn't really care for Christian Dior's styles at the time. All that ugly A-line stuff. Later, I realized that A-lines are very figure-flattering and that's why they were so popular.

Yves Saint Laurent, however—now, there was a designer. I liked everything he did. I was very simpatico with the man's style. He quickly became my idol in the fashion world, and I read everything about him I could get my hands on. He led the pack in initiating women's fashions and had started the whole luxury ready-to-wear movement over thirty years ago when he opened the first Rive Gauche shop on the Rue de Tournon.

He plunged skirt lengths below the calf when miniskirts were all the rage. He brought the peasant look to haute couture, along with pop-art prints, vinyl raincoats, and visor caps. He also introduced fisherman's shirts, turtlenecks, and pea jackets to haute couture and popularized the safari suit, the long scarf, and hip boots. I loved his fashions. *Très magnifique!*

In school, I always tried to tie in a sewing project with my various class projects. For a world history report on Mexican culture, for instance, I made a sombrero, a serape, and a Mexican dress. I even brought maracas and had a whole presentation. The teacher loved it, and so did the kids.

I think teachers liked me because I really liked them and loved almost any subject. I was just a sponge for knowledge. I would sketch not only fashion but anything else we were studying in school. The teachers seemed to be intrigued as to what I would draw next, and they were very supportive.

I fantasized constantly about being a fashion or costume designer. My brother James would give me a lot of sketch pads, and I took them with me everywhere. I was so preoccupied with it, you'd have thought I already had a job somewhere in the fashion industry. Every Sunday, I'd buy the *New York Times* and study the fashion section.

I read that every designer has a signature *croquis* (pronounced krō•'kē, the French word for a small, rough sketch), which is the one-dimensional "model" they always use to illustrate their designs on. By fourth grade, with lots of practice, I developed my own signature black croquis, who had lots of attitude. I called her "Vera." I would sketch Vera in every style imaginable.

I would also create my own miniature models out of plastic or paper bags and stuff them with hosiery, packaging materials, cellophane, or anything else I could find. Then I'd make whimsical outfits for my crudely made models. Fresh flowers would be made into skirts, and I'd make my own buttons out of plaster of paris, bubble gum, clay, and even wax. Fascinated by colors and textures, I'd pick flowers and leaves from trees and bushes on the way to school so I could study their textures which ranged from a scratchy burlap to a fine velvet.

With my love of costumes, Halloween has always been my favorite event of the year. In my family, we knew a money tree didn't grow in our backyard, so we made our own costumes from scratch. It was a fun family tradition, and we made unique costumes out of the materials at hand. For that one special evening, just using our own imaginations, we'd suddenly turn into aluminum-foil robots, papier-mâché ants, cardboard garbage cans, raggedy hobos, Hollywood divas, and even Amazon natives with skimpy tunics made of leather and twigs.

We even made our own Halloween bags for candy. An old pillowcase served as a sturdy sack that could carry lots of Halloween booty. We went trick-or-treating all over the neighborhood. It was safe and fun to do that back then. We knew everybody in the neighborhood and they knew us—even though we were always surprised that our costumes didn't give us anonymity on Mischief Night.

Angie and I would also put on little fashion shows at home. We'd set up chairs for the audience, which sometimes included only Katie, and I'd dress Angie up for her trip down the fashion runway. Later, we'd present a puppet show with our sock puppets. Mom's clothes were sometimes redesigned for our fashion shows, and she threw a fit one day when she discovered I had added bows and glitter to her good black skirt. I made up for it, though. I'd help Mom choose her outfits and accessorize them.

Back then, my mother gave you style, even though we lived in the inner city. She gave you diva glam. Glamorama, child! It was like Motown happening every day at our house. She's very conservative now, preferring a print mode and classic navy suits, but in her younger days, she was notorious for turning heads.

Mom could give you any kind of look. She let you have it. When Marlo Thomas was doing *That Girl*, so was my mom. I remember she also went through a leather phase, along with a *Shaft*-inspired period with black bell-bottoms and tight tops. She had a *Partridge Family* outfit, too. For a while in the seventies, she even had that muumuu thing going on, with African dashikis. And polyester out the door. She was friends with Poly and Ester, let me tell you. They were best friends. Looking back, of course, polyester was the hottest new thing.

What my mom had, though, she made it work. We used to call her "the Flying Nun" because she had so many hats. I remember her wearing a very sophisticated Halston look—a wide-brimmed peach sun hat, with a peach-and-white-checkered leisure suit, a peach patent bag, and peach satin strappy shoes. Girlfriend, she was a shout-out.

Mom loved expensive clothing, but she couldn't afford it. She found a way to wear lots of designer labels, however, by buying at thrift shops, and she always managed to look like a million dollars on bargain-basement prices. She believed in quality and always inspired me to search for beauty in fashion.

Being the youngest boy, though, I had to wear tons of hand-me-down clothes. This was hard since, even in elementary school, it was important to me to dress nice and as fashionable as possible in school. Mom couldn't afford to buy us expensive new clothes, so we all had to shop at a local discount store. Man, they had cheesy stuff. Trust me, you didn't want your friends to see you go in there.

One day, Angie and I were walking home from school in the winter with one of our friends when I slipped on the ice and fell. I was wearing a long, bright orange-colored jacket that had been bought at that discount store. My prone body on the ice brought nothing but shrieks of laughter from Angie, who loudly declared that I looked like a giant Cheez Doodle lying there. I realized then the fashion danger of wearing a long, bright orange, and tacky, jacket—you can fall on your ass and look like a jumbo-size Cheez Doodle.

I really fell in love with school at Roosevelt Middle School in Roselle. The teachers there were fabulous and the spirit was strong. Going to school at Roosevelt was a celebration every day. It was a fabulous experience because everyone there was so high on learning. After twenty years, I can still remember every word of our school song.

I enjoyed every subject I took. Art, English, music, science—it didn't matter. Everything interested me. Roosevelt had a strong coed sewing program that I couldn't wait to get into. The school also had its own woodshop; a printing shop, where we made our own paper and stationery; a plastic shop, where we made things like key chains out of Plexiglas; and a mechanics shop.

We made sugar cookies in our home ec classes, and we had an incredible chorus that sang everything from Gershwin to the Fifth Dimension's "Up, Up and Away." At Roosevelt, I also participated in a band where I learned to play the clarinet and then the tuba. Child, I was the tuba in the tuba. I was jammin', honey. I loved performing in the concerts.

In sixth grade, I also fell in love with Calvin Klein and Brooke Shields. Nothing got between her and her Calvins, remember? I wanted to be like Gloria Vanderbilt and have my own jeans line just like she did. Sergio Valente jeans were all the rage, too, and so were jeans by Pierre Cardin. I knew all the labels.

Even while I copied the designers in my sketches, I started to develop my own style. I didn't have much money, so I would prowl through resale shops and the Salvation Army to find interesting fashion statements to wear to school. The Salvation Army people knew me so well, they'd save some of the better stuff for me. Our minister and his wife would even pick out for me some of the best vintage clothes the church received through donations. Everybody knew I loved clothes.

Angie hated to go shopping with me in retail stores, though, because I would always inspect everything on the racks and decide that I could make them cheaper or that the craftsmanship wasn't worth the price. I would shop in retail stores for ideas, rather than for purchases. I wanted to take what was selling in the shops and give these fashions my own spin.

I was into self-expression . . . big-time. I'd create my own outfits with my primitive sewing skills and thrift-shop finds. I remember that Mr. Muscatello, a guidance counselor at Roosevelt, once told me in the school hallway, "Anthony, I like your style." I really appreciated the compliment since I thought Mr. Muscatello was a classy guy.

Meanwhile, Mom was getting more and more worried about my preoccupation with fashion. She hadn't yet discussed the situation with Dr. Choi. First, she sought the advice of the Glenns. Mr. Glenn, bless him, advised Mom to "just let Anthony be himself."

I often showed the Glenns my sewing projects and made them little presents. I didn't know until recently that Mrs. Glenn always kept a special shelf in her house which she dedicated to the little gifts I made for her. Jeffrey met with her recently and she told him about it. It meant a lot to me to hear that. The Glenns will always be special in my heart.

From the sixth through the eighth grade, we spent a whole semester each year at the Battin Career Center in Elizabeth, now called Battin High School. There, we would learn about various careers from the professionals themselves. Scientists, newscasters, real estate agents, artists, writers, and every other conceivable professional would come to our school to tell us all about their field. All the other schools in the area would send their students, too. We were very multicultural and everyone valued one another.

In Elizabeth, there were over fifty-seven different ethnic groups represented in the school system, but there were never any serious racial problems. We considered ourselves to be one family and we supported one another's cultural holidays. On St. Patty's Day, we all wore green, you know what I'm saying? It was the perfect learning place. We didn't have no dashikis walking down the hallways—please. We all sang "We Shall Overcome" together. And we did.

I went to Hamilton Middle School for seventh and eighth grades. While Hamilton was an older school without a lot of the modern conveniences, it had great teachers. Mrs. Brenda Salter was my eighth-grade English teacher. She was an attractive, very manicured black lady with a mushroom hairstyle—this was the seventies, after all. She dressed incredibly well and loved fashion. She had done some modeling since her early teens, and in addition to teaching, she sponsored fashion shows for various organizations and fund-raisers.

At the beginning of the school year, she asked all the students to write down their favorite magazines, hobbies, books, food, and other information so that she could get an insight into everyone's personality. On mine, I wrote, "I would like to be Yves Saint Laurent. I love *Vogue* and *Elle* magazines, sewing, fashion. . . ."

When I realized that Mrs. Salter also loved fashion, she became one of my all-time favorite teachers. She was one of my first mentors, and we developed a great student-teacher relationship. Outside the classroom, I called her Aunt Brenda. She often refers to me as her godson, and so many people heard me refer to her as my "aunt" that they really thought she was related to my family. If I had a problem or a question my family couldn't answer, I'd get on the phone and call Aunt Brenda. She was an artistic soul, like myself, and I could count on her to tap right into wherever I was emotionally.

Aunt Brenda wanted to encourage my interest in fashion, and she would occasionally ask my mother if she could take me to the Short Hills Mall so I could see the fashions of Yves Saint Laurent, Anne Klein, Calvin Klein, and all the others. This mall was very upscale, with marble floors and top-of-the-line merchandise. I would take in every detail of the designer clothing, from the lined skirts to the exquisite buttons. After exploring the racks, Aunt Brenda and I would enjoy lunch together at the mall before she drove me back home.

She also invited me to participate in the fashion shows she sponsored for women's organizations, churches, schools, and charities. I modeled in several of them, and then, in high school, I asked her if I could submit some of my own fashions to be in the show. Aunt Brenda was always enthusiastic and supportive about my goals, and I'll never forget that. I would show her my designs and she loved them. Once I had completed my creations, I'd call her and say, "Aunt Brenda, you gotta come see this!" Luckily, she lived close by, because I called her a lot.

I made her little daughter, Erika, who was two or three at the time, clothing for her Cabbage Patch dolls. When I was about fourteen, I made Aunt Brenda a black and white herringbone skirt and jacket, with rhinestone buttons. I was so proud of that suit, and she praised it as if I had given her an Yves Saint Laurent original from Paris, even though I'm sure it still had straight pins sticking out of the crooked seams.

With my eye on the Paris design houses, I knew that French was an important language for me to learn, so I tried to do my best in Frank Mazza's language classes. Mr.

Mazza was a gentle, patient teacher who made me believe that one day I could master another language fluently. Through his Latin classes, I learned that time flies with *Tempus fugit* and my motto became *Carpe diem*—"Seize the day."

Another great teacher who was a role model for me was Edward Nelson, the music teacher at Hamilton. He had a Cary Grant type of elegance about him and such a passion for music that it came through to his students. I learned to love musicals and even opera from him. To this day, when I think about poor Carmen's death at the hands of her lover, Don José, in Georges Bizet's *Carmen*, tears come to my eyes. Better than a soap opera, child. Erica Kane in *All My Children* didn't have nothin' on poor Carmen's problems.

At Hamilton, I also ran track and took mechanical drawing class. James Carter, the mechanical drawing teacher, was really tough on me. I think I was too eccentric and creative for him, and he wasn't into fashion at all. While I loved to freely sketch, I just could not get into mechanical drawing. I'd erase my work so many times I'd have holes in the paper. I was horrible in that class. I never did understand mechanical drawing and T squares. I guess it just didn't allow me to flow creatively; I felt hobbled by the unyielding parameters of it all.

I wondered why I couldn't be a little more left-brained like the other guys in my class, but it just wasn't me. My frustration in Mr. Carter's mechanical drawing class was one of the reasons I felt different from all my classmates. Some of the other students, instinctively zoning in on my particular individuality, sometimes went straight for the jugular with their verbal taunts aimed in my direction.

I had to endure being called names at school from the very beginning. The most horrible thing is to be called "fag." That word still stings today, and I started hearing it when I was about eight. In grade school on up, it seemed like all of us who were different—the overweight, the gay, the smart geeks, the special people—hung out together so we could support each other.

I always felt different, even from the rest of my family. I sometimes wondered why I wasn't more like my own brothers, who were naturally interested in sports and cars. I just wasn't, though, and I had to go after my own interests alone. I always heard music they couldn't hear, and as much as they loved me and I loved them, I often had a hard time explaining to them the rhythms I was moving to. Even the fact that I was a twin didn't totally suppress the nagging feeling of alienation I subconsciously felt.

Because I liked to sew and create fashion, the guys in my classes would never pick me to play basketball or soccer or any other sport. I was always the last one to be picked, and it was so humiliating. The guys never included me in any of their other activities, either. The girls liked me, though, and that made my social life enjoyable.

I think because I was different from most kids, I was drawn to learning about people who were also somewhat askew from the norm but who had used their uniqueness to great success. I read everything I could on famous entrepreneurs like Thomas Edison, Henry Ford, and Frank Lloyd Wright, and I was inspired by them all. These were people who marched to their own drummer, often enduring criticism for peculiar notions that were sometimes just ahead of their time.

What people don't often remember is that these great individuals all had lots of failures to their names, too, in addition to their tremendous successes. I really identified with their struggles and was especially fascinated by

Thomas Edison. Edison also had hundreds of failures but never gave up; his success is an enduring monument to his faith and determination.

Edison's main lab and mansion are still in nearby West Orange, New Jersey, and I used to go see it all the time. This was a place where nothing was too impossible to be achieved. In spite of conventional skepticism, Edison invented the phonograph and motion picture equipment, as well as early electric light and power equipment, among many other achievements.

In the main lab, which is three stories high and 250 feet long, there were machine shops, an engine room, glass-blowing and pumping rooms, chemical and photographic departments, rooms for electrical testing, stockrooms, and a library with ten thousand volumes. Four one-story labs were set at right angles to the main building. Edison kept meticulous records of his work and I was inspired to follow his example.

Close by Edison's West Orange laboratory complex was his twenty-nine room Queen Anne–style mansion called Glenmont, with its clean-lined gables and balconies. I loved to tour this incredible home, walking up the wide staircase to grand rooms that still boast stained-glass windows, rich chandeliers, elaborately carved wood paneling, and frescoed ceilings. Most of the original furnishings from Edison's residency have remained: damask-covered furniture, animal rugs, imported statuary and paintings, as well as gifts the Edisons received from around the world.

Whenever I'd visit Glenmont, a feeling would envelop me like some entity had taken over my body. It was a warm, engaging feeling of success and passion. It was as if Edison were saying to me, "Come in, come in. You're a creator, too, and you're welcome in this house."

Edison became a spiritual mentor to me. I would often go to his graveside behind Glenmont and ask him to pass on to me some of his courage. In my daydreams, I pictured myself listed among the giants in the business world and fantasized about running my own company. I'd be a fashion designer with my own labels and my own employees. I was more than determined to see this dream come true.

6

In the House of
Antonio Fierce

All the hot designers at the time were of Italian influence. Sergio Valente, Giorgio Armani, Valentino, Gloria Vanderbilt by Murjani, and Oleg Cassini reigned supreme, so in junior high I created a designer name for myself—Antonio Fierce. Jeffrey had always described me as "fierce" because I was so determined in everything I did. My brothers and sisters laughed, but I thought my clothing was fierce, so I loved my new nom de guerre. I signed my sketches "Antonio Fierce" and created Antonio Fierce jackets, shirts, slacks, and even socks.

By eighth grade, I was a sewing fool, making everything under my own self-styled label. Jeffrey was in the Army at the time, and when he'd come home, he got a kick out of my Antonio Fierce persona. He still calls me that today, in fact. At one time, I actually considered legally changing my name to Antonio Fierce.

At home, I'd escape into my *atelier,* which is French for "workroom." I often used Jeffrey's attic bedroom, even though he had deemed it off-limits to everyone. That's why I liked it, though, because it was totally private. There, in my secret atelier, I would imagine that I was the head designer for the House of Fierce.

And I *was* fierce, girlfriend. When I showed up at school in a burlap cape and baggy pants, people said, "Who's that?!" The answer, of course, was Antonio Fierce. Fierce Clothing, Inc., honey. I'd make my own label tags out of paper. When the kids teased me about my style, I'd just show up the next day in an even more outrageous outfit.

Whenever it rained and we kids were stuck at home, my brothers would busy themselves with their mechanical toys, while I'd dream of Paris and my original designs gliding down a runway.

"I had to pull everything out of myself for this collection," I'd sigh to the reporters at my fashion show.

Coco Chanel was a role model for me, too. Coco was born to poor parents, and after her mother died, she and her sisters were placed in a Catholic orphanage by their father. At the age of eighteen, she was placed in a convent boarding school as a charity student. In spite of that, Coco thrived and achieved huge success through her perseverance and ingenuity. She was an inspiration. I believed that if she could make it, so could I.

Coco took the negative elements of her life and worked to turn them into positives. Forced to wear drab uniforms throughout much of her young institutionalized life, for instance, Coco set out to radically change the style restrictions between the social classes. She took a traditional maid's uniform with the white collar and pleated navy skirt and transformed it into high fashion. She actually created a version of the maid's uniform that was of haute couture quality. She did the same thing with wool gabardine.

As a designer, Coco Chanel was simply ahead of her time. She somehow anticipated what women would need to wear for their more active roles during the First World War and thereafter. She introduced mobile, efficient, unadorned fashions that allowed the freedom of movement that men enjoyed in their clothes. Her skirts had functional pockets and were flared or pleated. While Coco's skirts were relatively short, she didn't believe in showing the knees. They were elegant in their simplicity and women loved them.

As soon as Raymond got his driver's license, I would constantly hit him up for rides to downtown Elizabeth, which is still full of small, individual shops reminding me of a small European town. When I was seven or eight years old, I began my expeditions downtown to Wolper's Fabrics. Mr. Wolper thought I was crazy but loved my enthusiasm and encouraged it.

For me, his shop was like going to a candy store. I'd be in a state of ecstasy, exploring this vast smorgasbord of color and textures. It was seventh heaven. Mr. Wolper would show me all the best fabrics and tell me about them—which ones were from Italy, Africa, France, or Belgium; which ones were machine-made or handwoven. . . . I would be totally enthralled.

"That fabric is gorgeous," I'd tell him, as I lusted for every exotic texture he showed me.

It was "showtime" when I went to a fabric store, honey. I would roll out the fabrics and pin them up on Angie or whoever else was with me, creating instant fashions for everybody in the store, including Mr. Wolper and his employees. While I was there, I considered it to be my atelier and everyone in it to be my models. I'm sure a lot of people thought, Who is this child who thinks he's Yves Saint Laurent?

After I had unrolled half the bolts in the store and played with at least fifty different fabrics, I'd finally go up to the counter and ask Mr. Wolper to cut me just half a yard—which was all I could afford. Mr. Wolper would always slip me another half yard and give me remnants to play with. I was his biggest fan.

My designs were sometimes inspired by the most unlikely of sources. At the local bakery, I studied how they decorated their cupcakes, which looked like upside-down ball gowns to me. I felt wonderfully free to create and express myself and it was a magical time. I dreamed of working in Valentino's court and with other designers. By this time, I was also inspired by the fitted suits and gowns by Dior.

By seventh grade, I was making clothes for myself and for friends, as well as pillows, curtains, and anything else that could be sewn. I was always drawing and designing in my spare time. I loved to shop just to see what was selling on the clothing racks.

Around this time, Angie introduced me to her friend Cherub Khan, who was a tall, awkward, skinny girl with braces and glasses. We hit it off, though, and the three of us became great friends. Cherub was shy and quiet like Angie, but I'd enlist her to let me make her clothes and we spent a lot of time together.

In the summers, when I'd go to Virginia to visit Grandmother Toy, she would encourage my aspirations to become a designer. She herself was a wonderful seamstress who had made all her daughters' clothes. Grandma Toy always believed her grandchildren could achieve anything we set out to do.

"Anthony, don't sit on the sidelines," she'd tell me. "Do what feels right for you. Follow your dreams."

My grandmother was a groovy girl. She'd take me on the weekends to Dan River Mills, where we would buy slightly irregular sheets to use as material for the fashions I had sketched. For generations, some of my Virginia relatives had worked in the mills, passing the shuttle to create fanciful sheets and fabrics for the fashion industry. With the fabric they produced, I would create whimsical designs, imagining that I was a great designer in a Paris couture house.

One time, I selected sheets with a Laura Ashley–style rosebud design. Without a pattern to work with, I took these sheets, sewed them together, and cinched them up to make 1950s-style summer dresses. I also made the petticoat and everything else the dresses needed to make the look complete.

My grandparents' farm was a refuge for us from the pressures of the city. It was a simpler place where church was still the social center of the community. Religion was important to them; Grandma Toy didn't miss her Sunday church. My Grandfather Joe, a wonderfully sweet man, had two basic sets of clothes: his work overalls, and his dress overalls, which he would wear to church every Sunday with a freshly starched white cotton shirt under it and with freshly polished black dress shoes on his feet.

I loved to listen to my grandmother's family stories, learning about my heritage and also about many of the crafts that have been woven into the rich tapestry of our family traditions. One of my fondest memories is of myself as a small boy sitting with Grandma Toy as she sewed rag dolls to put in the children's Christmas stockings. I learned that our ancestors, utilizing whatever materials were at hand, would make dolls out of rags and socks with buttons for eyes.

After my Grandfather Joe passed on in 1979, Grandmother Toy began keeping time with an elderly neighbor and friend I'll call Nelson. She'd go over to his house in the evenings, and we kids assumed she and Nelson were always just watching television over there. I mean, what else would old people be doing after the sun goes down? When we asked that question, we were surprised by her quiet but amused response.

"Grandma got to have companionship, too," she replied, with a twinkle in her eye.

Everyone loved Grandmother Toy. She could make people laugh and had lots of old sayings like "Stay single, let your money jingle." Grandma Toy lived the way she wanted to live. She loved her Dr Peppers, which she drank by the case, even though her physician advised her against it.

She was the respected matriarch of the clan, and we all thought she was invincible. Looking back on the many summers I spent on my grandmother's farm, I realize that I had gained a wealth of wisdom and joy from her. For one thing, I learned to appreciate life's simple blessings; for another, she taught me that a person's success can be measured by the road he walks.

7

Moving On

My father, Ramone Moya, lived mostly in Mexico after he left our family. He was in his mid-sixties then. All I could really remember about his life with us in Elizabeth was that he loved to play cards and dominos. When I was thirteen, we heard through my godfather that my father was seriously ill. I wrote several times a year to the people in Mexico who were taking care of him, but rarely heard from them.

My mother started dating William "Pete" Hankins, a truck driver, when I was in sixth grade. Angie and I were about twelve years old. A widower, Pete was sixteen years older than my mom and had thirteen children of his own, mostly grown. Only two of his boys, Jay and Chris, were in high school and still living at home.

Pete didn't understand what my sewing was about at all. I had girls coming and going to the house all the time for fittings, since I was making prom dresses and other clothes for them. I was always sewing and, to my mother, he would grumble continuously, "What's with this kid?"

Mom would tell me not to pay him any mind. Pete wasn't a happy man at that time anyway. He had lost his first wife to cancer, and he sometimes took his frustrations out on the people around him.

As his relationship with my mother progressed, it looked as if marriage might be in the cards for them. Pete's grown children initially gave my mother a hard time when they learned she was thinking of marrying their father. When Raymond found out Mom planned to marry Pete, he took it hard, too. He gave Mom a rough time about it for a while.

Kevin, who was sixteen, took the news really hard. He couldn't stand the thought that a man—any man—was going to take Mom's attention away from us. We had always been a team, and now someone else was going to be demanding her precious time. Kevin couldn't stand the thought and ran away to Virginia to stay with our Uncle John there.

James accepted the news philosophically.

"You need to do whatever makes you happy, Mom," he told her when Mom asked him what he thought about the idea of her marrying Pete.

Finally, Raymond decided, too, that it was time for Mom to have her own happiness after sacrificing so much to raise us kids. If marrying Pete was going to make her happy, then Raymond would accept it. Mom's decision to marry Pete wasn't so hard on Angie and me, probably because we were the youngest and most amenable to new situations within the family.

Mom and Pete were married in 1981 by Bishop Saunders, who presided over the church in Newark where Pete, and now my mother, attended services. The bishop and his wife were wonderful friends, as well as leaders of the community. For the ceremony, Mom wore a beautiful gown, Angie was a flower girl, and Sarah Davis was maid of honor.

We held a big reception at our house, with a wedding cake and long tables of food. Pete's children came, even though they weren't thrilled with the marriage. People come out when there's food, honey. Everyone had a great time and shook their booty till the wee hours; then Mom and Pete left for their honeymoon.

After Mom married Pete, we moved to his house at 424 Linden Street in Elizabeth. Linden was a turn-of-the-century cobblestone street. Unlike on Third Avenue, our neighbors on Linden Street were blue-collar black folks. Not very many people there had much money.

Pete's home was a big old Tudor-style house from the late 1800s that Angie and I liked a lot. It was huge to us, with six bedrooms and two staircases, including a formal front staircase and a maid's back staircase, which we thought was so cool to have. The house reminded me of the ones in that Judy Garland movie *Meet Me in St. Louis,* but without all the ornamentation. You could just imagine, though, how fine the house had been in its heyday.

In the early days after Mom and Pete's marriage, that house held a mess of emotions. There was a lot of tension there, with all these people trying to get along with only one bathroom and many different mealtimes. I inadvertently contributed my share to the tension when I caused the tub upstairs and, on another day, the fish tank, to overflow. Mom tried valiantly to avert conflicts, though, begging everyone to please keep peace in the house. We all tried our best to make adjustments to our new home as calmly as we could.

While Mom maintained strict discipline with her children, Pete's style was more lax. He often talked a big game but never really followed through. Mom didn't allow Katie to have her first date until she was a senior. Angie was also in high school before she was allowed to date.

Pete's children had grown up with a much looser set of rules. We got along well with Jay and Chris, though, and that helped our families to blend together. Kevin, after seeing that Mom was happy in the marriage, eventually came back to the fold.

In her new household, Mom still called the shots. Until we were in high school, we had to be back in the house by dark. During our years at Elizabeth High School, we could be out until 9:00 P.M., unless we had parental consent for a later curfew. Mom also gave us all a sex education talk early in our lives. She didn't wait for us to learn that stuff on the street or in the school yard.

Mom didn't want to start her marriage by sleeping in the master bedroom, which my stepfather had shared with his first wife, so they chose another bedroom. I lucked out and got the master bedroom, which was perfect for all my sewing projects. It had lots of room and was soon filled with my sewing machine, worktables, several old dress forms for fittings, ironing boards, and everything else I needed. I had bought one old dress form at a Singer shop and found the other at a garage sale. My room was a mess—it looked like a clothing factory.

I loved it, though, except for one night when I had a ghostly encounter that scared me to death. I had been sewing all evening in my room until I finally fell asleep. When I woke up later in the night, I initially focused my eyes on my sewing table and then noticed something strange on the ironing board that was at the foot of my bed: a curvaceous woman with long, wavy black hair, dressed in 1930s clothing, was stretched out on the board—eyeing me seductively with a vamp's stare.

I screamed and fled from the room in a streak of terror. Angie's light was on, so I ran into her bedroom, where, thank God, she was still up reading. Man, I was freaked! Gasping for breath, I told her what I had seen. When Mom heard about it the next day, she just laughed and said, "It must have been a witch riding your back, Anthony."

I don't care what anybody says, that house was haunted! When I was young, I had heard that spirits linger in houses, and I think death definitely leaves a feeling on a place. Old man Poe built the house at 424 Linden Street at the turn of the century and died right in the living room. I think he and his relatives have been walkin' that house ever since, honey. I would hear doors open and close, whistling sounds, footsteps. . . .

Our dogs would act crazy inside that house, too, barking at unseen figures. One of them, Bear, would growl every night as I was about to enter my bedroom. I think Bear knew a ghost was in there. It was the actual master bedroom, after all, and I think the former residents of the house were still comfortably occupying that room. To me, the house was possessed.

After I saw the ghost, I told Bishop Saunders about it and he came over the next week to bless the house. Yes, he did, child. He sprinkled that holy water and prayed over every room. I prayed, myself, that this blessing would take away the spirits from the house. Most of the time, I felt that Bishop Saunders' efforts had succeeded. The house seemed quieter, except occasionally when I was home alone on dark and stormy nights. . . .

* * *

By this time in my life, I was already seriously career-pathing and destining, determined to be the next Willi Smith, who was a young, hot, African-American designer in New York. I'd spend hours and hours sewing in my room. Mom was worried about my spending so much time slumped over a sewing machine late at night, but I had a clear vision of my career even then.

"Ma, I'm not going to always be sitting at a sewing machine," I finally told her when I was about fourteen. "Someday, I'll be able to just sketch a design on a piece of paper and give it to someone. I'll have people sewing for *me*."

My stepfather, though, became an obstacle to me and my goals. Pete was really, really negative toward me. He's not much of an optimist anyway. He just has a different twist on life than we did in my family. Pete fought in World War II, and especially for his generation, my interests were bizarre. While Mom had always accepted my interest in sewing, Pete never took me seriously when I told him I was going to be a fashion designer one day. He's from the old school, I guess, where men aren't supposed to be into sewing. Since my career goals seemed beyond his comprehension, our relationship was full of friction.

I don't mean to give the impression that I don't like my stepfather. He's very supportive of my work now, and I really respect him because he's always been a devoted husband to my mother. Pete Hankins is a good man and has treated Mom well. They're best friends, and I don't ever remember them fighting. Even now, after so many years, I know he'd walk on water for her. They still go to church together and talk enthusiastically with each other like they've just met. Back then, however, Pete and I were at constant odds with each other because he just couldn't fathom that my goals were valid.

By seventh grade, I had already made my mind up that I was going to be a fashion designer and was working every day toward that goal. Pete was very vocal about the fact that he thought I was wasting my time and would never amount to anything. It hurt a lot, and my mother had to do things for me on the sly. I tried to keep myself centered by listening to Langston Hughes tapes and Barbra Streisand albums. I think my stepfather also resented the fact that I was getting attention from teachers and other people in the community because of my talent—a talent he considered totally useless for a man to have.

Most people in the family supported my goals, though. One of my new stepbrothers was really, really flamboyant. He was really out there. His name was Willie Jr.—named for my stepdad. He was a really nice guy who happened to be gay and later died of AIDS. He worked for a paper company, and he'd send me lots of pads and markers and encourage me to design, design, design.

Willie always took an interest in my goal to be a designer. He understood me and I appreciated that. People in the neighborhood would help me, too, giving me dollar bills, even twenties and fifties, so that I could buy my supplies. I was really blessed to have their support.

I explored the mall extensively and studied the designers' fashions on the racks. To quench my thirst for information on fashion, I also often went to the library and asked the librarians to order specific books for me. I'm probably responsible for the fact that the library in Elizabeth has so many books on fashion.

I read everything I could about my idol, Yves Saint Laurent. I imagined myself working in the House of Saint Laurent on

Avenue Marceau in Paris—the model of which, I'd read, was the salon of Princess Mathilde, the aunt of Napoleon III, who had a town house on the Rue de Berri.

I was impressed that Yves Saint Laurent had made a name for himself at the age of twenty, turning ordinary materials into high fashion. Saint Laurent was ahead of his time in that he stressed the importance of ready-to-wear lines, realizing that haute couture represented less than 5 percent of the turnover of any of the Paris houses.

8

Stylin'

I didn't start designing clothes under my real name until the ninth grade. American names were leading the pack of designers then and included people like Calvin Klein, Perry Ellis, Ralph Lauren, Donna Karan, Bill Blass, and Willi Smith. I would create original clothes for Angie and other girls to wear to school, and I loved to improvise. I made miniskirts with bright fun buttons, pinafore dresses, skirts, pants, pleated wool skirts, gowns, everything. I kept the house buzzing with the activity stemming from my design work.

After we moved to Linden Street, I became good friends with a girl I'll call Tina. Tina was very artistic and could draw anything; in school, we'd share our fashion drawings. She also had an incredible singing voice. She'd perform in every talent show, trying to get discovered, and I'd create the costumes for her performances. Tina would wear feathers and buy these crazy hats. . . . I loved her flair.

She would get up on that stage and really let loose with her singing. She was so hot, she was on fire. Child, she was a better singer than Whitney Houston. In church, Tina would be front-row singing and she'd blow out that church! Jesus heard her for sure. Lord, that girl could sing.

"Tina, you're going to be a star, you're going to make it," I always told her. "If anyone's going to make it out of our group, it's going to be you. I know it, girl. Tina, you need a singing contract!"

Tina's father owned his own company, and he would give her money, sometimes as much as $200 a week. She would share the wealth, and this worked out well because Tina and I loved to shop.

The summer after eighth grade, Tina and I were bike-riding in the neighborhood when a car suddenly hit her. I watched in hopeless horror as Tina flew over the top of the car and landed, unconscious, on the ground with a broken leg. Neighbors and ambulances came running. When she went home from the hospital a week later, she was in a leg cast.

After the accident, Tina started hanging out with a wild crowd that included a fast girl in the neighborhood from New York City who dressed like a woman of the night in tight pants. This girl wore extensions in her hair and threw wild parties that were rumored to be sex orgies with crack addicts.

Tina's new friend lived by a park around the corner from Linden Street, which was known to be full of drug dealers. Most of us kids stayed clear of that park when the drug dealers were there. Even so, it was definitely a rougher crowd on Linden Street than on Third Avenue. Our mother didn't allow us to hang out on the street. She made sure we were kept busy at our own house. I was always sketching and creating, so I had no time to get into that much trouble.

Unlike the strong parental role models on Third Avenue, some of our friends on Linden Street had stressful situations at home—alcoholic and drug-addicted parents, with little discipline or supervision. I think Tina was trying to escape from her own family situation. She dropped out of school in ninth grade, and I didn't see much of her after that. News from the grapevine told me she was gone on drugs. It made me really sad to think that my friend may have succumbed to the negative elements of the neighborhood.

As Angie and I began high school, the neighborhood started to go down even further. I hate to say it, but the Haitians moved in and hated the blacks who were already there. Drive-by shootings occurred after that. The Haitians wore weird colors and even weirder prints in a style that can best be described as hodgepodge eclecticism. They had nappy hair and no fashion sense. Believe me, if someone called you a Haitian in my neighborhood, you were ready to fight.

After Angie and I left for college, my parents moved out of the neighborhood just in the nick of time. The neighborhood just sucked people right into the cesspool. My family was really fortunate because we were always able to escape neighborhoods before they became "projects."

I missed Tina, but soon a cool girl named Valerie Green grabbed my attention. She was a senior when I was a freshman, and we called her "Punk Rock Val." I was sittin' on our old-fashioned porch, drinking Hi-C, wearing my pink and navy shorts with my pink Turtle shoes, when Val first came around the corner to our house, with her hair swept up along with her attitude.

She wore an oversized light blue Ralph Lauren oxford shirt, tight-and-tapered Levi's jeans, a big Western belt with a silver belt buckle, pointy cowboy boots, and cat's-eye glasses. Her shiny lip gloss shimmered in the sun as she thoughtfully chewed her gum. Man, she was so cool. I loved the way she dressed and I wanted to hang out with her.

"Girl, you got it going ON!" I shouted to her from the porch. "I love those boots you have on."

Punk Rock Val and I quickly discovered we were on the same wavelength and were soon hanging out together all the time. She had her own sense of style, but she had been ridiculed for it, like I had been for mine. She and I would go to the grocery store, wearing our bandanas. We'd buy a Mrs. Smith's apple pie, add cinnamon and ice cream to it, and have a feast while we watched MTV and read our new *GQ* magazines. I read every issue of *GQ* faithfully. I was developing my own sense of style and was influenced by Val's free sense of it.

Val and I traveled all over New York City, exploring museums, department stores, restaurants, and everything else. We were always comparing the fashions we saw on the street wherever we were. If I saw someone wearing something that looked tacky, I'd say, "That looks cheesy." People used to call me "the King of Cheese" because I had such definite opinions on what should be classified as "cheesy."

Val, though, was always on the cutting edge with fashion—she was just a shout-out! She would always catch the wave before we even knew it was time to go to the beach. Punk Rock Val was into Mary Janes before Mary Janes even knew they was happening, child.

I looked like a male version of Punk Rock Val. Together, we went through half a dozen fashion themes. We'd wear stuff like golf slacks and status symbols like oxford shoes and penny loafers. Val and I also loved to wear Alan Flusser golf shorts, and I made a ton of Hawaiian shirts to wear with them when we went through our "Tropics" period. We were part of the reason Hawaiian shirts became the rage in our high school.

Our "Pretty in Pink" stage, though, stopped traffic, honey. I'd show up at Elizabeth High School wearing pink knickers, a pink-and-white-striped shirt, a pink tie, and cranberry penny loafers. They called me Amadeus Benjamin Franklin. Yes, they did. I was entertainment personified at school and I loved the attention.

I was sewing lots of stuff then and was also influenced by Spanish styles. Being half Cuban, I made friends with the Spanish students in school. Even though my father was gone, I was still in touch with my Cuban roots. At Manning's, a Cuban-owned men's shoe and clothing store in Elizabeth, I always noticed that the customers really *dressed* in that store. I'd be clocking the looks in my head, then I'd go to the Salvation Army and Daffy Dan's, a local designer discount store, to knock it off. I loved to wear this funky burlap jacket that I had made, or my old-man coat that I had bought in a thrift store.

I always tried to wear a different look every day. I might come in one day as a Frenchman, wearing a natty beret; the next day like a Hollywood star, hiding my identity behind my Foster Grants; the next like Buckwheat, with oversized sweaters—or maybe I'd come in as a Preppy Poster Child, with my khakis, polo shirts, and deck shoes with no socks. One day, I even came to school in an English riding outfit I'd made.

I was also big into hats—all kinds, like bandanas, Arabic-style headwear, and fedoras. I loved to wear my beige fedora and duster topcoat, as well as capes and pilot jump-suits. Anything for a look. I was drama personified, girl-friend. It was like a really fun show. Every day, I would dress as a different type of person with a whole new sense of style. I was a jazzy jeff, man. I turned the mama jama out at that school! Sometimes I'd change costumes twice a day. Most of the students and teachers really enjoyed it. They loved my originality.

Although I had lots of friends in ninth grade, there was a group that ridiculed me. If I wore my beret or my Michael Jackson high-water pants, I'd sometimes hear someone hiss, "Look at that fag," as I walked by. I tried not to pay much attention to them, but those words felt like a sharp stab in my back every time. I made up my mind, though, to ignore them because I knew they didn't know any better. I loved hanging out with Cherub, Tina, and Punk Rock Val. I adored women, so how could I be gay?

As a freshman in high school, I was excited about enter-ing a new phase of life—a real coming-of-age period for me. For ninth grade, we attended classes in a building called Jefferson House, which was separated from the main campus of Elizabeth High School. I was involved in a lot of school activities and was also beginning to see the fruition of my design work. I welcomed the chance to really develop my craft and style. From ninth grade on, I plotted to get academic attention so that I could get into college.

I used the high school library to read up on everything I was interested in. There, I became friends with Mrs. Har-riet Anderson Mayner, who was the school's educational media specialist. Her office was right off the library. I'd bring her the outfits that I had created on my sewing machine at home. She took a look at all my crooked seams and knew I needed some formal training. My uneven and amateurish workmanship left something to be desired.

"Anthony, I love what you're doing, but you need to take some sewing lessons," Mrs. Mayner advised me. She recommended Mrs. Janet Papetti's sewing class, which I promptly enrolled in for my sophomore year. Meanwhile, Mrs. Mayner was a constant source of inspiration. At school, she also ran an art workshop that Angie and I were involved in. We would put on variety shows for which we'd re-create scenes from musicals like *The Wiz* and *The King and I.*

Every other year, though, the workshop would present a fashion show featuring both students and teachers as models. Angie, who was normally quiet and shy, surprised everyone with her natural flair for the runway. She would suddenly become a diva on the runway, thin and beautiful, holding her head in just the right, proud position—as if she'd been born to model for couture houses. Angie just had that air about her that caught everyone's eye. Once she got on a runway, girlfriend, an attitude would come over her and she'd just do her thing. It drove the guys wild.

I'd often tell Mrs. Mayner about my fashion dreams, and she was always a positive force, saying, "Go for it, Anthony. They'll either say yes or no, and you've got a fifty percent chance of a yes. You may get some noes, but if you keep trying, you're bound to end up with some yeses." Mrs. Mayner was right. I did end up with some yeses!

I plotted my life in levels. In addition to Mrs. Papetti's sewing class, I took fashion illustration and art classes. I was busy in a variety of student organizations and was also determined to have a competitive fashion portfolio. I went AFTER what I wanted!

In ninth grade, I took an art class that was taught on a college level by Mr. Larry Walker. We studied all aspects of drawing and painting, color theory, and art history. It was a great class and I was really into it. Mr. Walker allowed free expression in his class and didn't believe in pigeonholing his students. I looked up to Mr. Walker and would ask him a million questions a day.

I'm sure at times he regretted it, but he allowed me to be who I was—and I *expressed* my free self in his class, child. I guess you could say I was the catalyst for discussion in that class because I was always arguing my point of view. Mr. Walker liked me anyway. He always told me he loved the funky ways I would dress for school.

For the first time, I felt like I was more of an artist than just a designer, even though I always managed to sneak my fashion interests into whatever project we were studying. I also brought my sketches in to show Mr. Walker. Through his class, I was developing patience, tenacity, and an artistic love for everything. It was my first real serious opportunity to create something that wasn't always fashion-related.

Wherever there was an opportunity at school to create something artistically, I was there volunteering. I made friends' wardrobes, shaping their image based on their own ideas and mine. I had confidence in what I did and imagined myself as a grand salon designer. This vision empowered me, girlfriend. A lot of fashion is about drama, in my opinion. You've got to have that flare. I never dwelled on where the creativity was coming from. I just concentrated on channeling it and fueling my creativity.

Angie and I became members of the Color Guard, the coed drill team that marched with the band, and I loved the pageantry of it, as well as the competition between the drill teams. We went together to all the practices, every morning and three times a week in the evening. Cherub was also a member of the drill team, and I loved being with a group of people who were all concerned about putting on the best show.

After several rehearsals, when everyone would be exhausted, I'd still be ready to go again. My rallying cries were, "Have some pride in your stride!" and "Get some pep in your step!" Angie, especially, would groan and accuse me of having too much energy for my own good, but I usually loved every minute of practice. It was invigorating. Our team won some awards and I finally knew what it was like to be part of a winning organization. I developed a lot of self-esteem through my participation in the Color Guard, along with a sense of purpose as a team player.

9

Rough Times

Ninth grade, however, was a real challenge because I was suddenly just one face out of almost a thousand in my class alone. After eighth grade, students from Hamilton and at least four other middle schools were funneled into Jefferson House for ninth grade. Some of these new kids just didn't understand me, but I was involved in so many activities at school that I didn't really have time to worry about what they thought of me.

As a freshman, I was already out to change the world, so I decided to run for sophomore class president. I tacked up my carefully hand-lettered campaign ads and posters, handed out flyers, and passed out personalized buttons and pens with slogans on them that said, "Vote for Anthony/I'm Your Man/You know I Can."

I really worked hard on my campaign, but some of the students who didn't know me very well trashed my posters and flyers, threw my campaign pens down on the ground, and refused to take the campaign buttons I offered them. Some students even referred to me with insulting gestures, like the limp wrist. I thought this was the highest insult. One guy even walked up to me out of the blue and said, "I can't stand you. I'd punch you out right now if I could."

As much as it hurt, I forced myself to ignore all the insults and taunts. I had my own agenda, and that was to be a great class president. I was going to give it my all, no matter what. It helped immensely that I had a solid group of friends who always stood behind me, giving me constant strength. These were not only girls but also guys—straight guys, at that, who understood my creative flair and weren't threatened by my untraditional take on malehood.

During this trying year, it gave me encouragement to know that Yves Saint Laurent himself had endured the same kind of taunts as a student and that this torture only made him stronger in the end. Barbra Streisand, too, was regarded as different from most people in school. She was considered a loner, arrogant and aloof. But a few fellow students who knew her recognized that it wasn't all self-involvement with Barbra. She just had a lot more adult matters on her plate than most other people her age. Barbra had a professional goal by the age of fifteen and she went after it with a vengeance.

I wasn't going to let a few taunts stand in my way. I tried to ignore these incidents because I knew what I was doing was so right for me. I had straight friends like Michael Kagdis, Eddie Wilchins, Herve Ernest, and John Waters who accepted me. They were obviously secure within themselves and appreciated me for who I was. There were other guys, as well, who were friends and stood up for me in high school. They didn't tolerate anyone calling me names.

My brother Raymond and stepbrother Jay were also always there for me. Once, when I was out on the practice field with the Color Guard, some kids from the band were again calling me "fag." Raymond was practicing football nearby, but after hearing that these guys were giving me a hard time, he and some of his football buddies went up to them and introduced themselves. Raymond identified himself as my brother and told them that if they continued harassing me, they'd hear from him personally. It was great to know I had my brothers looking out for me.

When my election opponent, Nancy Joseph, and I gave our campaign speeches, hers was funny while mine was very serious. Surely, I thought, the students would see how dedicated I was to our alma mater. Later, however, when the votes were counted, I was shocked to realize that Nancy was the clear winner.

It was crushing, absolutely devastating, to lose. Before this defeat, I had thought I was all that and a bag of chips. I remember being quite subdued after the votes were tallied and I realized that I had lost. As I walked, dejectedly, to Mr. Walker's class, I was stunned to see that on one of my campaign posters that I had taped to Mr. Walker's door, someone had written, "Ha, ha, the fag lost!"

Fuming, I tore down the poster and stalked into the classroom—just in time to hear one of the guys in my class muttering under his breath, "I'm glad that fag lost." That was the last straw. I asked Mr. Walker if I could speak to our class. My fighting spirit returning, I wanted to show them that I wasn't defeated after all. I'll always be grateful to Mr. Walker, who allowed me to talk to my fellow students and give them a piece of my mind. I got everything off my chest *that* day in class, child.

"At least I was trying to do something positive," I told them. "And I intend to run again. I'll be back. You can make fun of me now, but I'm going to win the next time. And at least I don't just sit around and do nothing. I want to bring a lot of great things to Elizabeth High School."

I took a deep breath. No one stirred. You could have heard a pin drop in that classroom.

"Yes, I was upset today," I admitted, "but I'm still determined to make it. I'm getting involved and you've got to get yourselves involved, too. Don't wait around for someone to come to you. At least I'm doing something. I want to make things better for our school. Don't you want that, too?"

I was so emotionally involved in that speech, you would have thought that Martin Luther King was standing behind me. I wanted them to believe in my vision for Elizabeth High School. It was a speech of empowerment for all of us, and I meant every word. I may have been a funky clotheshorse, but I had a serious side and damned if they didn't see it that day. Mom always said I was a mouthpiece, and at least I wasn't afraid to stand up for what I wanted.

After that, some of the kids who gave me trouble seemed to have a grudging respect for me. I wasn't just "that fag in the weird clothes."

I developed more of a thick skin after this experience. I got over it fast because I had too much else to do to worry about it. The only way I could get the kids to take me seriously was to get involved in school activities. I started speaking up for the rights of students and joined the cafeteria committee. Over the next four years, I signed up for just about every club and activity that school had to offer. I was determined to make my voice heard.

When you're one in over four thousand kids, it takes some doing to be noticed. As the only guy in the sewing class, however, it's easy to get attention. I won the girls over first. They started asking me if I could make them different things. The guys were jealous of the attention the girls were giving me, and a few of them even decided to enroll in the sewing class, too.

Not only had I lost the election, but things at home weren't going quite right, either. Val had graduated as I started ninth grade and had enlisted in the Marines. I felt lost without her for a while. My stepfather, too, still didn't understand my drive for a career in fashion and made it clear that he thought I was wasting my time—how could I possibly think I could become a fashion designer?

I didn't listen to him because I knew there was more out there in the world than this working-class neighborhood. I wanted to explore the world and all the finer things in life, but my goals weren't all about money. I had a passion for fashion, and I was going to make it work. I knew I wasn't meant to live my life under the industrial smokestacks of Elizabeth, New Jersey—just like Barbra Streisand knew as a teenager that she didn't want to live her life in a tenement apartment in Flatbush.

Barbra hadn't let criticism and setbacks stand in her way. She ignored the fact that her stepfather never seemed to like her and that her mother didn't believe she was cut out for a show business career. She tried out repeatedly for a spot in her high school's elite choir, but the director was unimpressed and refused to accept her. Undeterred, Barbra set out to win over the director by actually recording two songs. Armed with this small demo disc, she finally persuaded the director to accept her into the choral club.

When one avenue wouldn't work for Barbra, she would simply find another way to get where she wanted to go. I gained a lot of inspiration from her. I'd listen to her *Funny Girl* album over and over, singing "Don't Rain on My Parade" right along with her.

"How can you wait for your ship to come in if you never send it out?" was my brother Jeffrey's philosophy, and I wholeheartedly agreed with him.

Looking back, I can see that Pete's comments to me were positive in that they only made me more determined to show him. At the time, however, my stepdad and I just weren't getting along and the tension was building. I had a blowout fight with him one day and that was it. I just couldn't take it anymore. I stormed out of the house and took the bus to stay with my brother James for the weekend. James lived in Roselle, five miles away. He sat me down and we talked and talked. James is intelligent and artistic himself, so he understands creative people.

James reminded me that there would always be people ready to give me a hard time. That's just the way life is. Our mom's philosophy, he added, was the same as Martin Luther King's—that you can do anything you set out to do as long as you have an education. James also brought up a quote from Senator Robert Kennedy, who once said, borrowing lines from George Bernard Shaw, "Some men see things as they are and say, Why? But I dream things that never were, and say, Why not?"

He also gave me several books to read on self-esteem that he personally valued. One was *Jonathan Livingston Seagull* by Richard Bach. I really identified with Jonathan's wanting to fly high and being criticized for it. Although ostracized from the other seagulls, Jonathan stuck to his dream and eventually taught the other gulls to fly high, too.

You know, it's the messengers in your life that can make all the difference. People that bring you positive messages usually have a very strong inner peace themselves. That was James. He's very insightful, calming, and analytical. There's a quiet, doctorial way about him. He reads an awful lot and has a wonderful inner spirit. Over the weekend, James went to my parents and had a talk with them, too.

The books that James gave me were fuel for my soul. They were my secret ammunition. After I read those books, which I keep with me to this day, nothing could stop me. Things began to click for me, and I started focusing on Anthony. What would it take for me to be a better player in life? At last, as I concentrated on centering myself, my stepfather didn't irritate me like he used to. When he'd make me mad, I'd just go sew up another creation. I decided that people would either love me for the way I was or they wouldn't. Simple as that.

I also got a lot of inspiration from Bishop Saunders, who was always very good to us. Our family went to his house for prayer service every Tuesday night, and we kids would go over there sometimes after school. If I had a problem in school, I always knew I could go to Bishop Saunders to talk about it.

His house was like a safe haven, and talking to Bishop Saunders and his wife, whom he called "Mother," was like therapy. Under his guidance, I studied the Bible and religion began to have a personal face for me. I've always liked hanging out with older people, anyway, and talking with Bishop Saunders helped me reach for a higher level of spirituality.

Mrs. Saunders sang in her husband's church, and at home, he loved to accompany her beautiful voice with his fine piano playing. They'd invite us to sing along with them and he taught me piano. "What a friend we have in Jesus," they'd sing, loud and clear. I remember he'd often still be wearing his church robes at home. The church was his life, although he did make time to go fishing every morning at the Port of Elizabeth. A big man, at least six foot six, he always rode his bicycle everywhere. I don't remember him ever driving a car.

It was still a strain, though, to be myself when my step-father and others thought I should be something else just because I was a male. I stood my ground, but sometimes it felt like maybe I should be a little more mainstream. I just wasn't interested in the stuff my brothers and stepfather were interested in, however, so there wasn't any use pretending. They'd just have to accept me for who I was.

Besides, I was busy making clothes for what seemed like half the people in Elizabeth. "Anthony, can you make this dress for me?" "Anthony, can you fix these pants for me?" It was exhausting. I was even making outfits for the teachers. I didn't want to say no to anyone, but somehow I managed to get it all done.

Cherub, by this time, had blossomed into a beautiful, graceful swan in high school. I adored her and fantasized about spending the rest of my life with her. We were tight friends and hung out together constantly. I'd often get her to try on my new creations; her beauty and grace as she carefully modeled the gowns made me yearn to have her by my side always.

"Girl, we're going to hit the fashion world together!" I'd tell her. "I'll be the designer and you'll be my top model. We'll do it all together!"

I don't think she took me seriously, but I meant every word. It really was my dream.

10

Team Player

In tenth grade, we all transferred over to the huge campus of Elizabeth High School. There was uniqueness and diversity in our multicultural class. I had gone country western prep by this time, wearing boots, chinos, and camp shirts from L. L. Bean. Even though my fashion style was taming down most days, everyone still anticipated what I'd be dressed in when I entered the classroom.

My sophomore year, I decided not to run for junior class president because my freshman-year campaign defeat still stung as strong as a bee's sting. I was also immersed in so many school activities, including school plays, that I didn't have time to get another campaign going. One year, we did a skit from *Oklahoma!* in which Angie and I played a black version of the lead characters, Laurey and Curly, spoofing the musical's dance routines with our own exaggerated twirls and dips. We also did a hilarious skit that was a take-off on *Airplane!* which we called "Scareplane."

I wanted to do everything I could to develop my portfolio, so I offered to create costumes for the drama department whenever they were gearing up for a new production. Mr. Robert Young directed the drama group in high school, and I'd sketch out costumes and then create them once he had approved them. I made sure the new costumes blended nicely with the rented ones and I was especially proud when my costumes won some awards. It made all the late nights of intensive sewing worthwhile.

My senior year, we put on Shakespeare's *Midsummer Night's Dream*. It was the school's first Shakespeare production, and the faculty didn't know if it would be well attended by the students. To everyone's surprise, it turned out to be one of the most popular productions of the year and even won numerous awards, including one for costuming.

Helping me immensely to perfect my skills was Mrs. Papetti's sewing class. There, I was formally critiqued for the first time and corrected on a lot of my form. It was hard because a lot of the things I had been doing on my own were wrong, but I was excited to be finally learning how to sew correctly. If I hadn't taken her class, I'd probably still be sewing crooked seams.

Mrs. Papetti advised me that if I could sew and understand all the mechanics of each job in the factories, it would greatly aid my career as a designer. She was so right about the importance of learning every part of the industry. The competition to become a designer is tough, and because of that, Mrs. Papetti showed us films once a month that featured all the different jobs in the fashion industry, from the buyers and sellers to the designers, cutters, patternmakers, and textile people. Everyone up and down the fashion career ladder was included.

She also made sure we had access to a lot of research material, so that we'd be able to connect the importance of her sewing class to our professional lives. Mrs. Papetti was wise enough to know that a lot of us could actually carve careers out of sewing-related jobs. She was very career-oriented herself and didn't want to be considered just an old-fashioned sewing teacher there for the benefit of future housewives.

Sometimes, when I felt like I might have to drop her elective class because I was loaded down with required classes, Mrs. Papetti stressed that, with my particular career goals, it was important for me to be able to demonstrate how to execute my ideas, in case they weren't understood verbally or in a pattern. I had to know how to make it all myself. I knew she was right, so I always made sure her class was on my schedule.

I was so proud of the first pair of pants I made in that class. It was a skintight, pull-on pant with no elasticity. It took no less than fifteen minutes of hard tugging to get them on, and then you had to almost sew yourself in to keep them up. Mrs. Papetti, of course, pointed out this impractical aspect of my creation, and, properly chagrined, I had to take it all apart and redesign it.

I always wanted to do things too quickly and Mrs. Papetti had to constantly encourage me to slow down. She taught me how to first follow a pattern and *then* improvise on it—rather than the other way around. I always wanted to change the patterns to create my own original version, but she taught me to first understand what the original patterns called for.

Another aspect of Mrs. Papetti's class was learning how to repair garments. Teachers and friends would bring us their clothes to repair in class and would pay us a certain amount for each item. Whatever money we earned went into a class fund to buy our materials. Some of the kids, like myself, also took extra repair work home for money that we earned for ourselves.

We all got to know Mrs. Papetti very well because she also served as the advisor to our senior class. She followed our class from sophomore year to graduation. I was always in her classroom after hours, using the sewing machine to finish up play costumes, Color Guard uniforms, prom dresses, flags, and everything else. Antoine Blalark, our Color Guard instructor, was also madly sewing there at times. Even the football players would come in with repair requests for their uniforms. Mrs. Papetti loved the attention that Antoine and I brought to her sewing class. We had more students coming to her class than ever before.

I'm forever grateful to Mrs. Papetti because she taught me the basics—the 5/8-inch seam, zippers and sleeves, waistbands, buttonholes, hems. . . . We learned all kinds of tricks that we could do on the sewing machine, like "stitch in a ditch"—an invisible machine stitch that tacks a facing down in a shoulder seam. It's invisible because it's sewn down an already existing seam. I practiced all the aspects of making garments a million times until I could do them in my sleep.

We had so much fun in that class because Mrs. Papetti was wise enough to make sure we made clothes that could be completed in a day and proudly worn the next. We also learned how to make our own clothes from fabric that we chose ourselves. We made pants, tops, dresses, skirts, shorts, prom gowns, and everything else we could find in a pattern.

I wasn't the only one in class who wanted to design his own clothes. It seemed like everybody had original ideas.

Poor Mrs. Papetti: we always wanted to do things differently from the norm in our quest to be junior designers, and she had to help us figure out how to execute our various ideas. I flourished in her class and loved to get everybody else motivated. I was always raring to go.

Antoine was also full of design ideas. He sewed well but needed help getting it all done. He would describe his ideas for uniforms to me and I'd sketch them to create the look he wanted. I also designed a patch for competition for our Color Guard jackets, as well as band uniforms during our junior and senior years. I especially loved the girls' varsity outfits—very retro.

One year, Antoine and I came up with a New Wave design of baggy pants, but these seemed to hide the performers' leg movements too much. We learned from our mistakes and went high-tech the following year: lightweight black jumpsuits with black, gold, and red lamé outlined with sequins. We won awards for some of our costumes.

In the spring of my sophomore year, I inherited a part-time job from Raymond, who was graduating from high school. He had worked as a court administrative assistant in Elizabeth's Union County courthouse, and when Raymond left, he recommended me for the job. I ended up working there in the summers, as well as two days a week during the school year until my senior year. I was on a work-study program and I'd race out of school at noon to get to the courthouse.

In my new job, one of my duties was to order supplies for all the judges and personally deliver them to all the departments. Each judge had his or her own list of preferred supplies. I would also make sure each of their books had the updated dockets, or laws, added to them each year. It was fun working with all the divisions within the court system.

One of my duties was erasing tapes of court business and I'd beat out a whole roomful of those tapes in record time. My boss loved me because I got them done so fast. This task taught me to be detail-oriented—what if I didn't erase them thoroughly? I always made sure I did my job well.

I got the nickname "Roger" at the courthouse because when they asked me to do something, I'd say, "Okay, roger, over and out." I'd always do whatever they asked me to do without complaining or claiming it wasn't in my job description.

When I first started working at the courthouse, Pat Tomei was the person I reported to. She was a young woman, about forty-two years old, who dressed really well. Pat was really cool and she was always there for me. She'd give me motivational books like *All Things Are Possible—Pass the Word,* by Barbara Milo Ohrbach, which contained positive-thinking quotes from famous people past and present. I still have that book in my office today and refer to it often when I need to hear an encouraging word.

If I was a little down about something, Pat was sure to ask, "Is everything okay? Honey, let's go have a soda and talk about it." Once we were sipping our sodas, we'd talk and talk and she'd always find a wonderful thing to say to cheer me up.

Around this time, I was saving up my money to buy a new sewing machine because I was still using my old Singer at home; I really needed a new one with more features on it to work on my portfolio creations. I had my sister's formal prom dress and all these other important projects to do. But it seemed that I never had enough money to buy the new machine. How was I going to get everything done?

One day at work, I was really upset and was crying salty tears to myself because I still couldn't afford to get the new machine. Pat could tell that my spirits had sunk lower than a mole's hole. She stole a few concerned glances at me and said, "Anthony, let's go make some tea and talk."

"What's wrong?" she asked, once we had our hot cups of tea in our hands.

I told her how I needed the new machine to finish the prom dresses I was working on and to prepare my portfolio for my college interviews. I had decided that I really wanted to attend Pratt Institute's School of Design in Brooklyn because, unlike other fashion schools, Pratt had a traditional college campus and I really wanted to experience that. Pratt also had a wonderful reputation and was close to home. I wanted to interview with them ahead of time to make sure I was on the right track. I wasn't going to leave a single stone unturned, so I was determined to show them my portfolio my junior year.

I needed to have certain samples done to get into Pratt, however, and my old machine just wasn't up to the task. I had picked out a new machine that would purr right through these projects, but I just didn't have the money to buy it. I poured out my heart to Pat. Those violin strings were singin', honey. Pat asked me how much the machine was. The model I wanted was $150—a mountain of cash to me at the time.

"Oh, baby, I'll loan you $150!" she exclaimed. "You can just pay me back something every week."

I was shocked and, for once, speechless. It was the first time anyone white had ever given me anything. Pat had nothing to gain, but she loaned me the money anyway.

Once I recovered my voice to thank her, we made our informal loan arrangement and she handed me the money! I raced down to the Singer store and bought the sewing machine I had been salivating over. When I brought the new machine home from the store and set it up in my room, my parents eyed it suspiciously.

"Where'd you get the money for that new sewing machine?" they wanted to know.

"Pat To-mei Gave Me The Money For This Sewing Machine, O-kay?" I said in a firm tone that told them I didn't want to hear that I shouldn't have borrowed the money from Pat. Where there was a will, there was a way—and my friend Pat had helped me find the way.

I had agreed to pay Pat back twenty dollars every week, and each week she'd deduct the amount I paid her from a ledger pad she kept at her desk. Once I had given her the last twenty, she marked the loan "paid in full" and gave me a big hug, along with a little gift—a pink pin cushion. She told me, "Anthony, you'll go real far. You'll make a lot of great things on this machine."

I showed Pat the machine that I had bought and she was so proud of it. She also wanted to see all the gowns I made. I had that sewing machine up until the time I went to Paris and it was lost in customs. I was bummed out when that machine disappeared because it was the first one I ever got on my own.

Anyway, as soon as I had that new machine humming, word got around the courthouse about my sewing aspirations. One day, Judge Frank Fitzpatrick came to me and said, "Anthony, you sew, huh? You want to hem some pants for me?"

That man paid me some big ol' cash to hem pants for him—ten dollars a pair. He was so nice and wanted to help me make some money for school. Pretty soon, everyone at the courthouse was bringing their sewing in for me to work on, as well as articles on fashion design they had saved for me.

When I worked for "Judge" Frank Paul, an assistant to the trial court administrator, he would also put articles about designers on my desk. He was extremely supportive and wonderful to work for. He would ask me to make his bank deposits for him every week—a very big trust. We're talking his personal paycheck. I was to bring him back a certain amount and put the rest in his other accounts. He really trusted me and that meant a lot.

Judge Paul allowed me to do more and more as time went on, and I learned to be very detail-oriented. Every day before work started, he would ask how everything was going for me in school and at home. He also wanted to know if everyone in the courthouse was treating me right. He'd occasionally call my mom and let her know how well I was doing.

The supply cabinet that I used at the courthouse was in Dawn Bowers' office. She and I hit it off great. She was ten years older than me, but we became close friends. I'd show her my sketches, and she commissioned me to make her an evening gown that was black, with a silver top. One sleeve was silver, while the other was black with silver flowers. The hem was also lined with silver.

The gown looked fabulous on her. She turned my head in it, girlfriend. Yes, she did. I even asked Dawn if she'd go with me to my senior prom. She was flattered, saying, "Oh, Anthony, you just made my day! You do realize, though, that I'm ten years older than you and they'll probably think I'm your chaperone."

While Dawn couldn't see herself going to a high school dance, I did bring a bottle of Moët with me later on when

I went to her house to discuss two wool skirts she wanted me to make. We had a great time toasting and sipping.

"This is a good way to make a sale," Dawn told me, laughing, as she sipped the wine. She also commissioned me, for a small fee, to make her a suit dress that was a paisley print with a lace collar and pearl buttons. Dawn told me recently that she still has it today, along with the evening gown I made for her for fifty dollars. Judge Alexander Menza, bless him, told her then, "You know, that dress is easily worth three hundred dollars because it's an original."

Whenever I would get a little depressed that I wasn't advancing fast enough in the fashion field, Dawn would give me a pep talk and remind me to relax, saying, "It's going to take time, Anthony. You're doing fine. Most successful people that you read about are in their forties and you're barely twenty. Be patient. You have to pay your dues, too."

Thanks to Dawn and other friends, people were soon calling quite often to commission me to make them outfits. I'd go over to their houses to discuss what they wanted made. I would make these house calls, with my supplies in a black bag just like Dr. Welby, traveling by foot or public transportation to get there.

As I struggled to raise money through scholarships to attend Pratt, Dawn called the appropriate faculty members and recommended me. Everyone else I knew at the courthouse also looked after me. They wanted to know about my report cards and my plans to attend Pratt. They helped me fill out my financial aid forms for college and gave me financial tips for the future.

"Always save ten percent of everything you make," they advised me.

Even the young hot-shot attorneys were nice to me. They knew the judges liked me, but the attorneys were nice strictly on their own account and were very supportive of my design work. A lot of the courthouse ladies would drive me home during snowstorms, and they gave great birthday parties for me.

Their confidence in me taught me to be a leader. They let me make my own judgments about ordering supplies and I had a lot of autonomy in my job. I enjoyed everyone there and didn't mind working my butt off for them. I always tried to do my best, being careful, for instance, not to interrupt courts in session to deliver supplies.

"You were always a gentleman," they told me.

I'm still in touch with some of my old friends at the courthouse. Judge Paul is retired now, but he called me recently and said, "People don't believe me when I tell them that I knew you, Roger." They were such wonderful people in my life.

11

In the Running

In eleventh grade, I started getting down with a bona fide career path. I knew exactly what I wanted to do and it was time to get totally serious about it. I even toned down my daily fashion statements. In my junior year, my school clothes were totally prep—Izods, button-downs, chinos, and gabardine slacks. I still cut loose and surprised everybody some days, but mostly I wanted people to know I wasn't just out for fun.

I was the only guy in home ec class my junior year, but that didn't bother me. By this time, I didn't get teased about it much because everyone understood that I just had this peculiar talent for creating clothes. Even they realized that my purpose in life had been cosmically chosen for me. I was making clothes for a lot of the students and teachers then, so they all liked what I did anyway.

In sewing class, I really concentrated on the technical work of making garments correctly. I started looking at everything with a critical eye. Where I had always been in a rush just to create, I'd now take the time to do it right. I'd do a hem a hundred times until I got it right. Working at the courthouse had taught me to be patient, methodical, and detail-oriented, like the law clerks and the judges. In anything you do, I learned, you should take the time to do your homework and make the right decisions.

When I was sixteen, I really started making garments that people would cherish—beautiful dresses with yards and yards of gorgeous fabrics. I considered myself an inventor of gowns. That feeling of invention is still with me today. I created a prom gown inspired by Elsa Schiaparelli for my friend Meredith Hyman which I called the "Vamp" dress. It took me a month to complete this one, and while we were involved with the fittings, I got to know her boyfriend Emil Nems, whose family was to greatly help me in just a few short years.

The Vamp dress had a black sequined bustier, with rhinestones, colored stones, and appliqués of fuchsia, red, emerald, and purple scattered throughout the bodice. I made hot pants for it out of black taffeta that had "attitude wings" on the cuffs. Attached to the back of the hot pants on a snap was a big Darth Vader cape, out of black taffeta, that went from the waist to the floor. The sleeves were black leather gauntlet gloves. *Very* vampish. Wearing that dress, Meredith was just *gone*. She looked stunning in it.

It also took me a month to complete a new prom dress for Angie, which was inspired by none other than Lena Horne's gowns in the movie *Stormy Weather*. Child, I loved Lena Horne in anything. Whenever I felt lost, like Dorothy in the land of Oz, I'd visualize Lena in her role as Glenda the Good Witch in *The Wiz* coming to my rescue. I imagined her as my guardian angel—one who could belt out

"Stormy Weather" like no one else on the face of the planet.

I created my own patterns for the gown, which was a sweet creation of white chiffon and organza with an illusion sweetheart neckline, a cathedral collar, and tapered, puff angel sleeves. The sheer sleeves were covered with rhinestones that formed a peacock pattern. The full-bodied, fitted bodice came down to the high hip and was covered with silver rhinestones. The arc of the bodice formed two half-moon shapes from which cascaded yards and yards of chiffon.

At the bottom of the skirt was a gathered ruffle, and underneath the chiffon were layers and layers of organdy and tulle so that the dress stood out. The challenge was sewing on the fifty-two pearl buttons down the center back of the gown. I used to put pearls on everything back then. For this gown, Angie wore long pearl earrings and a crown of roses in her hair. Then, to complete the ensemble, I made a fan of roses and lace for her to hold. Angie looked like a beautiful bride in this dress.

I also made a gown for Cherub which had a Grecian neckline that draped from shoulder to shoulder out of slippery purple charmeuse. The dress came down in a wonderful, fitted column with very simple, clean lines. The sleeves were all purple and gold velvet burnout on chiffon. There was no back to the gown, but I created a gold lamé cocoon cape that just wrapped around her body. It was fabulous, dahling, and Cherub looked fabulous in it.

She and I were spending a lot of time together, although her parents didn't allow her to officially date yet. We'd laugh all the time, talk on the phone for hours, and write notes to each other in class. We were confidants. Cherub sat in front of me in some of our classes, and I couldn't keep my hands out of her beautiful hair. She was tall and thin, with long, curly hair and a beautiful exotic look that brought out the best of her mixed family heritage—a background that included black, East Indian, Portuguese, and South American ancestry. Cherub was shy, so her parents, hoping to bring her out of her shell, enrolled her in modeling school. Aunt Brenda also encouraged her to model to help build her confidence.

Angie, like Cherub, was fast becoming an attractive girl, and in high school Raymond and I were keeping a sharp eye out for her. She didn't know it then, but Raymond had warned all the guys on his football team not to even THINK about messing around with his sister. I also kept an eye out for guys who might be setting their sights on Angie. She never could figure out why the guys she liked never seemed to like her. She thought it must be because she was unattractive. The guys were definitely interested in Angie but knew they'd face serious repercussions if they tried to make time with her.

When Angie and I entered the main high school as sophomores, Raymond thought he'd head off the tide of male interest in Angie by fixing her up with someone he personally approved of. He handpicked a guy from the football team whom he thought was suitable for Angie to date and brought his friend home to meet his sister. Raymond's plan didn't work, however; Angie wasn't very receptive to the poor guy he'd chosen. She might have been a little shy, but she wasn't going to let Raymond pick her dates for her.

Angie soon found her own romantic interest. She and Juan Guzman became good friends and dated through high school. Juan was a nice guy whom we grudgingly approved of. From time to time, however, they'd have a fight and Juan would need a little help in smoothing things over with her. I'd coach Juan on what Angie would like and give him tips on how to relight the romantic flame.

"Buy her flowers and put them in her locker," I would whisper to him in the school hallway after I found out that Angie, in a huff, had left him standing alone in her wake. I'd tell him what kind of flowers she liked and what kind of music she'd melt to. Juan had his work cut out for him. Angie may have been quiet, but she was opinionated—definitely not a pushover for an easy relationship.

Meanwhile, I was crazy about Cherub. I told her again that I planned on marrying her when I graduated. Since we were only about sixteen years old, she just laughed and didn't believe that I was serious. But I was. I thought about her constantly and she was always in my future plans. If I was going to Paris in my dreams, she was walking down the Champs-Élysées with me.

For the time being, however, I had to settle with just going to the junior prom with my love. Cherub and I had a great time, and as we danced, she looked like a princess. The theme song of the prom was "Almost Paradise," which had been recorded by Mike Reno and Ann Wilson, and every time I hear that song today, I still think of Cherub, looking like an ethnic Audrey Hepburn in *Sabrina*, dancing the night away.

Audrey Hepburn also inspired the dress I created for Angie that same year for our winter formal. Mr. Wolper had this gorgeous black brocade displayed in a glass case in his fabric store. This material was so expensive that no one had ever bought it. I'd bet it was probably twelve dollars a yard. I was salivating for that fabric for Angie's gown, which had a velvet bustier with rhinestones, along with a brocade skirt and a big taffeta bow for texture. I showed

Mr. Wolper my sketch of the dress and he loved it. He made me quite a deal on the brocade, essentially giving me the whole bolt for twelve dollars! I was ecstatic.

Angie and Juan had broken up for a short period, so she and I planned to go to the winter formal together. Mr. Wolper wanted to know what I was going to wear myself. I told him that I had planned to rent a tux. Oh, no, no, no, he said. I had to make myself at least a jacket to match her gown. Inspired, I made myself a whole black brocade suit.

Angie and I felt like Krystle and Blake Carrington, from *Dynasty,* at the winter formal. We danced with everyone and kept the deejay spinning LPs till way into the night. To our surprise, we were selected king and queen of the ball, and I was honored that Mrs. Papetti was the one who crowned us.

Angie and I were two of the best dancers on the block. We'd do the hustle all the time, as well as other dances we learned from watching *Soul Train* and *American Bandstand.* We knew all the twirls, turns, and dips that you could shake a stick at. Fred Astaire and Ginger Rogers had nothing on us.

I noticed that the top dancers on *Soul Train* often wore bizarre styles. Only in California, I thought, could you get away with dressing so abstract and wild like that. The Pointer Sisters were hot, too, with their white handkerchiefs and forties retro look. I first saw them when they appeared in the movie *Car Wash.* Man, they were sizzlin' in that film.

While I was in the school library one day talking to Mrs. Maynard, she introduced me to another student, a sophomore named Eddie Wilchins. Eddie and I found out we had a lot of friends in common. His main interest was studying music, since he was a gifted jazz and rock guitarist, but when I found out he also loved looking at *GQ* magazine, we connected and talked about men's fashions for hours. We became great friends.

Our principal, Dominic Parisi, who was like a father to everyone, allowed me to use the gym auditorium to put on a fashion show that year. Eddie helped me produce it, and we enlisted Cherub and other girlfriends to be the models. Fellow students also helped us with the music and creation of the backdrop, while my friends Garth Bracey and Willie Sierra volunteered to be the photographers for the show. I was a whirlwind of activity, child—the Energizer bunny couldn't even keep up. We had a great turnout, and I was proud of our efforts.

By my junior year, I had become involved in so many school activities that everyone knew me, or at least knew who I was. Mr. Parisi encouraged me to run for senior class president, and my opponent was a friend named David. The competition, though, put stress on our friendship. He wanted me to drop out of the race, but I knew it was my turn to shine. The student body seemed to be pulling for me to win the election, so this campaign was one that I really enjoyed. I made signs and the usual promotional baubles with campaign slogans on them that said, "I'm Not Here for Fun or Fashion—All I Want Is a Little Bit of Action!"

By now, I was known as "Happenin' Hankins," and when it was time to give our campaign speeches, I couldn't resist "dressing" for it. I came on stage wearing these baggy black harem pants with a green satin shirt—my Yul Brynner outfit. I had relaxed enough about myself to have more of a sense of humor when it came to student politics. I didn't take it any less seriously, you understand, but I wasn't afraid to inject a little outrageousness into it. It sure helped get the students' attention. Listening to a guy give a speech in silk harem pants is not something you forget in ten minutes.

I socked it to 'em, though, girlfriend. I was drama personified. During that speech, I was like Elizabeth Dole in the '96 Republican campaign: I went down into the trenches and talked with the troops. I worked that crowd like a bad rag. I'd go right up to an old friend and say in a rap staccato, "Madinah Hawkins, you've known me forevah. I'm here for ya, so who could be against ya?"

Even though I won the election this time, I also won a severe case of the hives. I suppose I had taken on just too much, even for me. In addition to the excitement and stress of organizing the campaign, I was still extremely busy with extracurricular activities and nervous about being accepted into Pratt. I really, really wanted to go to Pratt. I put everything I had into my portfolio and then some.

The stress in my life was starting to show up in itchy physical symptoms. The hives wrapped around my middle, and Mom had to buy me all-cotton shirts so my tortured skin could breathe. Even though my body was constantly on fire from the hives, I still managed to keep working at the courthouse. It was awful, though. Lord knows how I suffered.

Hives aside, good things still continued to happen during my junior year. Nancy Shields did an article on me for the local newspaper, the *Daily Journal,* with the headline DESPITE SOME NEEDLING, HE HAS DESIGNS FOR BETTER LIVING. I remember that headline! She talked about all my activities and expressed amazement that I still had creativity left for fashion design. It was a front-page article, and I was so proud when Judge Paul congratulated me with, "Way to go, Roger!"

I was so determined to be successful as a designer that I gave out cards to friends at school to be redeemed when I had achieved my goal. The cards read something like, "I'm going to be a famous fashion designer someday, and when I make it, I'll make your wardrobe for free." I wonder if anyone kept those cards.

Kevin took me to Pratt for my admissions interview, and I had his car stuffed with my creations. Honey, that car was weighted down. I took fifteen to twenty suit bags hung on several portable wardrobe racks. Each suit bag probably contained over six pieces. I also had my portfolio, résumé, recommendations, school records, and everything else with me. I was nervous but exhilarated.

For the interview, I was wearing what I called my "uniform" back then—black slacks, a black jacket I had made, black shoes, and a white top. Even now, I love to wear this combo when I'm on the road putting on trunk shows. It's a great clean look and hides nervous perspiration well. Lord knows I needed that protection on this particular day.

This trip was the first time I had gone to New York by car, since I usually took the train. I enjoyed seeing the sights, like the city's skyline and the Brooklyn Bridge. We pulled up to the Ivy League–looking gates of Pratt and I took a deep breath. I had spent quite a bit of time working on my portfolio and sample boards preparing for this moment. I had asked everyone I knew for their opinion, but now the only thing that mattered was how the Pratt officials would react to them.

It took both of us to wheel it all in for my interview with Pratt's admissions director, a casually dressed black guy who reminded me of Smokey Robinson with glasses. He was stunned to see my extensive presentation, which included band uniforms, prom gowns, dress suits, sports-wear, and everything else I had created. It filled the room and threatened to spill out into the hallway. I proudly took him through every phase of my fashions.

When I had finished with my presentation, I waited breathlessly for the director's response. He told me he was very interested in my work, and then I heard the magic words: "Come back when you're ready and we'll get you in."

I was accepted! I was the happiest guy in the world. Kevin and I finished out the afternoon touring the campus. Now I could breathe without a respirator during my senior year because I knew I had already been accepted into a major fashion school.

Junior year quickly faded into summer. On a peaceful Sunday morning in July, as my mother was preparing to go to church, the phone rang. I was upstairs but heard my mother loudly groaning, "Oh, no. . . ." I knew instantly that someone in the family had either died or been severely injured in an accident. I wondered if the call could be about Uncle Johnny, who was suffering with cancer.

To our shock, Grandmother Toy had passed away. Invincible Grandmother Toy. . . . How could she possibly be gone? In my mind, that concept was not in the realm of possibility, but it had happened. My grandmother had fallen in her house, and although she had no outward injuries, she had passed away in her sleep that afternoon. She was sixty-four years old.

Mom was heartbroken and hurried on to church to pray for Grandmother Toy. I worked through my sadness by making Mom a black skirt with a black and white blouse to wear to the funeral in Virginia. It was strange to be at Grandmother Toy's house a few days later and not have her heading up the family table. Her funeral service was held at the old country church she had always attended, even though the temperature inside felt like 110 degrees from the sweltering summer sun. Mom, although she grieved, remained composed and carried herself with a quiet, stoic dignity that I think is typical of Southern women. It's not proper to lose emotional control in public.

Still, how could she and her sisters finalize my grandmother's life so calmly? It was hard for me to accept then, but as I've gotten a little older, I've come to realize that death is just another phase of life. I knew Grandmother Toy was at peace, but I still missed her profoundly. I wasn't the only one, of course. After she died, her companion, Nelson, was heartbroken and he soon followed her into heaven.

Senior year, my relationship with Cherub had been on my mind constantly and I really wanted her to know just how much she meant to me. At the end of gym class one day, when everyone was lining up at the door to escape to their next class, I suddenly got down on one knee to her and proclaimed, "Cherub, you're the love of my life and I want you to marry me."

Cherub was stunned, to say the least, and I could hear students whispering in shocked tones behind me.

"Anthony, this isn't the time or the place!" Cherub cried, when she finally found her voice. She pulled me up and fled for the door where the other kids were filing out. I trailed after her, hoping she'd respond in kind to my heartfelt declaration. Cherub, embarrassed by my sudden confession, simply pretended that it hadn't happened as she made her way into the hallway. I looked after her helplessly, wanting to plead my case, but she hurried off to her classes, trying to avoid the gossipy whispering that was still buzzing all around us. I loved her, though, and I didn't care if the whole school knew.

Since we had different classes after gym, we had to go our separate ways. For the next few days, we avoided seeing each other, but after that things returned to normal and we just pretended it had never happened. I didn't tell Eddie about it, but he knew that I was a little down about something. When Eddie and the other guys went to New York City to cruise for chicks, I preferred to stay home and work on my projects.

I loved my friends and school work, my goals were set in my mind, but something still wasn't quite right with my life. I'd always been different, and while I enjoyed being a "singular sensation," sometimes it weighed heavily on my mind that I couldn't be more like everyone else.

Eddie sensed that something was eating away at me. He pushed me to accept myself for who I was. I had a right to be what I wanted to be and what I was born to be, Eddie told me. In order to be balanced in my self and career, he advised, I had to make peace with it. He encouraged me to continue pursuing my dream and not be concerned about what other people might think of my unusual style and drive.

As senior class president, I worked on a beautification program with the city; arranged for our class to go to the Statue of Liberty and Ellis Island, which had just been restored as a museum; worked with the Board of Education closely; and planned pep rallies and get-togethers. It was a hard year since I was juggling so many projects.

A "B" student, I had a moment of panic as a senior when I learned that members of the National Honor Society would get special recognition at graduation. Oh, God, I thought, as senior class president, I should be earning that. I set out to make sure it happened and spoke out so that other students would also be informed early in their high school years about the requirements of the National Honor Society. This was a roster I wanted to make sure I was on.

I also fought to change the location of our senior prom since it was going to be three major highways away from the school. It was a frustrating fight, and many times I was in danger of losing my cool over it. I was ultimately on the losing end of this issue, and I was tempted to let a few people in the school know the anger I felt about the situation.

Before I could let the volcano inside me erupt, however, Mrs. Mayner calmed me with her usual words of wisdom. She taught me that there is always a mature way to go about trying to change things, and she'd slow me down whenever I got too hyper or excited—reminding me that I should always behave like a professional and a gentleman.

When Mrs. Mayner felt I was going overboard on an issue, she'd take me aside and say, "Now, listen, Anthony, be careful how you treat people. The people you pass on the way up are the same people you pass on the way down."

Another one of my goals for senior year was to be voted "Best Dressed" in our yearbook. Everyone knew this contest was really between me and my friend David Mitchell, who was our senior class vice president. David was a spectacular dresser, and we had a good-natured but intense rivalry to be named "Best Dressed."

People told me I was going to win because my opponent's shoes were sometimes scuffed up. I wore beautiful clothes all year, honey. There was no way I was going to get on Blackwell's list. Every two weeks, when I got my paycheck from the courthouse, I'd go right to my favorite stores to buy some clothes or fabric. My efforts paid off—I won the "Best Dressed" distinction for posterity.

All too soon, though, it was the end of senior year. We quickly filled the pages of our yearbooks with personal notes and letters from friends and teachers. At the courthouse, Pat Tomei asked me what I needed for school at Pratt. I thought about it for a moment and realized I could use a trunk to store all my supplies in my new dorm room.

"Oh," she replied casually. "Well, maybe you'll get that."

A week later, Pat and my other friends at the courthouse threw a graduation party for me and I received a beautiful trunk, along with a lot of sewing supplies. I was so touched. These were such great friends and I was really going to miss them.

While I had been accepted into Pratt, Angie had chosen a different path. Jeffrey and James had both gone into the Army after high school, while Raymond had enlisted in the Air Force. Angie was an outstanding student but was afraid she couldn't afford college. Restless and ready to see the world, she delayed college by enlisting for four years in the Air Force. I think Mom was relieved that her baby girl was going to be in such a highly structured environment after she left home. I'm sure she thought Uncle Sam would take good care of Angie.

Our graduation ceremony was held in our high school's huge gym. I gave a welcome speech to everyone and then nervously tripped over the words to "The Pledge of Allegiance." Still, Mom sat very tall in the audience, beaming with pride. She had been determined that all of her children graduate from high school, and she had helped us meet that goal. Anything we did after that, she often told us, would be extra icing on the cake for her.

As I watched Angie and all my senior friends walk down the aisle to receive their diplomas, moving their tassels to the other side of their mortarboards in the traditional "pomp and circumstance" rituals, I couldn't help feeling sad that our childhood was officially over. It was time to grow up. I was scared but determined to succeed in life. In my head, I kept singing the words from Mary Tyler Moore's television theme song, which gave me the courage to believe that, like Mary, I was going to make it after all.

12

Life at Pratt

Angie left home in July, bound for six weeks of basic training in San Antonio. It was the first time in our lives that we had been apart from each other, but in a way, we were both ready to develop our individuality. I had always been the mouthpiece for the two of us, so now it was time for Angie to exercise her own voice. Even though it was sometimes hard to deal with the fact that we were no longer together, it was our chance to explore the world and we were excited.

I looked forward to my first fall at Pratt and concentrated on earning money for school. After a busy summer running my own little sewing shop in a space the Singer store allocated to me, it was time to pack up my sewing machine and move to the campus for my first year of college. I had never been away from home for very long at all, so I had to take a deep breath and just do it. I was ready for an adventure but glad to know, too, that Brooklyn wasn't that far from Elizabeth.

Checking into my tiny dorm room, I quickly unpacked my footlocker that my friends at the courthouse had given me for graduation. I set up my sewing machine and planned to make money by offering to alter clothes for the other students. I was determined to be the best fashion major there ever was at Pratt.

I arranged everything in my dorm room with the utmost care. Growing up, I was somewhat obsessed with organization. Angie can testify that even my socks were organized in neat little rows in my dresser drawer—all arranged by color, with each pair in individual Baggies.

On the second day of school, I had to register for my classes. At orientation, I was standing in a long line for my classes in this huge gym when I spied a gorgeous girl with beautiful olive skin and long dark hair standing with her father on the other side of the gym. While I was wearing funky clothes, this very wealthy-looking girl was wearing an Adidas warm-up suit and Jack Purcell sneakers—but no socks, just like me. Both she and her father just radiated class.

Normally, I would have assumed she'd be out of my league, but somehow I instantly knew "that girl" and I were going to be great friends. I don't know why I thought this. I had no idea what major she was because she was already through registering. Yet I noticed her out of hundreds of people, and I knew.

I also knew she was going to help me emotionally get through school. We were going to weather all the storms together. She just had that look on her face of someone who really cares. When I looked at this girl, I could see her inner soul. I felt like we had known each other in another life. She knew it, too, because she noticed me as well and flashed me a big, knowing smile. Somehow, our souls recognized each other.

We didn't meet then, but sure enough, she was in my first class, which was "Light, Color, and Design," on Monday morning. She introduced herself immediately. Her name was Andrea Antonioni. She was a fashion major, too, and we were to be in almost all the same classes our freshman year.

At the end of our first class session, the instructor told us that we needed to pick up our supplies at a certain art store, Canal Paint, on Canal Street in New York City. I was going to have to take the train to get there, but Andrea immediately offered to give me a lift in her car, which turned out to be a convertible VW.

As we drove to the store, I confessed to Andrea that I thought we had a soul connection—I had felt it in the gym during orientation when I had first seen her. I shouldn't have been surprised when she confessed, too, that she had sensed the same thing—so strongly that she had mentioned it to her father.

"Now, there's a brother who's on target," she told me she had thought that day. "I loved your haircut and the way you were dressed. I knew you'd be a cool person."

Needless to say, Andrea and I became inseparable friends. She's still one of my best friends—so giving and caring. Originally from Argentina, Andrea had been raised in Connecticut. Even though her family was wealthy, she was a superhard and dedicated worker who wasted nothing. Andrea made her own money, working as a waitress in a diner.

In friendships, everyone brings something to the table, and Andrea brought organization and thriftiness. She helped me learn how to stretch my meager budget for supplies even further. Andrea had beautiful supplies that she shared freely. Until I met her, I wasn't artistically organized. Andrea had a sketch pad for shoes and separate ones for blouses, pants, dresses, and accessories.

She helped me with my sketches, and I did all her English essays for her. She'd make A+ on them, while I'd make B's. I never figured that out, except that she had beautiful handwriting and I guess the power is in the pen. For fun, we'd dress up and go out on the town imitating all the big-time designers. Child, we had attitude, attitude, attitude.

One of our instructors was Michael Renzuli, who was a great teacher. Mr. Renzuli had worked with a lot of design companies, so he knew what he was talking about. He was an inspiring, life-altering person. He taught us that a designer is a director who is in charge of everything, so he asked us all to make believe that we were already designers. It was obvious to everyone that Andrea was a great patternmaker and just a natural for this industry.

Mr. Renzuli taught us a lot about respecting the soul of the fabric. "When we cut the fabric with scissors," he would tell us, "we're breathing life into it—giving birth to it."

Andrea and I took our "birthing" of the fabric very seriously and often worked together since we were on the same wavelength. We inspired each other all the time. With her fiery Latin background and my naturally high rpm's, our combined energy was so strong it was almost like spontaneous combustion! Work sleeves rolled up, we'd be immersed in our projects for hours on the floor of my dorm room, surrounded by our patterns, tracing paper, toolboxes, straight pins, and fabric.

One day, we left our mess on the floor to go grab a quick bite to eat in the cafeteria. When we returned, we were shocked to find that my roommate, Ian, was working on his own art project and had spilled plaster of paris all over the floor, dangerously close to our fabrics! We freaked out. What if our projects had been ruined?! We discovered that Ian's mess had indeed damaged a corner of Andrea's material. While Ian and I got along as friends, his habitual sloppiness really worked on my nerves. After this incident in which he almost ruined our projects, I moved to another dorm room.

During my first semester at Pratt, I also worked at WilliWear, designer Willi Smith's company, for a two-month nonpaying internship, and it went really well. Willi Smith was a young African-American designer from Philadelphia who had started his own company in 1976. I was in awe of Willi, who was one of the industry's most successful black designers. I found him to be a very warm, understanding person, and I am thankful that I had the chance to know him before his untimely death due to an AIDS-related illness in 1987.

Mark Bozek was my boss at WilliWear. He was so nice and classy—tall, handsome, and very well groomed with tortoise-rimmed glasses. He was very conscientious and would sit down with me to talk or come by often to make sure I was doing okay.

At WilliWear, one of my duties was to list all the fabrics and styles we were working with on "war boards." I also assisted in planning the line, developed sweater packets to go to the Orient, and sat in on fabric meetings. Even though I was just a college student, I was often asked for my thoughts and opinions on projects, and that meant a lot to me.

At school, Andrea and I noticed a poster about the Fashion Society on campus and we both decided to join. The society held a fashion show every year at Pratt, so Andrea and I worked as a design team to create gowns for the show. Our gowns included a black column sensation with a side sash and bow, along with avant-garde creations in balloon and mushroom shapes. Andrea modeled one of our ball gowns on the runway and she looked gorgeous.

I met her parents at the fashion show. Her father was a vice president of Latin-American affairs for IBM, and her mother had been a famous model in Paris. They had a beautiful house then in Greenwich, Connecticut, and her parents invited me to visit them. Paul Newman and Diana Ross were neighbors of theirs, so you can imagine how fabulous their house was. I love her family and still talk regularly with them.

Even though we were just freshmen, Andrea and I soon became top officers in the Fashion Society, all because of a drag queen's busy schedule. That's the honest truth. A gay guy I'll call Spencer and a friend of his were in charge of the society at that time. Spencer's specialty was impersonating Grace Jones singing "Slave to the Rhythm" and "La Vie en Rose." He was actually very good at it and performed as a drag queen all over New York. His friend helped him backstage with his costuming, hair, and makeup.

Spencer had his own *La Cage aux Folles* thing going, honey. He would compare notes with Andrea on everything from makeup to panty hose and bras, and he'd often ask to borrow our gowns for his performances. Andrea and I soon found ourselves dressing drag queens! It was hysterical. When Spencer's performance schedule became so demanding that he and his friend didn't have time for their official duties as officers of the Fashion Society, they handed their titles to Andrea and me since we were so active within the organization.

As officers of the Fashion Society, Andrea and I would produce fashion shows to raise money for the society's activities. We'd stay up late in the studios, working on our own creations and helping others create their fashions for these productions. Sometimes we'd be laboring away until 3:00 A.M. Juniors at Pratt were expected to create three pieces for the major fashion show the school held at the end of the year, including lingerie, sportswear, and career wear. Seniors are expected to create at least five pieces—three sportswear samples and two evening-wear samples. It's a grueling student schedule.

While Andrea and I were soul mates at school, her heart was already taken by Gregory Sebaoun, a young French student she'd met in high school while he was in her hometown as an exchange student. He had gone back to France at this time, and Andrea missed him terribly. She'd come crying to me when they hit lows in their relationship.

I always told her she had plenty of time for Mr. Greg. Now, however, she needed to concentrate on school. When I finally had a chance to meet Greg, Andrea warned me beforehand that he was typically French—distant at first with people he didn't know well. Greg and I liked each other immediately, though. He loved the fact that I made Andrea laugh so much.

One night, as I was getting ready to join Andrea and some other friends to celebrate my birthday, there was a knock on my door. A female cop, who looked tough as nails, asked for Anthony Hankins. I identified myself and she told me that I was under arrest for stealing designs from WilliWear!

I was stunned—how could anyone accuse me of something like that?! "No, no, no—something's wrong—I didn't do that!" I muttered, in shock, as she handcuffed me right in front of everyone I knew in the dorms. It seemed that in this horrible moment, all of my friends were standing in front of my door. My life was flashing in front of my eyes. This had to be a case of mistaken identity, but such a mistake could ruin my career plans!

The cop ordered me to sit down while she asked me some questions. Suddenly, a chair appeared in the hallway and the cop handcuffed me to it. What was going on? As I opened my mouth to protest my innocence to the cop, I noticed a strange grin on Andrea's face. Wait a minute. What is this?

The crowd in the hallway was getting thicker, as strip music started and this bogus female member of New York's Finest began to bump and grind in front of me, slowly removing her blouse! As part of her routine, the stripper lit matches that were attached to her nipples, and as the honoree, I was supposed to blow them out. I'm sure my face turned all shades of fuchsia. I knew Andrea had been in on the stripper caper, and I shot her a look that told her she was dead meat.

While I enjoyed my internship at WilliWear, I needed to find a job that paid. Susan Jones, the dean of the School of Fashion, told me that New York designer Homer Layne, who had studied with the legendary couturier Charles James, was looking for an intern for a paid position. It was haute couture work and Homer was very particular, she said. I'd need to show him some of my garments that involved intricate sewing.

"You're a good sewer," Susan told me, "but Homer has strict standards."

I knew Susan was telling me the truth about Homer Layne. Other people had told me he was very picky, picky, picky. . . . He was supposedly really difficult. Homer had the rights to the Charles James ball gowns and was responsible for taking care of the Charles James collection at the Brooklyn Museum.

I had read about Charles James, who had died in 1978. In the 1940s and 1950s, James was considered the greatest American couturier—a dressmaker without par who raised fashion from an applied art form to a pure art form. That was how his professional equal, Christóbal Balenciaga, was reported to have described Charles James. He was a genius who approached the craft of dressmaking with an extreme attention to detail. Charles James was America's answer to the couture geniuses in Paris.

Homer Layne himself had won a lot of awards, and anyone who worked for him really had to be on their toes. I needed an internship that paid well, however, and this job paid ten to fourteen dollars an hour, so I really wanted it. Susan set up an appointment for me to meet with Homer Layne in his studio at the Chelsea Hotel.

On the way to meet him for the first time, I was really, really nervous. I took three of the best ball gowns I had made for Pratt—a balloon dress with a column skirt, a black taffeta ballgown, and a prom dress with pearl beading on it. I was afraid, though, that Homer wouldn't like them. With his sophistication, he'd probably consider them too juvenile and frivolous.

As I traveled across town on the subway's G train from Brooklyn, weighted down with suit bags filled with taffeta and beading, I kept envisioning that Homer Layne, as a bona fide heir to the world of haute couture, would be working in his New York atelier, which, of course, would be a supercool, upscale designer space.

When I got to the Chelsea Hotel on West Twenty-third Street, between Seventh and Eighth avenues, where

Homer Layne had his studio, I was surprised to see that it was an old, archaic hotel that had been turned into an apartment building. The lobby was furnished with faded, musty furniture and threadbare curtains. I took a surprised breath as I entered the lobby and surveyed its tired ambience. This place had definitely seen better days.

Asking for Homer Layne at the hotel desk, I was directed to the fifth floor to find his apartment. There, I found a note on his door for me: "Anthony, I went to the museum. Will be back soon. Homer." I noticed his handwriting was very nice and neat.

The hallway air was stale and stuffy, so I decided to wait for him outside on the hotel steps. When Homer arrived to meet with me, I was surprised to see that he looked very proper and British—like the Monopoly man—with his raincoat neatly draped over his arm. He had a little mustache and seemed to be in his mid-forties. He was five foot five, with a receding hairline, sandy brown hair, blue eyes, and about a thirty-six-inch waist. He fiddled with his keys to get into the door and invited me to follow him in.

His apartment served as a small working studio as well as his residence. The first thing I saw was a large cutting table with big grids on it. In the living area, there were two sewing machines—with a cat nestled on one. I also noticed a radio, several mannequins, a desk, and a sofa that I later learned had belonged to Charles James, along with a big-screen TV. Some of the apartment's furnishings and antiques, though, were covered with dust sheets.

The sound of classical music from the radio filled the apartment. I looked at this eccentrically filled space and wondered what I was getting into by applying for an internship here. As I took in the details of Homer Layne's studio, he studied my portfolio and the prom gowns I had lugged all across New York City to show him. Every once in a while, I would hear him comment to himself, "Oh, this is interesting. . . ." Was he finding my work just "interesting" with a boring period after the word—or "interesting!" with an exclamation point?

I tried not to disturb his concentration as he looked over everything I had brought, and hoped he didn't notice that I was trying not to fidget nervously. I heard him mutter, "My, my, my . . ." as he inspected the ball gowns I had created. What did "My, my, my" mean on a scale of one to ten? Was he impressed with my work or just trying to let me down gently?

To my relief, Homer offered me the internship, and I was thrilled. He warned me that the hours would be long and tedious, but I didn't mind that. I knew I'd be learning a lot about the craft of haute couture from working with Homer Layne. I had heard that he was a wiz at patternmaking, for instance, and that everything he did was very accurate and precise.

At first, I was nervous about working with Homer, but he really wasn't intimidating at all. My impression of him was that he was very much like a Southern gentleman. I found out later that he actually was from the South originally. He reminded me of a Felix Unger type from *The Odd Couple*—very proper and accommodating but not outgoing at all. Homer was a laid-back teddy bear who never copped an "I am the designer" attitude.

I also found out he loved cats and dolls, just like me. He even talked about being raised on a farm. Homer always filled his studio with fresh gardenias and classical music; because of him, I grew to appreciate these things.

I'd work with Homer all day on Fridays and Saturdays, then part-time during the week after school. The hours were indeed long and grueling. On the weekends, I'd sometimes work from 8:30 A.M. until 9:30 P.M. or 11:00 P.M. After school, I might work from four o'clock until midnight. Homer was working on some Revlon commercials for Bradford C. Moody, a young designer from Texas who was in charge of a collection of gowns for Bergdorf Goodman. Bradford had commissioned Homer to create all these gowns because Bradford's style was a lot like Charles James'.

I ran errands for Homer, picked up trim, pressed and prepped garments, answered the phone, made patterns, and cut fabrics—learning Homer's precise system. Barbra Streisand's rendition of "Putting It Together," the Stephen Sondheim song from her *Broadway* album, was often running through my head, and like the song says, I really realized that every contribution definitely has its importance in the scheme of things. There was no unimportant task in the creation of these gorgeous gowns.

After a while, I also started doing some design work for him, as well as preparing fabrics, sketching, and sewing. As we worked, Homer would explain how everything was done in a gentle, singsong voice, saying, "This is the way we do it. . . ." He would also tell me stories about the demanding and mercurial Charles James.

Homer, too, was a challenge in his own quiet way. He had all these different techniques and rules, many of which involved a lot of hand-sewing. He would hand-knot every finished seam, for instance. He wouldn't just backstitch to finish it. Such meticulous work took hours upon hours to complete.

Before I started working with him, I was always rushing and taking on more than I really could, doing more than I was asked to and never really understanding what I was doing. I was just going through the motions. Like Mrs. Papetti, here was someone who explained everything. Everything had its purpose. This is really important, especially when you're a creative entity. All that energy needs to be focused and channeled.

Through my work with Homer, I was also able to meet some of New York's finest citizens. Maria Cuomo, Mario Cuomo's daughter, came in one day with her business partner, Judith Agisim, to meet with Homer. Their company was called C&A Associates and they handled Homer's public relations. Maria was a very beautiful uptown girl, chic and tanned. She wore very little makeup and her nails were polished, with a French manicure. She wore a fitted green avant-garde dress that was Italian-looking and of very good quality—accessorized with pearls and black, expensive-looking shoes.

As they settled in for the meeting, Maria suddenly realized that she hadn't put enough money in the meter for her car. I offered to run down and put the money in the meter for her. She really appreciated it and started chatting with me when I got back. She asked me what I wanted to do career-wise, and I told her my fashion plans.

Even though her father was the governor of New York then, Maria didn't have an attitude. Always very cheerful and unpretentious, she kept a very low profile. With her quiet personality, she usually let Judith do all the talking. Judith was very outgoing and just all over the place— charming, engaging, always with a pleasant smile on her face. She and Maria both appreciated high fashion and loved to survey Homer's creations when they were visiting. They were tremendously supportive.

"Homer, what are you making?" they'd ask. "Let's see it. Oh, my God, how fabulous!"

After three months of seeing Maria and Judith on a weekly basis, we got to know one another and they gave me recommendations of people I should contact in the fashion industry. I took those recommendations and I networked, child! I worked that phone and went to every event—invited or not. My goal was to meet as many people in the industry as possible, and I probably worked it twenty times harder than most people.

I figured that if I could get into one cocktail party, I could get invited to three more from that—especially with my gift of gab. I talked my way into high-society parties, girlfriend. Yes, I did. I made some great contacts at these soirees. Even when I didn't feel like going to events, I made myself go and made sure I came home with a stack of business cards. I found that it was easy to network as long as you smiled and were excited about what you were doing.

I networked everywhere, even in my hometown. I stayed on campus during the week but liked to go home on weekends as often as possible so that I could continue creating my own fashions in Mom's basement. Kevin had moved out on his own by that time, and his apartment was near Mom's. He would pick me up at Pratt on Fridays and take me back Sunday night.

After my freshman year at Pratt, I was determined to put on a fashion show in Elizabeth during the summer, to raise money for school. My high school friend Eddie was all for it and agreed to help me send out invitations and press releases. The managers of the Singer store had also agreed to let me have the show there.

The rehearsals with the models went great. I had gathered a wonderful cross section of women in Elizabeth to wear my fashions. Some were high school friends, and others were older ladies I knew from church. From the second floor of the store, they would descend downstairs, mark the runway to the front door, then sashay back up. It was going to be so hot! The music was also sizzling and included Brazil 66, Barbra, and even Handel's *Messiah*. We're talking class, girlfriend.

We decorated the store and filled the main floor with chairs for the audience. In the foyer, we had a display board that featured all the prints and solid fabrics the audience would be seeing. We even offered hors d'oeuvres and a cocktail hour before the show.

As the audience filed in, we peeked down the stairs from our upstairs dressing rooms and were stunned to see fifty or sixty people there! The place was packed. Our families were in the crowd, and so were people who knew us from school, like Mr. Walker and Mr. Parisi. Eddie, scouting the crowd, reported back that there were even reporters from the *Star Ledger* and the *Daily Journal* there! Our press releases must have worked!

Unfortunately, for a while I was mortified to think that that might be the only thing that was going to work right that evening. Some of our models were late, and others who couldn't make it sent replacements who didn't exactly fit the dresses they needed to be wearing. They also didn't know the routine we had worked out for each model. Adding to the tension, our emcee for the evening still had not shown up. By the sound of the coughs and murmurs emanating from the audience, the natives were clearly getting restless.

While frantically pinning dresses around girls who were a size smaller than the outfit, I sent Eddie downstairs to try and stall the audience. I was flipping out. Everything seemed to be falling apart at the last minute. How could I get anyone to take me seriously as a designer if my show was a colossal mess? I tried not to think about the reporters in the audience. Please, God, I prayed, send me some help!

He must have heard me praying because our emcee walked in at that moment and rescued Eddie from doing his stand-up routine at the microphone. The models were also ready to roll. Finally, everything fell into place and the music started. To Barbra's song "The Ladies Who Lunch," the ladies of Elizabeth strutted their stuff down the stairs to the main floor and the runway. It was a rush to see the positive reaction from the crowd.

Everyone loved the fashion show—impressed, I guess, that a kid my age could pull it off. I had the biggest smile on my face as I watched the fashions that I had created floating down the runway to oohs and aahs from my hometown friends.

Child, that audience gobbled up my designs. I had tons of orders for the dresses and suits, which I was making for between fifty and seventy dollars. Mr. Walker was impressed enough with the show and with my portfolio to give me a donation toward my school expenses. This strong show of support from my hometown friends meant the world to me and still does.

After the show, Eddie and I went out to a diner to celebrate. Eddie was jazzed about our success and described to me his vision for the future House of Mark Antony—for which we could produce a fashion show called "The Fall in Rome." He even came up with a campaign for this "Mark Antony" line. Eddie was such a good friend. He wanted to see me succeed as much as I did.

Returning to Pratt for a new semester, I was asked to sew up an haute couture garment for Bradford C. Moody because Homer was on vacation and Bradford thought I could do it, along with the help of Barbara Clark, a friend and fellow design student. We met with Bradford in Manhattan and he offered to pay us $1,000 for our work. Heading back to Brooklyn on the G train, Barbara and I studied the dress pattern and said to ourselves, "Piece of cake. Like taking candy from a baby. We could whip this thing out in two, three hours, tops."

As we started to cut out the dress, however, we realized that Mr. Renzuli's description of breathing life into the fabric was more than true. In our case, our fabric suddenly became the Bride of Frankenstein! It just went crazy. First of all, the peplum on the skirt was not lying right at all. We tried to press it and the hem just refused to lie flat.

"Oh, Barbara," I cried. "We cut the fabric on the wrong grain! And we don't have any more fabric, so we gotta make this work, girl!"

I also couldn't get the neckline on the blouse to do what it was supposed to do. We even messed up on the lining of the skirt and had to tack it down. Everything was going wrong. We struggled and struggled, wrestling with materials that didn't want to behave.

Barbara and I ended up staying up all night—madly sewing like Lucy Ricardo and Ethel Mertz. We were so tired and drunk with exhaustion that we did everything wrong and had to correct it all. Through my delirium, about the only thing I remember hearing Barbara say, over and over, was, "Damn, Anthony, we messed up again! Damn!"

We finally got the thing stitched together, snatched an hour's sleep, and then caught the train to deliver the dress to Bradford in Manhattan. We didn't even have time to clean up or take a shower. Barbara and I felt like we had screwed up so bad, but Bradford seemed pleased with the results and paid us our money. We couldn't believe we were being paid for that mess.

"That dress is going to fall off that woman," we said, laughing, as we rode the subway back to Brooklyn.

My new roommate, Paul Morgan, and I became friends with a female student, Tracy Green, who was the residential advisor on our floor. She brought everyone together, regardless of race or background, always believing in the power of a positive attitude. She often offered people herbal tea and cookies in her room, which she had decorated all in Miami kitsch with plastic pink flamingos and palm trees. It was so cool. I loved it. Tracy really brought out the whimsy in everything she did or said. She could always make me laugh.

"You're as cute as a Calvin Klein button," she'd say to me.

Tracy also had a great flair for merchandising, and we hung out together a lot, trading ideas. She was from an upwardly mobile family in Atlanta, but she knew how to handle herself. One day, Tracy and her girlfriends were on the subway coming back from a shopping trip when they were mugged. The muggers, however, had picked the wrong targets.

"I wasn't about to let them take my new outfit from Macy's," Tracy told us afterward. "We beat them up just like they stole tomorrow."

We were so proud of them and helped them celebrate their victory over the muggers that night.

Tracy decorated our floor's bulletin board every week and was really good at it. She was very artistic, and for Black History Month, she really went all out, filling the board with pictures of famous African-Americans. Soon after she completed this presentation, however, we were stunned to discover that someone had defaced the pictures with the words "Nigger, please." Not only that, but half of the pictures had been torn off the board.

Tracy was crushed and wouldn't come out of her room for days. She thought the culprit must have been someone from our floor who knew her personally. We held a meeting, though, and agreed that it must have been someone from outside our circle.

"We celebrate all nationalities here," Tracy said, still hurt. "I made up the board because I thought everyone would appreciate it."

And we did appreciate it. Except for this one incident, I don't remember anyone ever calling anyone else names. As college students, we were all on the same creative wavelength and too busy exploring new areas of our own inner selves.

In my second year at Pratt, for a project in my "Light, Color, and Design" course, I was supposed to design a dress with a sculpture around it. I decided to do a Hula-Hoop dress, and when I described my idea to Homer, he said, "Wow, you're really going to do that?"

The Hula-Hoop dress was a strapless white dress with orange polka dots, with an overlay dress of clear plastic made from the same pattern. In the plastic hem was a Hula-Hoop, which made the dress stick out. It was accessorized with Hula-Hoop buttons, Hula-Hoop earrings, a Hula-Hoop bracelet, and a Hula-Hoop hat. The clear plastic hat sat on the head with a Hula-Hoop on its outer edges like an orbit encircling a planet.

I was sewing on this project into the wee hours, working on the Hula-Hoop dress everywhere—even on the train. People stared at me like I was crazy. Looking back, I don't know how I got that thing on the subway and everywhere else. I just made it happen through sheer willpower. When you're determined to do something, you just find the strength to do it. People on the train would ask me what I was doing, and I'd say, "It's my homework. I'm a design student." They laughed when I explained that I was making a Hula-Hoop dress. I had to work with the plastic material by hand, trying to sew it around the Hula-Hoop. I also had to cut a Hula-Hoop by hand to make the earrings and other accessories from it.

When it was all done, though, it was definitely worth the effort—the Hula-Hoop dress was incredible! This one black girl at Pratt, Joyce, a senior design major, loved the dress and wanted to model it for my class. Joyce was very flamboyant. She wore turbans every day and once came to class in a full-length mink coat that she had modeled for a furrier. *Très dramatique.* She thought she was Leontyne Price, okay?

When she saw the Hula-Hoop dress, she said, "Child, that thing is too fine."

She modeled it for my "Light, Color, and Design" class and really worked that classroom, strutting in that dress and throwing her hands up like Diana Ross singing "Stop! In the Name of Love." She was crazy.

Then Miss Thing led everybody through the school cafeteria, showing off the dress to much applause for her performance. She also sashayed right into Professor Ono's class. Professor Ono was a strict Japanese instructor who hated interruptions while his class was in session. He was a fabulous professor but also a hard taskmaster. He would rip your stuff apart until you got it right. I think he was trying to prepare his students for the difficult, high-pressure world of the design houses.

"Professor Ono," Joyce called out loudly, "what do you think of Anthony Mark Hankins' creation?"

I held my breath. Professor Ono lowered his reading glasses, perused Joyce in this wild ensemble, and tried to hold back an amused smile.

"Not bad, not bad," he conceded. I let out a sigh of relief.

Since Homer had seen the patterns and all the sketches for the Hula-Hoop dress, I invited him to the formal fashion-show presentation of the dress, and he assured me he'd be there. I suppose he wanted to see this crazy thing for real. Sure enough, he showed up for the event.

Tracy Green modeled it for the show and actually got the Hula-Hoop spinning in the hem so it looked like it was spinning in space around her. It was fabulous. This dress stopped traffic, child. Everybody came by our classroom, saying, "What is this Hula-Hoop dress we've heard about? We gotta see it."

"Anthony, you're too much," someone at the presentation said.

"Good job," Homer told me afterward, and I was proud to have his endorsement. I gave the dress to Tracy after she modeled it for the presentation because she was so cool in it. Recently, I found out that Tracy still has the Hula-Hoop dress.

"You'd better be giving that dress some prime real estate in your house, girlfriend," I told her.

13

Leap of Faith

I wanted to know more about haute couture, so I went to the Caroline Pratt Library on campus and did more research. I read more and more about Yves Saint Laurent, whose style I loved most, and about a school in Paris that Homer had told me about, the École de la Chambre Syndicale de la Couture Parisienne. The Chambre Syndicale is similar to our trade unions; it governs the Paris fashion houses, setting the standards and rules of the industry. The school, or *école,* was founded in 1929 by the Chambre Syndicale to provide talent and skilled labor for the Paris design houses. It is the only school in France for the training of haute couture designers.

When I read about this school, which Yves Saint Laurent and Karl Lagerfeld attended in the 1950s, something clicked for me. I wanted to work at a French design house and master all the techniques for the haute couture style of dressmaking. I wanted to learn how to make these Rolls-Royces of dresses. They were the most intricately designed pieces of clothing in the world.

In my dreams, I wanted to work with Yves Saint Laurent in Paris for a time, before starting my own company there. I'd stay in Paris until everyone there said I was hot, then triumphantly bring my collection to New York and blow everyone out in America—just blow all the other designers right out of the water. Child, even Bill Blass would be declaring, "This kid is ruining business."

Bolstering my dream, Homer was always telling me, "You're very good at this, Anthony. You should go to Paris. Patrick Kelly's there and you'd be great there, too. You have such a good sense of color. You should apply to that school in Paris."

Patrick Kelly was a young African-American fashion designer whose own life closely mirrored my own. By the time he was in his early thirties, he was a sensation in Paris, with his whimsical and sassy clothes. His signature style was incorporating multicolored buttons and bows on most of his creations—a look inspired by his grandmother, who had started using buttons everywhere on clothes to distract from the fact that she didn't have matching buttons.

Kelly designed for women of all sizes and shapes, just like I have always wanted to do. In *People* magazine, I read that he wanted women to feel they were beautiful just the way they were. To look great wearing his fashions, they didn't have to have perfectly shaped bodies. To prove his point, when he showed his fifth collection in Paris, he even included a model who was eight months pregnant.

Before Patrick, everything was taken so seriously, but he had fun with it all. His dresses had a whimsical, folk-art sense about them that was fresh and currently turning Parisian fashion critics inside out! They couldn't get enough of this brash young African-American. While he always wore denim overalls decorated with bright buttons, his clients were *très chic,* including Bette Davis, Madonna, and Princess Diana.

Like Patrick Kelly, I knew my sewing machine was my ticket to Paris. It had opened so many doors for me already, and now it was going to somehow take me around the world. With Patrick as a role model, I could see myself in Paris. It made my resolve to go to school there even stronger. I learned that the École was very prestigious and that the selection process was very difficult. It is the best of all schools for fashion design—the most prestigious, internationally.

"You're crazy," people told me. "You can't get into that school."

They thought I was trippin'.

"You're not getting into that school," my friend and roommate, Paul, challenged.

"You watch me," I told him.

My instructors couldn't believe my plans, either, and they thought I couldn't get in. Pratt's fashion school was difficult enough, they reasoned, so why did I think I could make it at the École? Patti Choi, a career counselor at Pratt, was all for it, though. She believed in me.

"Go, get outta here," she encouraged me. "Do it! Explore!"

Most people, however, were saying, "Come down to earth, child."

Homer, though, still thought Paris was a great idea for me. So did Maria and Judith. Paul believed in my plan, too, after a while. Since we all thought we'd have to do something different from the crowd in order to get noticed as designers, why not that?

I've never been traditional, and I decided that if I ended up starving on the streets of Paris, well, at least I had gotten there. I had nothing to lose and everything to gain by going. I looked at Paris as a great opportunity. I was young and wanted to test the waters.

At Pratt, I had learned a lot while exploring friendships and expanding the theatrical part of my personality. After two years there, though, I felt like I needed a new challenge. What I love about fashion is that you are able to do something new every season. Most people wait for tomorrow, but I've never believed in waiting. I did wait, though, to tell my parents about my plans to attend the École until I knew there was a good chance of my getting in.

I hate it when people say to me, "You're so young to have done all these things." I've tasted life and done a lot in a short time. Homer always told me to have patience, but I always felt that time was running out fast. I don't know why. Maybe it was because I had already lost my father and my grandparents.

I knew that my portfolio would make or break my chances to get into the school, so I burned the midnight oil making sure it was flawless and full of drama. I used a variety of materials to make my renderings come alive in my portfolio, like actual fabric samples, hosiery, and hair for my croquis sketches.

I wanted to make my portfolio so exciting that you couldn't wait to turn the page. I learned a lot about creating outstanding portfolios from studying those that three architecture student friends of mine at Pratt were submitting. Their portfolios were amazing—almost 3-D in their inventiveness. They used actual building and decorating materials in their renderings to make them realistic.

I learned how to use wallpaper samples for texture and background, as well as papier-mâché, metals, fabrics, lace, and other materials. I also learned to layer and get the action going with 3-D effects on my portfolio pages. I had fun with it. Nowadays, students can use computer technology to help them create phenomenal portfolios. Some have even created exciting pop-up art. It's hard to forget that kind of creativity.

I believe that you've got to develop your own style and let it show in your portfolio. You know when someone has spent a lot of time and care working on something. It's worth spending a little extra money on your portfolio since it will be your calling card. I used the best portfolio case I could afford, as well as the best-quality markers, acid-free paper, vellum, and fabric samples. Since high school, I've tried to best my own portfolio every year.

My sophomore year at Pratt, I sent my portfolio off to Madame Olga Saurat, the director of the École in Paris. I handwrote the letter since I had read up on French culture and learned that the French like letters that are handwritten. In her response, she wrote that she had reviewed my portfolio and approved it, but would like to meet with me in person to see if I would fit into their school system. I was really excited. I didn't want to leave Homer because I was learning so much, but at the same time—PARIS, okay?

I still didn't tell my parents about it, though. I knew the school was expensive, but I didn't know how much. I just told myself that somehow I was going to do this. Then I found out how much the École tuition was—$10,000! How was I going to raise that kind of money?! They wanted it up front, too. When I tried to figure out how I could raise that much cash, a lot of panic set in. How was I going to do it?

The next time I saw Judith Agisim, I told her about the École and its tuition, asking her for suggestions. She gave me a list of people to contact, like designers Calvin Klein, Victor Costa, and Louis Feraud; as well as others like Susan Sokol, then president of Calvin Klein; and Sarah Lemiere, the costume designer for *The Cosby Show.*

Sarah was really cool. Just an awesome person. After I contacted her, she invited me to have lunch with her at the Plaza, after which she gave me a tour of the Kaufman-Astoria Studios in Astoria, New York. She looked at my portfolio and gave me some helpful advice. Sarah also introduced us to Claudette Roper, who handled PR for *The Cosby Show,* and invited Angie and me to be part of the studio audience at a taping of the show. We were thrilled, especially when Claudette gave us the VIP treatment, inviting us backstage to meet Bill Cosby himself and the beautiful actress Phylicia Rashad, who played his wife.

I felt numb as we made our way backstage past the busy stagehands and thick, round electrical cables to Bill Cosby's dressing room. We were going to meet The Man himself! I couldn't believe it. As we were introduced to Mr. Cosby, I hoped that he couldn't tell how nervous I was to meet him. His warmth, however, instantly put us at ease. He enjoyed teasing Angie, telling her she was far too pretty to have a twin who looked like me. He had us laughing like crazy. A few moments later, we met Phylicia Rashad and she was also just as wonderful to us. I was surprised that they were both so down-to-earth.

Meanwhile, I was doing everything I could think of to raise some money, but nothing worked. It seemed that nobody was giving grant money to fashion students then.

None of the black organizations were willing to help me, either. I also wrote to the governor and to all the well-known people I could think of, even Whitney Houston, but no one responded.

"Please give me ideas on how I can raise money for tuition," I asked everybody. I was sincere in my requests but didn't even get a "Dear John" letter in reply. Judith was sympathetic to my frustration.

"Judith, I gotta get some money, I gotta get this going!" I told her in a cry of desperation.

"Call Christy Ferer," Judith suggested. "She's a fashion correspondent. Christy knows everybody."

I called Christy as fast as my fingers could dial the number and, with Judith's referral pulling strings for me, made an appointment to see her and show her my portfolio. I knew it would help to get my story on the airwaves in order to raise the money for Paris, so I also tried to contact Rolonda Watts, who at that time was a television reporter doing "Slice of Life" segments on our local New York City *Eyewitness News*.

"I'm a local fashion designer and I'm going to Paris, but I need media coverage to help me do it. Please do a story on me," was the spiel that I left on Rolonda's answering machine. She didn't call me back at first, so I just kept leaving messages for her. I also faxed her letters, determined to persuade her to let me meet with her.

"You gotta tell my story," I begged her. "Please give me an opportunity to show you my stuff."

Who is this Anthony Mark Hankins guy? she must have wondered.

Meanwhile, I was really nervous going into the city to meet Christy. She had a very gutsy, raspy voice over the phone, and I thought she'd be this tense older woman. I got there before she arrived, so people in her office took me into a room and let me watch some of the television pieces she'd done. When I saw her tapes, I was surprised to see that she was young, vivacious, and cute. I also realized, with a shock, that her pieces were on the *Today* show. Oh, my God, that's huge, I thought, stunned.

When Christy arrived, I showed her my portfolio and nervously waited a moment for her response. She said she thought my story was really moving and she wanted to do a two-part piece on me for the *Today* show—the second part of which was to be filmed in Paris as I started school there. She would make arrangements with her film crew, she told me, to come to Elizabeth on that next Tuesday and Wednesday.

When I returned home, in a daze from hearing Christy's positive response, I was stunned when Rolonda also called me from Channel 7 and told me that she'd like to meet with me finally. I couldn't believe my luck. The stars in the heavens were definitely in perfect alignment that day. Even though Rolonda jokingly claimed I must have left hundreds of messages for her, she told me she liked my energy and agreed to do the story.

Since not one but now two television film crews were about to descend on our house, I finally decided it was time to tell my parents about my plans to attend the École. They were astounded by my new goals for school and amazed that there was going to be television news coverage of my plans.

"How did you get the *Today* show to come out here?" they wanted to know.

When the news crews began to arrive, I could see it finally dawning on my stepfather that maybe I might be on to something after all. News vans and electrical cables lined

Linden Street. Our neighbors were hanging out in their yards, leaning over their fences and staring our direction, asking one another what was going on at the Hankins house. Had somebody killed somebody over there? They couldn't figure out what story big-time news crews could be covering on their street.

My mother was nervous about how I'd handle myself in an interview, but when Christy and, later, Rolonda put their microphones in front of me and the cameras started rolling, child, I started talking. I caught a glimpse of Mom silently expressing her surprise at my ease in front of the cameras. Here I was, only seventeen and talking to a television camera like I was Montel Williams. I loved talking about my craft, and being interviewed about it was not a nerve-racking experience at all. The camera liked me and I liked it.

"I think somebody dropped me from the sky into this household," I told Christy in the interview. I proudly showed her and the cameras some of my work, including a bubblegum prom dress, a crab-back jacket, princess puffs for prom gowns, and a vamp bustier—"à la Hankins."

"I want to be known as the first true American couturier," I boldly declared, and went on to make other affirmations about my future. I was obsessed with making it, I confessed, and I was willing to burn the midnight oil all night long, just to get what I wanted. I wanted the world in my pocket. I didn't want just a little portion of Fifth Avenue. I wanted all of Fifth Avenue, and I was going to get my education in Paris in order to reach that goal.

In Rolonda's interview, she mentioned that I would be among the very few Americans, especially African-Americans, to ever be accepted at the École. Rolonda talked about my accomplishments to date and it seemed that my stepfather began to recognize all my efforts. Instead of thinking, That crazy kid is nuts to think he's going to Paris, my stepfather started wondering aloud to Mom, "How is Anthony going to live in Paris?" I was proud to finally get his blessing.

The *Today* show's film crews traveled from our house to Elizabeth High School, to Pratt, and even to the Port of Elizabeth for some local color. The *Eyewitness News* crew followed closely behind them. The Port of Elizabeth is one of the largest shipping terminals on the East Coast, with thirty-nine regularly scheduled steamship lines operating out of there. I guess the point was that a blue-collar job might have been more likely for my future.

After the television interviews were completed, I still didn't have the money for even the flight to France, and Mom was always asking me how I was going to get this "Paris money" that I needed. She worried, too, about how I was going to make it in Paris once I got there. I would say to her, "Mom, where is your faith?" I just always believed it was all going to come together.

"Let him go to Paris," James said. "The worst that can happen is that he comes back."

To earn money, I spent part of that summer in Elizabeth working for a camp in nearby Linden, New Jersey, where I taught kids arts and crafts. Those kids drove me crazy with their short attention spans, but it was fun. They even won a competition.

When the camp session was over, though, I was desperate for another job. A friend at school, a photographer, suggested that for the rest of the summer I go up to Montreal, where her parents lived. I could stay with her family, she told me, and learn some French, and she would line up some clients that I could create dresses for. I took dress patterns with me to Montreal and made haute couture dresses for her family and friends for just $100 a pop.

At the end of the summer, though, I had still saved only $1,400 for the school in Paris. Madame Saurat had written that the next step in the admissions process was a personal interview at the school. Just a quick meeting with her in Paris. Easier said than done.

I regarded the television pieces on me as having been nothing short of a miracle but, soon after the *Eyewitness News* piece on me aired, another miracle happened: a plane ticket to Paris arrived in the mail with my name on it! An anonymous person had sent it directly to my mom's house. The sender could have been a viewer from anywhere in the greater New York City area. I was stunned to see the plane ticket and knew that it was a sure sign from God that I was meant to go. Higher forces were surely at work here.

No one ever owned up to sending the ticket—not even the staff of the *Today* show, so I wasn't sure it was them. I have my suspicions, but it could have been anyone. I had read in interviews with Patrick Kelly that he had also received an anonymous ticket to Paris. Maybe there is a benefactor out there who helps young African-Americans achieve their dreams. To whoever sent the ticket, though: my heartfelt thanks because your generosity changed my life.

I called Christy and excitedly told her that I had received a ticket to Paris! She was happy for me, but I still had to raise some big money fast. I had already tried all the avenues I could think of. Even Patti Choi at Pratt didn't know what else to do. Christy suggested that possibly someone in Paris would help me.

Even though I had only saved $1,400 toward the school's $10,000 tuition, I knew after I received the plane ticket that I was meant to go to that school. I now had a way to get to Paris but there was still the problem of finding an affordable place to stay.

My leap of faith was again rewarded when my mother visited her church one day and mentioned to a family friend, Mr. MacKenzie, that I was planning to go to school in Paris. He told my mom that his son, Tom, a jazz musician, maintained an apartment in Paris and, because of his frequent traveling, would probably love to have me occupy it while he was gone.

My luck improved even further when my friend Emil Nems suggested that I contact his mother, Amal, who lived in Paris. She would be glad to help me, he said. The Nems were very wealthy interior designers who had a mansion in Lebanon but, because of the war there, lived in Paris. Emil's relatives also owned several buildings in New York City. His family was well connected on both continents.

It seemed as if everything was coming together for me to go to Paris. Even though the École had not fully accepted me into their school—I was still subject to the personal interview—I just knew they would accept me once I had gotten all the way over there. I wasn't going to take no for an answer. My mantra was, "I'm going to school in Paris, I'm going to school in Paris. . . ." I said it over and over again until I had no doubt that that was what I was going to be doing.

My friend Eddie's sister, Joan, it turned out, was also going to be living in Paris soon. She had been working for a French company in New York, and now the company was transferring her to their Paris office. When she heard that I was going over, too, we could hardly contain our excitement.

"Can you believe it?!" I screamed. "We're going to Paris—the City of Light! The fashion capital of the world!"

14

Bonjour, Paris

As I packed my suitcases for Paris, my mother watched with wonderment. Her baby was flying away—to the other side of the world. Mom and Katie took me to the airport and we all cried the whole time. I had never been very far away from home, and now, for the first time, the miles were really going to separate us. I knew my going to the École was the right thing to do, but that didn't make leaving home any easier.

I had planned to get to Paris just before school started. I still had faith that something was going to happen to help me with the tuition money. When it got closer to the time I was to fly to France, I was more and more certain it was going to happen. I just threw caution to the wind and knew I was going to be taken care of.

I had an inner peace about it. There are very few times you get that feeling. I knew it was my destiny. This was one of those decisions that I felt I could live with for the rest of my life. It was the right time, the right place, the right everything. Divine intervention was urging me to get on that plane. The school wants you, it told me, so you'd better show up. I had to take that leap of faith.

Faith was all I had on that trip across the Atlantic. I remember that I wore my blue blazer and black slacks on the plane. My mother used to say to me, "If your shoes are shined, your shirt is clean, and your tie is straight, you can get whatever you want." When I was in my polished mode, I called myself "Mr. Windex."

Even though I didn't know much French and I was up against incredible talent, I knew I was bringing racial diversity to the school. I didn't know what I could do yet, but I was going to make a difference in France. I was going to leave my mark on the tree of life.

When my plane landed at Charles de Gaulle Airport, Amal Nems was there to meet me. A beautiful, cosmopolitan woman with long black hair and Mediterranean brown eyes, she reminded me of Diane Von Furstenberg on a thin Diana Ross frame. She could have been a dancer.

Amal was decked out in a fabulous Yves Saint Laurent pant set with a silky, ethnic animal-print blouse, over which she wore a silver fox coat. She greeted me with an expansive, "Dahling, dahling, welcome to Paris!" After we collected my luggage, she asked, "What would you like to do on your first day here?"

Girl, I thought, I want to go see the House of Yves Saint Laurent! I didn't care about seeing the Eiffel Tower, the Louvre, none of that stuff. Amal asked me if I knew the address of the House of Yves Saint Laurent. It had only been tattooed on my brain since the age of ten.

"Five Avenue Marceau," I rattled off to her, without hesitation.

She looked it up on her little map, then put on huge sunglasses and leather gloves before gripping the wheel of her gray Volvo. As she drove through the city, I was totally in awe of Paris—a beautiful city, but noisy and full of traffic and people speaking a language I didn't know. I took everything in and for the first time knew what it was like to be a foreigner. This was one time I definitely felt like Dorothy after she had landed in the world of Oz. And one thing I knew for sure: I wasn't in Kansas anymore. With my limited French, how would I understand what people were saying to me?

The headquarters of Yves Saint Laurent looked like an imposing estate from the 1800s, stern and masculine in stone-gray with beautiful black awnings. The three-story town house is just a few hundred meters from the Seine and the Place de l'Alma.

Standing in front of the House of Yves Saint Laurent was one of the most incredible experiences I've ever had. I felt it was meant for me to be there. I didn't know how, but I just knew I'd be inside that building someday. I was going to find out every little nook of that building. I'd be a part of the activity there, too.

I stared at the House of Yves Saint Laurent for at least fifteen minutes with such an intensity that I might as well have been pressing my face up against the glass windows. Suddenly, I was aware that Amal must be wondering how she was going to pry my body off the building's brick facade, so I saved her the embarrassment and regretfully left with her, making a silent vow that I'd be back—soon.

The next mission of the day was to pick up the key to Tom MacKenzie's apartment on Rue du Docteur Heulin.

Eddie's sister, Joan, had already arrived in Paris for her new job with L'Aromarine, a French bubble bath and soap company, and she had checked out the apartment, thinking she might rent it with me since we knew each other.

Joan had stayed in Tom's flat for the first six weeks before deciding to rent her own accommodations. Since Tom, a musician, was on the road so much, he had left the key with Joan for me to pick up. I called her and asked, "Well, what do you think of the apartment?"

"Good luck," was her first reply. Not a good sign but, I figured, how bad could it be? I hadn't expected to be staying in a luxury suite anyway. I should have asked her more questions about the apartment, but I was so excited about just getting to Paris that the conversation quickly strayed back to what to see and experience in the city.

That afternoon, Amal drove me over to L'Aromarine and waited outside while I ran up to Joan's office to say hello and pick up the key. Joan handed it to me with real sympathetic eyes.

"If you ever need anything, call me," she said, which really meant, "You will, believe me."

Uh-oh. Another subtle hint. Now I was really wondering what I was in for.

As Amal and I drove across Paris to my new abode, I noticed the decline in the quality of the architecture and the increasing number of immigrants on the street. The closer we got to Rue du Docteur Heulin, the more Muslims and Africans I saw. This area was obviously a hub of immigrants; I felt like I had arrived on Ellis Island. Or, more accurately, maybe Senegal. Immigrants from all over Africa filled the streets.

It wasn't that the neighborhood was that bad. It was typical of any inner-city neighborhood. It was just that my vision of my very own Parisian atelier was totally blown. I had pictured sidewalk cafés, croissants and baguettes, wine and cheese . . . suave Frenchmen with berets watching fashionable women parade down the sidewalks. . . .

What I saw in my new neighborhood was Muslim women, always chaperoned, scurrying home from the market; African dashikis, turbans. . . . We pulled the car over by the address Tom had given me—24 Rue du Docteur Heulin. It was a dirty, nondescript gray-cast building that had literally been there for ages. Tom's apartment was actually a first-floor two-room tenement. As we stepped inside, the noxious smell of mildew hit our nostrils. This place definitely needed a long airing out.

The ambience was that of a damp, dark, cramped basement with the lowest ceilings I'd ever seen. From the front door, you first walked into the kitchen area, which was tiny and had, for some unexplainable reason, a shower in the middle of it. There was a shower drain in the middle of the peeling linoleum floor. If you opened the windows to the place, you'd see me taking a shower in the kitchen, okay?

We also discovered that the refrigerator was not only discolored inside but wasn't working, either. Off from the kitchen was a large rectangular room with a loft area above the main floor which contained a rumpled double-size bed.

The toilet was another horror story. It was *in* the common hallway. Not off the hallway, you understand. In it. You had to unlock the toilet, and when we did, cobwebs sprang up from all over it. Cold air rushing up, bugs everywhere. This toilet was worse than any outhouse I'd ever seen. As I tried to maintain my crumbling composure, Amal murmured, "Oh, no, Antony, oh, no. . . ."

I tried a light switch in the apartment. Why was I surprised that the electricity was off? Oh, God, I thought, how am I going to get the lights turned back on? The flat also just had a small electric heater—I could just imagine the cold winter ahead. There was one window in the front of the place, and one in the back, where there was a desk and a loft bed.

It was *un taudis,* a hovel, okay? I was totally upset. Now I realized why Tom never stayed in his flat. It was just the worst, worst, worst. Oh, well. . . . I had wanted to be in Paris. . . .

That first night, I had to clean my little hovel by the pale light of the streetlamp outside, since the electricity was still off. I found Tom's collection of cleansers; all of the labels were in French, of course, so I had to open each one to figure out what they were. I ripped up some of Tom's old discarded shirts for cleaning rags. The bed wasn't too disgusting. Joan had spent over six weeks in the place when she had first arrived in Paris, and she had left fresh sheets on the bed.

The kitchen shower was freezing cold—of course, no hot water. I tried to cheer myself up but just couldn't shake feeling depressed and alone. It could be worse, I thought. At least I had a place to stay, and that was better than no place. This was the first true challenge in my life, and I was going to have to meet it head-on.

After my numbing encounter with the shower, I needed some air but was afraid to leave my windows open while I slept because of the roughness of the neighborhood. Depression continued to settle on me like a dark cloud. I tried to fall asleep but it was impossible. I was an ocean away from family and friends. Suddenly, I felt hot tears streaming down my face. How could I have thought that I could just come over to Paris and make a big splash?

Would I soon find out that it was really an impossible dream after all?

I wanted to rush home to the safety of my parents' house but knew that wasn't possible. I had to talk to Mom, though. I had to hear her voice. I left my apartment and found a public phone nearby.

"You should come home," Mom cried, after I told her how horrible the apartment was. The idea was tempting, but I had come too far to turn back now. I knew I had to prove to myself, and to the fashion industry, that I could do the work. You can do anything you set your mind to do, Mom assured me. I already knew it, but that night, I needed to hear it from her.

She also suggested that I read the Twenty-third Psalm before trying to fall asleep again. Her advice was always on the money.

I had set up an appointment on my second day in Paris to meet with the renowned designer Louis Feraud, based on a recommendation from Maria and Judith. Feraud had opened a dress shop in Cannes in 1955, and his clients had included Grace Kelly, Brigitte Bardot, and Ingrid Bergman. He had also designed costumes for films before moving to Paris and setting up his own ready-to-wear organization. His fashions often had a South American influence.

Feraud was a handsome, distinguished, self-assured gen-tleman with salt-and-pepper hair. I held my breath as he glanced through my portfolio, lingering only briefly on a few pages. I was stunned when he dismissed my work rather cavalierly, saying, "This is not the kind of thing I'm interested in. Come, let me show you what *I* design."

He took me on a tour of his design room, introducing me to his staff and showing me *his* styles, which did not appeal to me at all. I thought his designs were overdone, with so many bells and whistles sewn on everything that, to me, his garments looked gaudy. I soon realized that the reason he really didn't like my portfolio was because my style was very Yves Saint Laurent. I'd spent so many years studying Yves Saint Laurent that his influence was apparent in my work.

The vibes with Feraud definitely weren't right, either, so I wasn't that disappointed. I knew there were other fish to fry, and I hadn't even gotten to the École de la Chambre Syndicale de la Couture Parisienne yet. I didn't know what would happen there, but I still had a feeling it would be something great.

I didn't have time that day to dwell on my disappointment with my meeting with Feraud because Amal's daughter Marianne, who was a twenty-six-year-old architecture student, was picking me up for the afternoon. Her mission was to show me how to get around Paris on the city's metro system. Marianne showed me how to purchase the tickets, read French maps, and follow the main routes. We rode the metro all around the city, and by the end of the day I felt like a "pro on the metro," okay?

That night, I had to get my portfolio ready for my interview at the school, making sure that every area of fashion was adequately covered—sportswear, sweaters, dresses, evening gowns, day coats, shoes, handbags, and jewelry. I also had to organize my résumé, grades from Pratt, photographs of my work, and all the fabric swatches to go with my illustrations.

I wondered if race would make a difference in the personal interview with Madame Saurat. The French were supposed to be open-minded. I had read the memoirs of

Josephine Baker, Paul Robeson, and James Baldwin and knew how they had been accepted in Paris. I also knew that Patrick Kelly was currently a hot item in Paris. It seemed like maybe it was even chic to be black in Paris.

I was determined to be there because of talent, though—not skin color. I had to be focused and ready to answer any question. My work would speak for itself. But that thought soon led to another horrible realization. What if I didn't make it, based on my work? Was I really worthy of this school? Even if I was admitted, would the school accept most of my course credits from Pratt? I wanted to transfer in on the third or fourth level since I was technically a junior at Pratt. What if I didn't pass the personal interview tomorrow? Would I have to use that return ticket home?

Hailing a cab the next morning with my fledgling French, I traveled across Paris to 45 Rue Saint-Roch, off Avenue de l'Opéra—a prestigious area in Paris, only blocks from Rue Cambon, where Coco Chanel had reopened her salon in 1954 after closing her original house in 1939. When my cab pulled up to the curb outside the École, I was surprised that many students were looking out the windows as if anticipating my arrival. Maybe they had heard I was coming—or maybe, I realized, they had been distracted from their studies by the sudden wail of the ambulance that had raced past my cab as I paid the driver.

The École, housed in a beautiful eight-floor pigeon-gray town house with black doors and gray awnings, looked magnificent. Inside the stately premises, I struggled to read the French on the directory in the lobby, finally making out "Office of the Director, 6th Floor." An elegant 1890s-era elevator, which reminded me of a gilded birdcage with black rails and a marble floor, carried me to the sixth floor, where a tall woman, whose stern demeanor conjured up visions of Lurch from *The Addams Family,* came up to me—addressing me in terse French.

I told her that I was Anthony Hankins and was there to see Madame Saurat, *la directrice.* Immediately, Lurch's grim demeanor melted just a touch.

"Monsieur Hankins," she said in a very thick accent. "I am Madame Saurat's secretary. One moment, please."

She disappeared behind two massive French ivory and gold doors. While I waited, I stared in awe at the walls around me, lined with designers' beautiful illustrations that made my sketches look like cave drawings.

My knees should have been knocking from nerves, but I was so excited that I almost forgot to be scared to death. I had made it to Paris! If Homer Layne and my friends could see me now—I was actually in the École de la Chambre Syndicale de la Couture Parisienne!

Suddenly, the massive doors opened toward me and an elegant woman with beautifully coiffed hair, dressed in a Chanel suit, emerged and beckoned to me with a smile so endearing that it made me feel I was the most important thing in her world at the moment.

"Good afternoon, Antony. I am Madame Saurat," she said graciously. "Would you please come into my office?"

I walked into her handsome office, where the decor was based on elegant shades of cream. Resting on the white plush carpeting was a huge Saint Bernard dog—gorgeous, fluffy, well taken care of. The walls were covered with pictures of Madame Saurat with all the famous designers, and I noticed awards mixed in with lots of crystal and glass ornaments on her shelves and credenza. Wow. . . . To me, it was like the office of an angel.

I thought to myself, Honey, this is high society here. Meeting Madame Saurat was like meeting the most upper-class French aristocrat. It reminded me of the movie *Gigi*—with Madame Saurat being Gigi's aunt. Although she didn't speak very much English, Madame Saurat graciously offered to continue the conversation in English for my sake. As she palmed through my portfolio, she would exclaim, "Ah-h-h! Ah-h-h!" and "Très bien. Très bien, Antony."

I was thrilled when she suddenly said, "Tomorrow you come to school. Your teacher will be Madame Miodowski. We have another American here. Michael. Michael Gregory. Michael will teach you French. You will sit next to one another and help one another."

The lady was class-y, okay? Class-y! CLASS-Y! Lots of savior faire and charm. She introduced me to Michael, who was to take me downstairs for a tour of the school. After we left Madame Saurat's office, Michael turned to me and said, "Is she not a jewel?"

Michael was also new there, and while English was indeed his first language, he was actually Australian. He wore schoolboy glasses and was tall and lean, with that tanned, healthy outback look. His brown hair was worn in a ponytail, and I noticed it was graying just a little at the temples.

We were both still in awe of simply being there, and as the other students milled around, Michael leaned toward me and confessed, "I've saved my entire life to be here. I've worked for years in Australia to afford to come to this school."

With this friendly admission, I suddenly felt a wave of insecurity surge over me. Michael and many of the other students were in their mid-thirties, while I was just nine-

teen. Maybe I *wasn't* worthy of being there. Michael had saved for years to have the money to attend the school.

My own tuition fee was technically due—a small matter of $10,000—and I barely had enough money to buy a new suit of clothes. I was still convinced, though, that God would not have gotten me all the way to Paris without a plan to let me attend the school, so I held my breath and asked God to please let me in on the plan soon.

Walking home from the École that day, knowing I'd finally been fully accepted into the school, I jumped up in the air and whooped for joy—which is not the Parisian thing to do, but I didn't care. I called Christy Ferer from a pay phone on my way home that day, as I had promised. I told her how excited I was to be in Paris and to actually know that I'd been accepted into the École, but there was still the problem of my not having any money for tuition. Madame Saurat was expecting a check from me the next day!

"Don't worry," Christy assured me. "I believe in you, Anthony, and I'm going to contact someone who might be able to help. We'll figure out something for your tuition. I'll call you tomorrow at the school."

The next morning, Madame Miodowski, a no-nonsense kind of woman, introduced me in very elegant French to the other students. "This is Antony Hankins . . . an American. . . . Welcome to our school." I had noticed that in France, everyone called me *"Ahntony."*

Madame Miodowski showed me my desk and the mannequin I was to use, then gave me a pin cushion for my wrist. Just as class was about to begin, Madame Miodowski's phone rang in the classroom. From her expression of surprise, I gathered that the phone didn't disrupt her classroom that often.

"Allo?" Madame Miodowski listened for a moment. "Antony Hankins?! Oui? Okay. . . ." In French, she asked Michael to translate for her. "Please tell Antony that Madame Saurat's secretary would like to see him upstairs in her office."

Oh, no. The tuition. I bounded up the stairs and reassured Lurch that I would have the tuition check in her hands very soon. I found out later that Michael had also nicknamed her Lurch. The French kids, once they'd seen the *Addams Family* series, also called her Lurch and thought this was the perfect name for her. She definitely had that Lurch edge.

I still didn't have the slightest idea how I was going to come up with the tuition money, but I was praying to God to help me. Between God and Christy, I had no doubt the miracle would occur somehow.

As soon as I had gotten back downstairs and settled in my chair, the phone in Madame Miodowski's classroom rang again. "Oui?" She asked a few more questions in French that I didn't understand, and then I heard her say, "Antony Hankins?" I was embarrassed to hear her mention my name again in the conversation.

"There's an important phone call upstairs for you, Antony, from New York," Michael translated. "A Christine Ferer."

I flew up the stairs two at a time.

"Listen, kid, I pulled some strings," Christy told me in her best conspiratorial tone. "I got you an interview with Joy Henderiks of Yves Saint Laurent. She'll be calling you sometime today. So smile, dress well, and be charming—she'll love you."

Later that day, Madame Miodowski's phone rang once more. By now, Madame Miodowski was getting tired of the whole thing. Her patience was clearly strained as she answered. "Allo? Oui? No! Joy Henderiks. . . . Yves Saint Laurent?! Antony Mark Hankins!?"

As Madame Miodowski shook her head in disbelief, she asked Michael to tell me that Joy Henderiks of Yves Saint Laurent was on the upstairs phone for me, adding coldly, "My, are we not the popular one today?"

It was the worst thing she could have said in front of the other students. I saw their jaws drop to the floor and their eyes narrow in suspicion. Why was this young black kid from America getting calls already from the House of Yves Saint Laurent?

"Hello, Antony," Joy greeted me through the phone line in a delightful English accent. "I spoke with Christine Ferer today and she had some wonderful things to say about you. I'd like to meet with you tomorrow, please. What time do you get out of school? We'll see what we can do for you here at Yves Saint Laurent."

I went back to class in a daze.

"You won't believe this," I told Michael. He was excited for me when I told him about the meeting at Yves Saint Laurent. Madame Miodowski asked Michael what had happened.

"Antony's going to Yves Saint Laurent tomorrow," Michael replied.

The other students gasped. Now they were really disgusted; they just hated me. They had all been slaving away at the school for years, and here I was, getting swept off to Yves Saint Laurent practically on my first day there. I didn't blame them; I would have resented me, too.

But I had no time to dwell on their opinion of me. Tomorrow I was going to the House of Yves Saint Laurent and I had to find some suitable clothes to wear. I remembered that my friend from WilliWear in New York, Mark Bozek, had given me a Hallmark card after I had finished my internship there. The note in the card mentioned a woman named Nancy at the WilliWear boutique in Paris who would help me if I needed it. Did I ever need help. Child, I felt like Cinderella going to the ball and hoped this wonderful woman would be my fairy godmother.

I called her up from the school and rattled on like a madman. "I'm a friend of Mark Bozek, and I'd like to come over and see you right away," I said. "I need an outfit because I'm going to Yves Saint Laurent tomorrow! I'll explain it when I see you."

I was obviously an American friend of Mark's, so she knew I wasn't totally crazy, but lord knows what else she thought as she waited for me to arrive. Luckily, Nancy was a fun, laid-back English woman. She reminded me of Bette Midler. Very hip and upbeat—ready for a party. I explained to her the whole situation and she couldn't believe I was going to YSL. This schoolboy wearing khaki pants and a plain old button-down shirt.

"You can't go there in that!" she exclaimed. "You have to have a WilliWear suit for good luck!" In a flash, she fixed me up with a whole outfit—midnight-blue pants, a suit jacket, and a white shirt. Honey, when she was finished dressing me, I looked good! Nancy also approved the results of her work as she studied my new, improved appearance in the mirror.

"You're a perfect size to model our suits," she said to boost my confidence. Yes, Nancy was another one of my angels. She didn't even charge me for the suit.

The next day at school, dressed to impress in my Willi-Wear suit, I watched the clock drag slowly on while I drummed nervously on my desk. As soon as class ended for the day, I beat it over to the metro for my journey to the House of Yves Saint Laurent. Soon, I was standing in front of this famous building, feeling the same déjà vu I felt before. Today, though, I was actually going to go inside the building—and this time, I had an appointment! I was going to meet with Joy Henderiks and give it my best.

Taking an extra breath, I entered the House of Yves Saint Laurent through its glass-door entrance and stepped into an opulent 1860s decor. The airy and spacious reception area inside was at the top of about eight grand steps leading up to a great hallway. The woman behind the desk was dressed in a black sixties retro dress. There were huge vases of flowers, beautiful chandeliers gracing high ceilings, and gilded cherubs holding sconces on each side of the expansive entry hall. To the left was a grand salon that showcased YSL's collections, with round burgundy settees for elegant reposing.

This was an opportunity of a lifetime. I took a deep breath, walked up to the desk, and told the receptionist, "Hi, my name is Anthony Hankins, and I'm here to see Joy Henderiks."

While I tried to appear calm on the outside, the inside of my head was a mess. One thought kept racing through my brain: My God, this is the House of Yves Saint Laurent—and I'm in it! Me, Anthony Mark Hankins, from Elizabeth, New Jersey. Unlike my meeting with Louis Feraud, however, this place felt totally right.

I sat in a gilded chair by the base of a staircase that led up to the second floor for about ten minutes before Joy came down to meet me. While I waited, I watched business-suited men and women rushing in and out, greeting one another with double kisses on the cheeks. Before I actually saw Joy, I smelled the scent of her sweet gardenia perfume, which wafted down before her. Her fragrance entranced me.

She seemed to float down the staircase, wearing a gray turtleneck sweater with slacks that had a real nice drape to them—very Yves Saint Laurent. Tortoiseshell pendants and a tortoiseshell bracelet; hair swept back in a tortoiseshell holder. She looked very Norwegian—blond hair, blue eyes. Gray suede slippers. Gold Cartier bracelet and necklace.

Joy met me with a firm handshake, her gaze warm but very focused. I think she was pleased to see that I was well groomed. She invited me into her small office (as senior vice president of corporate image for YSL—her main office, I learned, was in New York) and asked me at least 150 questions about my experiences, my school grades, my family, my goals. She made me feel that she was taking everything in with deep interest.

"Wonderful, fabulous," Joy would respond to some of my answers. I detected a soft accent. She was from Belgium, I would later find out. She took my portfolio and photocopied some items to show Yves Saint Laurent.

Finally, she said, "We have a scholarship fund that we give out each year, and it sounds as if you're very deserving. But before I can give it to you, I have to make sure that Yves Saint Laurent wants you to have it. I don't think there will be any problem, though, so don't worry about a thing. I'll arrange everything with Madame Saurat."

The phone rang in Madame Miodowski's classroom the next day. Someone from Yves Saint Laurent wanted to talk to me.

"I'm so happy to tell you . . ." I heard Joy Henderiks say from the other end of the line. Although most of what she said was a blur, I understood that Yves Saint Laurent had actually approved of a scholarship for me—enough to pay my tuition at the school! God had come through for me again. I had taken a step out over the ledge and He had supported me before I could fall.

I called my parents and Christy, telling them that my tuition was now taken care of. Christy was thrilled and said that the *Today* crew would be on a plane in two days to finish their story on me. A young American woman, Meg Morley, who worked for the NBC affiliate in Paris, would be accompanying me all over Paris with a film crew, Christy told me. Meg turned out to be lots of fun, and we became friends right away.

At the beginning of our school year, Madame Miodowski announced that we were all eligible, as well as expected, to enter Air France's international competition for young fashion designers called the Concours International des Jeunes Créateurs de Mode. This year's theme for the competition was to be a chic summer garden party outfit.

Of course, I chose something very difficult to make for the competition—a Marilyn Monroe–inspired dress that included a piqué jacket with embroidery on the sleeves, handmade buttons, and fabric that had to be specially dyed to get just the color I wanted. It was going to be a lined, strapless gown on bias pleating with six layers of pleated organdy so the skirt would stick out.

Madame Miodowski was already upset that I was an American and an intern with Yves Saint Laurent, and now I was taking on quite a challenge by completing this gown for the competition. I always tend to challenge myself in the extreme, but still, this was just my first year at the school. I'm sure she was wondering, Just who does Antony think he is?

For once, I agreed with Madame Miodowski—the dress was going to be a nightmare to create. It was also going to cost me a fortune for the supplies I needed to complete the dress. I asked Meg how I could possibly get all the materials on my meager budget.

"For the *Today* show," Meg suggested, "we'll go to this particular fabric store and tell them that we're doing this interview with you there and that they'll be on TV, so maybe they'll give you the fabric for free."

When the show's staff arrived at the school, it blew the other students' minds. It was Hollywood come to town. Lights, camera, action! Christy, Meg, and the NBC film crew followed me all over town—at the school, the markets, my flat, and the fabric store, which did give me the fabric I needed in exchange for the free publicity.

A lot of the students really resented the attention I was getting. They knew about the scholarship from YSL and wondered how I rated being the subject of a big television story. I knew I was in for it from then on. The other students would knock me down all they could. Even Madame Miodowski seemed very annoyed with all the media attention I was getting.

Christy also wanted me to go to Yves Saint Laurent's fashion show for his latest spring ready-to-wear collection so that she could film me actually meeting him. I wore my WilliWear suit, hoping that Joy Henderiks wouldn't notice it was the same suit I had worn for my interview at YSL. Christy instructed me to sit in the VIP section, third row from the runway. We arrived right before the show started, and I managed to take my seat just before the lights went down.

The fashion editors were buzzing, wondering who I could possibly be, but Christy had warned me not to talk to any of them. She didn't want anyone stealing her story. Christy didn't have to worry; I was too mesmerized by the action on the runway to talk to any of the fashion editors.

I couldn't believe I was there, watching a great master, a legend, introducing his new line. The clothing, the colors, the music, the backdrop—not to mention the models, with their expertly coiffed hair, makeup, and jewelry. . . . It was all so incredible. I had never seen a fashion show of this magnitude before.

As soon as it was over and the lights came back up, Christy grabbed me and pulled me backstage. We raced past the guards, with Christy shouting, "Let us through. I have Yves Saint Laurent's protégé here."

As the fashion editors crowded around Yves Saint Laurent, I got my first up-close glimpse of my idol. He appeared to be in his fifties, and although obviously revered, he was not at all pompous. I was surprised that his persona was actually childlike, almost bashful. Joy ran interference so Christy could have a moment with the designer. Over the din, I heard snatches of what she was telling him: ". . . the tuition for the École . . . Anthony Mark Hankins would like to meet you. . . ."

"It was a wonderful collection. Really beautiful and moving," I quickly told him in my fledgling French as I was thrust in front of my idol. He took my hand in a sincere greeting and graciously thanked me. Before I could catch my breath, my brief encounter with him was over. Yves Saint Laurent was cordial and friendly, but I was painfully aware of the throng still vying for his attention. Feeling light-headed, I wanted to get away from the crush of people as soon as possible.

The *Today* show cameraman had filmed our exchange from a respectful distance. Watching my introduction to Yves Saint Laurent being filmed with a television news camera, the fashion editors turned their attention momentarily to Christy, who was beaming.

"Christy, Christy, who is this kid?" they all wanted to know.

"You'll see him on the *Today* show," she answered triumphantly.

After Christy returned to New York, taking the camera crews with her, I settled into the rigorous, cloistered life of being a student at the École. I struggled to scrape up the money I needed to make my Marilyn Monroe sundress for the Air France competition. A friend of Joan Wilchins, Emmanuelle Jacomet, commissioned me to make her a little black dress like the one I had made for Joan. I quickly made it for her and used the money I earned to go back to the fabric store to buy my piqué. It also cost me over a hundred dollars to have the fabric dyed.

Emmanuelle was a graphics designer, and she helped me make the ceramic buttons for my Marilyn Monroe dress. Her father, who worked for the Paris Opera, had a kiln, and Emmanuelle and I fired the buttons in it. The three of us became great friends in the process.

I stayed up many late nights working on this dress, putting it all together. Nothing was turning out right, however; I spent twenty-four hours nonstop doing the hems alone. Adding to my stress was Madame Miodowski's criticism of my work. She belittled my efforts in front of all the other students. It seemed that everything I was doing was wrong—the draping, the collar, the design. . . .

It bothers me to this day, but I wonder if the main reason she ripped my work apart was just because I was American. As a student of Homer Layne, I think I would have learned how to set a sleeve in, you know? She gave me such drama on the bustier, and criticized my stitching, my lining, my hems. . . . She also had me use cheap, cheesy snaps inside the dress. Madame Miodowski didn't seem to care about that little detail, but I did. She drove me crazy. It was the hardest time of my life.

With every idea I had, she seemed reluctant to give her approval. As I was working on the dress, she told me I'd have to wait a week for the bias in the skirts to settle. What was I going to do for a week? I also did all the hand embroidery on the dress. She told me I couldn't possibly have time to complete all the embroidery, but I did it, girl-friend. I embroidered on the bus and everywhere I went, working through many sleepless nights to complete every-thing.

Helping me cope, however, were the relationships I was finally forging with my fellow students at the École. We really got to know each other through parties and other social events. Once they found out that I was a nice guy, we became friends and valued allies.

Even though I was often at the breaking point during my struggles at the École, being in France was liberating to a large degree. I could finally be who I wanted to be and freely plan for my future. While I studied at the École, I concentrated on my dream of one day being a famous designer. I had to have a name that would be recognizable. What about Anthony Moya? Or Anthony Moya-Hankins? Or, I thought, an even more sophisticated name might be Antonio Moya. I signed my sketches using any one of these signatures over the next two years.

15

Riding the Roller Coaster

Although my Paris flat wasn't quite what I had expected, the rent was practically nothing, so I really couldn't complain. I worked hard to turn my dingy apartment into a refuge from all the pressures of school. I opened all the windows as often as I could so fresh air would chase out the stale odors, and I swathed my little atelier with fresh coats of paint. Colorful French posters soon hid the cracks and holes in the walls, and I quickly made curtains out of bright fabrics to cover the windows so the drug addicts didn't have an easy view into my apartment. I bought small rugs to warm up the place, too.

Even though I had only been in Paris a short time, I had already managed to find some cute but cheap dolls and toys to liven up my space. I've always collected dolls from around the world, as well as toys, antique posters and post-cards, carnival glass, Depression glass, and African-American

folk art, among many other things. I'm very good at trading and haggling over prices, so no matter where I am, my
collections seem to grow.

The main room of the apartment really wasn't bad once
I got everything cleaned up. It was a huge space, actually,
with a large worktable—a perfect workroom for my school
projects. Once I had beautiful fabrics draped across chairs
and worktables, your attention was no longer on the dingy
floor or the cracked plaster walls.

When Joan came to visit me after I'd settled in, she didn't
recognize the place. It had been transformed. The dreary
apartment was suddenly bright and full of life! Gone was
the horrible stale, dank air that had originally greeted us.
When she had stayed there, Joan confessed, it had never
occurred to her that such an ugly space could be made so
appealing. Now she walked in circles around the place,
admiring my choices in cheap-but-chic student decor.

"Anthony," she exclaimed, "it's adorable! How did you
do it?"

Joan had not even attempted to fix up the place when
she had stayed there after first arriving in Paris. As a single
woman, she had been very uncomfortable with the stares
from the neighborhood's Muslim men, who didn't approve
of women going out at night unchaperoned. They assumed
that with her dark hair, she was Algerian, and they'd yell
at her when they saw her out alone. She told me that she
had wanted to yell back, "I'm not Algerian. I'm American
and Jewish, so leave me alone!"

Men had also followed her around, making her very
nervous. She didn't feel safe opening up the windows to
the apartment because she didn't trust the neighborhood.
Without fresh air in the apartment, the atmosphere within
remained stale and stifling. Joan had once gone out into

the hallway to use the locked bathroom, only to see some drug addicts who had wandered into the building, shooting up. That was the last straw for her. She had moved out of the apartment into finer quarters.

Ironically, now that we've both left that neighborhood, it's become a very chic, ethnic enclave known for its funky restaurants and art galleries. Then, however, it was simply full of very poor immigrants, and while my neighbors and fellow tenants were nice people, the added mix of drug addicts and prostitutes gave the neighborhood a dangerous edge.

Back in the States, the *Today* show piece about me aired on December 9, 1988. While my family and friends in Elizabeth marveled at my loud mouth boldly declaring, "I don't want a part of Fifth Avenue. I want all of Fifth Avenue," I was actually struggling daily in Paris just to conquer much, much smaller mountains. Far from conquering Fifth Avenue, I was barely able to master my lesson assignments—my mind had to translate them from French into English, sometimes with erroneous results. The French language still constantly tripped me up.

Although I needed to perfect my grip on the language, it wasn't as much of a priority as I had thought it would be. We were so busy putting together our individual school projects that sometimes I'd work for twenty-four hours straight without having to speak to anyone.

It was depressing to be so far away from home and just about everyone I knew. It was hard to subdue my boisterous personality to blend in with the more reserved French students. Getting acclimated to Paris, I was beginning to realize, was going to take some time. Everything looks similar to American sensibilities, but it is so subtly different that it puts you on an uneven keel.

While Americans are loud and boisterous, for instance, the French tend to be very guarded and reserved. They seem to talk very softly, sometimes in a whisper. It must have been a shock to my fellow students at the École when I arrived with my loud, shoutful self. I didn't have a choice but to try to tone myself down. I no longer arrived at class in outrageous ensembles, either. In New York City, someone could walk down the street in their pajamas and no one would notice; believe me, in Paris, it would have been a major incident.

Joan was an American oasis for me in Paris, and the Nems were another source of comfort. Amal was so sweet and invited me over for many a meal. I loved her Lebanese food, and I learned French from her teenage children, who still lived at home. We hung out a lot together, watching French television, playing card games, and grabbing hamburgers at a McDonald's there. I was surprised to realize that in France, McDonald's serves beer.

To help me meet life's challenges every week, Amal would read my fortune in my coffee grounds quite often. I'd drink her strong Lebanese coffee, then turn the cup upside down and let it drain. Amal would read the markings of the coffee grounds left in the cup's bottom.

"You're going to have good luck this week," she might tell me. "You will have a problem with an assignment, but don't worry, it will all turn out all right."

Quite often, her predictions would come true. It always amazed me.

While I was in Paris, my mother struggled to send me twenty dollars a week, along with a monthly care package of American-brand goodies that were hard to get in the City of Light—boxes of cookies, toothpaste, deodorant, potato chips, and other sorely missed items. I was always short of money, however, and often couldn't pay my utility bills. I'd wash my clothes in the kitchen sink instead of at the laundry. At one point, I was literally working by candlelight in my flat and went five days without eating. I was practically delirious with hunger but too proud to say so.

One thing that kept me going was remembering what I had read about Barbra Streisand's struggles when she was first starting out as a singer. She was making so little money that she couldn't even afford a city bus ride back to her flat after her gigs at night. Friends would invite Barbra over to eat because they knew she couldn't afford to buy groceries. Her costumes and clothing all came from thrift shops, where she bought each item for a dollar or two.

Barbra had stuck it out, and so could I. My stomach might wake me up at night with its rumbling, but I would just have to put up with it for a while. When I had no money, I would go down to the local grocery store and ask the owner, who was very friendly and nice, if he'd give me some food on credit, and he would always do that for me. I'd pay him back as soon as I had the money.

During that time, my friend Andrea from Pratt flew to Paris as often as she could to visit her fiancé, Gregory Sebaoun, whom I had met while we were attending Pratt. When Andrea and I got together in Paris, she took one look at my neighborhood and gave me a sympathetic hug. She also took a look at my skinny self and exclaimed, "Anthony, baby, what's wrong with you? You look thin as a rail. Oh, honey, let's go get something to eat!"

She took me to a hamburger place, and I tell you, that hamburger tasted so good! It was a salty hamburger, but we cried and cried over that hamburger. Bless you, Andrea, she was my girl!

*   *   *

Andrea's boyfriend, Gregory, and his family owned a denim company called Donovan in Paris. I had visited the shop and admired the jackets they had on their racks. One evening in November, Andrea and Gregory noticed that I didn't have a coat for the chilly air. At a carnival that night, Andrea and Gregory wanted to go on this crazy, souped-up ride that was skyscraper-high with gondolas that spun around on it. You could see all of Paris when your gondola got to the top of the ride. I was terrified of heights, though, and didn't want to get on that thing. If I wanted to have a bird's-eye view of Paris, I'd rather buy a postcard or get on a plane. Andrea and Gregory bribed me unmercifully to get on the ride, though.

"Anthony, you get on that crazy ride and I'll give you a jacket," Gregory challenged me.

Oh, God. He knew I needed a coat and didn't really have the money to get one. I considered the offer. When I looked up at the mechanical monstrosity that rose as high as the Eiffel Tower into the night sky, I broke out in a cold sweat and felt my breathing become shallow. But, I argued with myself, the ride was safe—nothing could really happen to me. And how long was it? Only maybe ten minutes long? What was ten minutes of terror?

With a dry throat and wobbly knees, I let them talk me into taking a seat on that evil ride. As the attendant locked us in, I prayed for an out-of-body experience. As the gondola we were strapped into rose higher and higher, my hysteria grew with each soaring view of Paris. Every time the gondola swayed, I thought I was going to pass out; I'm sure my soul was turned inside out for Andrea and Gregory to see. They hadn't realized that I had such a phobia of heights. I hadn't been exaggerating my fear to them. Every time they glanced over and saw my stricken face, they probably feared I might have a heart attack before the ride wound down and we mercifully reached the ground once more.

As we landed, Andrea and Gregory had to help my hysterical self off the gondola. I was sweating profusely and my heart was palpitating wildly. I had a hard time finding my normal speaking voice. But I had survived! The coat was mine. I didn't get it for nothing. I earned it. The very next day, I showed up at Donovan and told Gregory, "Child, I'm here for that coat!"

Andrea always knew how to cheer me up. After this trip, she sent me occasional care packages from New York, stuffed with treasures from home like Oreo cookies, canned hams, and anything else she could think of. When we went out together on her many trips to Paris to be with Gregory, I'd sometimes dress up to get a reaction from the staid Parisians, just like I had in high school. One day, I'd be dressed as a cowboy; the next, I might wear knickerbockers.

I also had fun with my new friends at the École. We'd pretend that we were already famous designers. I hung out with this black American girl named Sonya Quarterman, who was taking classes at the École, as well as interning with Patrick Kelly; and her friend Marie Chantal, a French girl who was a fit model. When we felt like kicking up our heels sometimes on Saturday nights, we'd call up exclusive nightclubs and discos that were hard to get into, like Les Bains-douches, and, in very proper English, proclaim that we were calling on behalf of Antonio Moya, a famous black fashion designer from America, who was in Paris and would like to enjoy their club for the evening. Would it be possible to leave his party's name on the list of admissions?

If the answer was yes, we'd dress up in our finest funky clothes, get on the metro, and formally announce our arrival to the club's doorman, who would look up our names on the VIP list and allow us in. Sometimes, we'd luck out and even receive VIP treatment inside, too, with the best seats, free drinks, the works. It was great to pretend for an evening that we were somebodies rather than stressed-out, struggling students.

Living on a less-than-meager budget soon began to take its toll, however. My health was starting to fade. Amal took action to help me when she realized I had lost so much weight. I didn't find out until much later that she had called Joy Henderiks at YSL on my behalf.

"You should see Anthony," she told Joy. "He looks horrible. It's a shame—he has no money for food. Can't you give him a job or something?"

The next day, I got a call at school. Joy had made arrangements for me to work at YSL three days a week. She told me to go see Christophe Girard, the *secrétaire général* of YSL-Paris. I was thrilled and nervous to be meeting someone so high up in the company, but Christophe's manner was friendly and engaging. After a casual interview, he finalized the offer for me to work as a paid intern at Yves Saint Laurent. I was to start working for YSL right after Christmas. I couldn't believe my good fortune.

At the same time I got the job at YSL, Meg also hired me to look after her kids three days a week. When I got off work at YSL, I'd go to her house to take care of her children. She would always make sure when I got over there that she had a table full of food. I think my friends were all in a conspiracy to take care of me. Meg was wonderful, and it was great to have a fellow American to talk to. I could go to Meg and she'd listen to my problems.

When collection time came around and I had to donate fabrics, she'd come up with something I could do to earn the money for the fabric—just like Pat Tomei and the sewing machine in my courthouse days.

"There's nothing in life for free," Meg would remind me. "We'll help you, but you need to earn it."

Around this time, a magical thing happened. My mother's good friend Mrs. Mildred Young, who was like my godmother, told her, "Mary, Anthony will not be hungry anymore. We're going to invest in that young man."

True to her word, Mrs. Young began sending me sixty dollars every week, along with my mom's twenty, so that I had eighty dollars a week for the rest of my time there. With such help from all these earthly angels, I was finally able to live in Paris a bit more comfortably. I could eat well, pay the rent, and get the power turned back on in my apartment.

When I started working at Yves Saint Laurent, it was incredible. Incredible, incredible. At YSL, there were seven or eight directors of separate ateliers, and each atelier specialized in one thing, like hats, shirts, blouses, suits, furs, men's wear, shoes, and so on. My boss, Frédérique, was in charge of evening gowns and silk. I was so grateful for the opportunity to work there, but a few of the kids at school really resented it when they found out about my internship. They retaliated by treating me coldly, criticizing my work, and occasionally giving me the wrong assignment information.

I was also still struggling with my limited French, which made my classes even more difficult. I wanted to answer in English because I was more comfortable with that, but I knew that I had to find the correct words in French. I soon learned the meaning of *faux pas* when I saw the color drain suddenly from Madame Miodowski's face as I described a garment to her.

I realized in horror, as I heard students snicker behind me, that a French word a student had "helped" me with must not have been quite appropriate. I found out later it was a word more suitably used in a brothel or a bathhouse. Fortunately, when Madame Miodowski saw how shocked I was, she chastised the students for setting me up.

Financially, my internship at YSL helped my situation immensely, but my work outside of school created another problem—exhaustion. There were teachers who didn't understand why some days I'd come in so tired, but I made 1,000 francs a month at YSL and really needed the money.

I centered myself, though, by listening to my Barbra Streisand albums. I must have played the song "Putting It Together" a million times. It reminded me of all the times I'd ridden the G train into New York from Brooklyn to work with Homer. I don't know how I had managed to put in all those hours interning, not to mention keeping up with all my class projects at Pratt, as well as my duties with the Fashion Society. "Putting It Together" made me realize that if I could do it all then, I could manage that type of load now. With this song as an inspirational mantra of sorts, I was able to get through many trying days at the École.

At the end of December, the entries for the Air France competition were being judged with a runway presentation in Paris. I wasn't able to attend the event because I was in Germany for Christmas, visiting Angie who was stationed there. I was told, though, that the model wearing my dress had done her best Marilyn Monroe imitation in it and that everyone had oohed and aahed over it. My creation had apparently received a good reception, but I was still crushed that it hadn't placed.

16

✂ -

In the House of
Yves Saint Laurent

My first job at YSL was in the evening wear atelier, where everyone was friendly and helped me as much as they could. I also made friends in other areas of the company. I had a card that entitled me to go into the YSL lunchroom for free and soon I became really good friends with Yves Saint Laurent's chef, as well as with his chauffeur and this young woman in the pattern room. I would never have connected those three but was surprised to learn that the chef used to be the chauffeur, the present chauffeur was his son, and the woman in the pattern room was the chauffeur's wife. They had known Yves Saint Laurent forever.

I had a project due at school and my newfound friends at YSL helped me get the materials for it. When I needed feathers for a dress, for instance, and couldn't afford to buy them, Frédérique would go to the trim department and come to my rescue. She not only gave me the feathers I needed but also left a box full of other trim goodies on my desk later. Everyone there looked after me. Joy would often come to visit Frédérique, but I think she was really checking up on me.

"Oh, by the way, how's my Anthony doing?" she would ask me, as she and Frédérique ended their conversation. Heading for the door, she'd call out, "Talk to you later, Frédérique—and see you later, Anthony." I'm sure Joy wanted to make sure I wasn't still suffering from malnutrition.

Meanwhile, our next project at the École was to make a smoking jacket, but I couldn't envision making just one. As usual, I wanted to be the overachiever in the class and create a series of three jackets. My proposal, however, first had to be approved by a small faculty committee headed by Madame Saurat.

"There's no way he can make all those jackets," one of the professors commented. "We don't care if he is an intern with Yves Saint Laurent, he'll be lucky to make just one and he wants to make three? It's crazy."

One thing I have since realized about the French is that many of them are born pessimists. The first time I would suggest a project, I'd get the answer, "No, it's impossible—it can never be done." The second time I would pitch it, I'd hear, "Well, maybe it could be done. We'll see." The third time, I might receive the go-ahead to do the project. Then, when the project turned out great, what would they say? "Oh, yes, I knew it would work."

I knew I could make it happen, I told the faculty members, and they reluctantly approved the project. Working my butt off, I did accomplish it all—even though Madame Miodowski fought me the whole time, as usual. These jackets turned out fierce, though. Each jacket's back was hand-embroidered. One jacket named all the major cities in the U.S. in beefy embroidery. "Free Nelson Mandela, Cry Freedom" and "A Day in New York" were the themes of the other two jackets.

I was killing myself to get them done, of course, sewing on sequins and madly embroidering on the bus, the train, in the lunchroom, and everywhere else over the two months we had to complete the jackets. I couldn't afford to hire someone to do the embroidering for me, so I was doing it all myself.

Finally, I finished the "Nelson Mandela" jacket. It was smokin'! Then I concentrated on the other two. A friend of Joan's knew an artist whose work I admired, and he invited me to visit with him in his studio. He helped me make these fun cartoon figures to go on the "Day in New York" jacket.

While I was frantically working on the jackets, I was also baby-sitting Meg's son Felix, who had the measles. I was sure I'd already had the measles as a child, so I wasn't worried about catching it. Unfortunately, I was wrong about my medical history and suddenly found myself suffering flat out with my own case of adult-size measles—right before the jackets were due. Man, I was sick as a dog. My face was broken out; I had a runny nose and puffy eyes, and felt tired as hell.

Meg felt terrible about it.

"What are you going to do?" she asked me.

"I don't know what I'm going to do, Meg," I confessed. "I'm just going to pray that it goes away."

Despite my constant prayers, I only got sicker. Itchy red bumps covered my body, and I suffered from a sore throat and a raging fever. I finally forced myself out of my sickbed to go to the École to tell Madame Miodowski that I was ill and couldn't finish my project. When the other students saw my swollen, bumpy face, they gasped. As I sat there waiting for a break in the class so I could tell Madame Miodowski about my illness, another student, Isabelle, who sat in front of me, studied the situation. Her husband was in medical school.

"Antony, you've got to see a doctor," Isabelle said. When I told her I had no money to see a doctor, she offered to call her husband. Isabelle took charge and picked up the teacher's phone, which was generally off-limits to students, to call him. Her husband suggested that she take me to a friend, who was also a doctor, for an examination. Isabelle took me by the arm and firmly told Madame Miodowski, "We'll be back."

After Isabelle's doctor friend examined me and wrote a prescription, I asked him how much I owed him.

"It's free," he replied. "You're in my country and you're a friend of Isabelle's, so don't worry about it."

I thanked him profusely for being so kind. He and Isabelle were saints. So many good things have happened to me—more than I deserve in one lifetime, I'm sure. When we got back, Michael, too, helped me out by loaning me some money so I could get the prescription filled. I took the pills, climbed into my sickbed, and prayed.

When I woke up the next morning, I was amazed. My face wasn't so swollen. It felt like my face again. I'm not a person who usually believes in the supernatural, but the next day I was back at school doing my work—feeling great. God had given me a miracle after all. I had four days until my collection was due and I was hauling.

"Isabelle, you're going to get the blessing of all time!" I told my friend.

I got the jackets finished two days before the presentation, which was held at a wonderful historic theater in Paris. The three jackets hit the spotlights simultaneously, with three models suddenly stepping out on the runway—wearing the jackets, along with tap-dance shorts, fedoras, and cool attitudes like three female James Bonds. Madame Saurat told me later that she was sitting by Pierre Bergé, Yves Saint Laurent's partner and the CEO at YSL. When the jackets appeared, he turned to Madame Saurat and commented, "Superior work." She reminded him that I was interning at YSL.

After the students' presentation, the École celebrated its sixtieth birthday by highlighting famous students' work like that of Courrèges, Issey Miyake, and Olivier Lapidus. Of course, Yves Saint Laurent's work was the showstopper at the end of the retrospective.

The next day, Janie Samet, the fashion editor of the Paris newspaper *Le Figaro,* did an article on the collection, illustrating it with fashion sketches, including one by Anthony Moya Hankins! Even Yves Saint Laurent himself noticed my work, and I soon found myself promoted to the Studio of Textiles at YSL. My friends from the sewing room were so supportive.

"You did it, Antony," Frédérique cried. *"Bien fait."*

In the sewing room, I had been guarded, protected, and loved. The Studio of Textiles, however, had a whole different atmosphere. There, I found myself being fed to the wolves in the design room because these people were determined to keep their positions and they wanted all the young designers moved out. No one was supportive in this atelier. They never gave me credit for my textile designs or my print choices.

Now I felt under siege at two institutions. At the École, Madame Miodowski seemed to think I was a total zero. In the Studio of Textiles at YSL, they laughed at my ideas for textile design. I knew how to pick my prints, but back then I believed them when they told me my choices were ridiculous. I thought I wasn't good at it.

What kept me going? I don't know. An inner drive, I suppose. I just had to get through this, I continually told myself. I concentrated on perseverance. I loved color and painting, and deep down, I knew that I had a flair for design, so why weren't my ideas appreciated?

I endured the reptiles in the Studio of Textiles for the next two months until I was moved to the shoe department, where, unfortunately, I encountered a new problem. My new boss, a woman I'll call Cecile, seemed to hate everything I did in that department and even accused me of copying other designers. I had made a bag for one of my school projects, and she actually accused me of stealing the idea. I admit that it was inspired by a shape the guy had used and it's a common practice to borrow ideas, but her criticisms went on for two months.

"I don't like these sketches," Cecile said to me one day after I turned in my work to her.

"Fine," I retorted. "I'll just take them with me then."

I made up my mind, though, to be better than she was. I asked Christophe Girard if he would move me out of Cecile's department. Christophe was a wonderful source of support, and soon I was moved on to the men's wear department. I had a good time there because the men weren't so catty. I worked my butt off, however, stacking the shoes and breaking down the sets of the fashion shows, among other duties. I loved the people in this department, and they really gave me a chance to shine.

Meanwhile, Madame Miodowski's constant criticism of my work was taking its toll on me. I was having trouble keeping up with all my projects for school, not to mention all the dresses I had been hired to make for people. It seemed virtually impossible to meet all my deadlines, and school pressures seemed to weigh heavier on my shoulders every day. Depressed, I was beginning to wonder how I would ever make it through to graduation.

Around this time, Joan invited me to a party at her place in honor of her brother Eddie, who was coming to Paris to visit for a few weeks. I was really excited to see a friendly face from home! Although I was suffering from major burnout, I told Eddie that everything was going fine. I was happy. But Eddie, as usual, could see right through me. A couple of days later, we got together at a café. Unbeknownst to me, Joan had told him she suspected that I was having a hard time. Eddie, never one to run from an issue, confronted me with it.

"Anthony, what's going on?" he asked me with his usual point-blank diplomacy.

"I'm just not fitting in here," I blurted out. "I feel like a fish out of water. I just can't assimilate. I'm still having trouble with the language, and Madame Miodowski hates my work. . . . It's too much. I can't do it all. I swear I'm going to quit and move to Memphis to be a preacher or something."

"Hang tough, Anthony," he reassured me. "You'll get it together. Don't worry."

We talked throughout the evening, and the next day Eddie came to visit me at the École. I introduced him around, and after he toured the school, we went for a walk through a nearby park. A familiar face from home was too much, and my bottled-up tension came swiftly to the surface again.

"I've always told everyone that I was going to be a fashion designer, and now I don't know if I can cut it," I confessed. "I don't want to go home a laughingstock, but I just don't know if I'm going to make it here.

"I'm going to quit," I vowed, and then repeated my earlier threat: "The next time you hear from me, I'll be living back in New York. I'm going back to the States."

Eddie, being a true friend, took me roughly by the jacket and read me the riot act.

"You're NOT going to quit!" he literally screamed at me. "You've only got three more months to go! Listen to me: you're staying or I'm going to kill you. You're not going to let yourself and your family down. This is what you are meant to do with your life. You've got too much talent to let it go."

Here we were, in this peaceful park setting, with Eddie jumping around me like a freak, screaming obscenities at the very thought of my leaving school. He was pretty vocal about it—the real conversation can't even be printed here. I'm sure mothers in the park were grabbing their children and scurrying to find the closest gendarme to report the crazy Americans having a confrontation in the park.

The day Eddie left Paris to go back to the States, I couldn't even give him a smile. I wished I could be going home, too. I knew deep down he had given me the right shock treatment to continue, but at the time, it was painful. I was still upset and unsure about my future. His words eventually did sink in, though, and somehow I found the strength to get through the remaining months of school.

Patrick Kelly also inspired me to go on. We had spoken over the phone and had met in social situations. He was very sweet and down-to-earth, and our tastes were eerily similar. Patrick and I were so alike that I thought we must be cosmic twins. When I first met him, I felt like I was looking in a mirror. Other people noticed it, too, and commented on it.

I attended one of Patrick's fashion shows in Paris, where Tookie Smith, Willi Smith's sister, was one of his top models. Tookie had started her modeling career working for her brother but soon was in demand with other designers because of her incredible spirit on the runway. She was jammin'. She would come out and just let you have it, throwing her hands up for joy and dancing down that runway. Child, it was like Josephine Baker had come back to Paris. The fashion crowds loved it, and Patrick, especially, wanted that same sense of fun in his shows. Tookie put passion in the fashion. It was *all* there, girlfriend.

After the show, I went backstage to meet Tookie, who took the time to introduce me to the famous fashion correspondent Elsa Klensch, who hosted CNN's weekly half-hour show called *Style with Elsa Klensch*. I was so touched that Tookie would take the time to do that. She certainly didn't have to; she could easily have just talked to Elsa about Patrick Kelly. After experiencing the exuberance of Patrick Kelly and Tookie Smith, I felt my old spirit of adventure returning.

At YSL, Frédérique was asked one day to oversee the fitting of a suit that the Duchess of York, Fergie herself, had commissioned. This fitting normally would have been handled by the head of the suit atelier, but he could not be present for some reason. Frédérique did not speak English at all and wanted to be sure to understand the duchess, so she invited me to the fitting as an interpreter and I was elated. Anthony Mark Hankins, from Elizabeth, New Jersey, was going to meet the duchess—Miss Royalty herself.

Sarah Ferguson was very congenial and polite. Since I was an African-American in such a French institution, the duchess was curious about me, and she asked about my background. Fergie was excited for me that I had gotten the chance to work at YSL. We enjoyed working with the duchess for her fitting, but I heard that her frequent weight fluctuations at that time presented a few challenges to the fitters.

I was also honored to be asked to work with actress Sigourney Weaver on an exquisite white Grecian gown that YSL was preparing for her to wear to the Oscars that year. This dress later made the pages of *People* and *Star* magazines, among others. Sigourney was a radiant person, and I was proud to assist her with the gown. As I later watched her, on French television, step up onto the stage at the Oscars in that gorgeous dress, I couldn't help beaming. I had hemmed that very gown that was now being seen on television by millions around the world.

(top left) With my twin sister, Angie, plotting our next adventure.

(top right) Another Sunday with Mom, attending Grace Temple Baptist Church.

(bottom left) Ugh! The fat years! I must have eaten too many of Mom's doughnuts. My brother James is seated next to me. Standing behind us are *(left to right)* Raymond, Jeffrey, and Kevin.

Trying to look cool in my Michael Jackson high-water pants on my eighth-grade graduation day.

Posing proudly in my Color Guard uniform in 1983.

Katie, our sister and Mom's second in command, with (*left to right*) James, Jeffrey, and Kevin at Christmas, 1985.

James and Kevin with our beloved Grandma Toy in Virginia, a few months before she passed away.

Angie and I at our high school winter formal, 1986, being crowned king and queen by senior class advisors Janet Papetti and Mike Villani. I made both our outfits.

Angie and I dressed for the senior prom, 1986. Her dress was inspired by Lena Horne's in the movie *Stormy Weather*.

PUTTING IT TOGETHER—PIECE BY PIECE

Designs I created while attending the Pratt Institute in Brooklyn, 1986.

An early fitting with my friend Cherub.

(*left*) My jackets being shown in Paris, 1989.

(*left*) One of my more recent designs.

A design I created as a student in Paris, 1989.

After a TV taping of the *Mike & Maty* show. The model on the far right is wearing the suit I made for my mom when I was seven years old, crooked seams and all.

MAKING THE CONNECTIONS

Meeting Yves Saint Laurent, with Joy Henderiks, in Paris was beyond exciting for me.

At the Home Shopping Network with designer Daniel Kiviat, our buyer Jenny O'Malley, her assistant Brian, and Ivana Trump.

Getting legal tips from Johnnie Cochran.

Saving the overtime for Gladys Knight.

Dionne Warwick giving me some sisterly advice. That's what friends are for!

It was an honor meeting Coretta Scott King, the First Lady of the civil rights movement.

Enjoying a hug with one of my favorite talk show hosts, Rolanda Watts.

Becoming more politically aware with Kweisi Mfume.

In the spirit with Susan Taylor of *Essence* magazine.

Mom and my stepdad, Pete, dressed up for an awards gala. I designed her outfit.

One of my favorite pictures with Mom, a beautiful lady.

Enjoying a limo ride with Angie. Sometimes dreams do come true!

17

✂ --

Au Revoir, Paris

Before I knew it, I had finished my program at the École. I was exhausted by the accumulated stress of the classes and projects. There was no graduation fanfare from the faculty. "Fine. Now go get work" was their simple attitude. The students, however, held parties in their apartments to celebrate the end to our monastic life at the École. We looked forward to utilizing our hard-earned skills in the Paris designers' ateliers.

Frédéric Castet, who was in charge of the fur division of Christian Dior–Paris, had contacted the school regarding its most recent graduates. While I interviewed with him and was offered a job, I decided that I wanted to continue my affiliation with YSL. It was exciting, though, to realize that other designers might be interested in hiring me and I was eager to finally become a professional in my field.

Christophe Girard, at YSL, had also taken a real interest in my fledgling career and often gave me books and articles on the fashion industry to read, along with extra work when I needed it. He believed in me and was a wonderful ally through all my trials and frustrations. He made sure I had a good seat at fashion shows so I could see the collections, and would invite me to join his set of friends for social engagements.

When Christophe invited me one day to join his crowd for an elegant evening at the theater, dahling, I realized in a panic that I owned nothing suitable for such an affair. I went to the men's wear atelier at YSL and asked my friend Bernard there to help me out. Faster than a flash, I was decked out in a wonderful smoked-camel suede jacket, with a scarf and a turtleneck underneath, a straight-leg pant, and suede boots that were as soft as butter.

Bernard and I admired the ensemble he had put together for me in one of the atelier's full-length mirrors. I looked like a million dollars and again felt like Cinderella going to the ball, since the clothes had to be back in the atelier the next day. The scarf was gorgeous and I wanted it so bad. I wasn't going to just take it for myself, though. I had too much pride for that.

Soon after I graduated from the École, Christophe asked me what I wanted to do and I told him that I wanted to learn about knitwear. I wanted to go to the south of France to work with Michel Paris, a knitwear designer whom I had met and admired. Michel's company manufactures sweaters for the designers in Paris, with YSL being one of his chief accounts. Christophe recommended me to Michel, who, being such a gentleman, formally asked Christophe if he could "borrow Anthony's talents" for a few months.

I was in seventh heaven as I traveled to Vaison-la-Romaine by train to spend the next few months in the south of France near Monaco to work with Michel. I had tons of luggage with me—everything I had owned in Paris. I felt exhilarated. I had graduated from the École and interned with YSL; now I was going to work with Michel Paris! I kept singing to myself "Let's Hear It for Me"—Barbra's triumphant song from *Funny Lady*. I was well on my way to tearing up the fashion world.

Meeting me at the train station was a representative from Michel's company, who was a jovial and proper fellow wearing a gray tweed flannel blazer with a paisley vest, tie, and lace-up leather shoes. He reminded me of a younger version of the actor Sebastian Cabot, who played the butler, Mr. French, in the television series *Family Affair*, except that he smoked cigarettes constantly.

"Bonjour, Antony!" he greeted me. "We're so happy to have you here!"

As we drove across the gorgeous landscape of Vaison-la-Romaine to Michel Paris' office, Mr. French, as I now thought of him, told me he was friends with Patrick Kelly. I was impressed with that, but on the downside, he was also friends with my nemesis at YSL, Cecile! Mr. French turned out to be friendly—often, too friendly. This Mr. French, I discovered, was gay and all hands, honey. I was definitely not interested in playing footsie with this man, so I played dumb with him the whole summer while deftly fending off his advances.

I can't help thinking that if I had slept with Mr. French, I might have gotten a better job with Michel's company that summer. As it was, I worked in Michel's factory for the summer and learned how to use the machinery, which was hard work. I had to learn how to count gauges and perform quite a few other technical tasks.

At first, they tried to have me run the shimatronic computer, which analyzes the sketch of a sweater, feeds the specifications in to a knitting machine, and—voila!—a sweater comes out the other end. Unfortunately, I was all thumbs with this mechanized system and my first sweater came out horrible.

Since I'm much better with handwork, I ended up mainly working on sketches in the design lab on projects for YSL, along with sweaters and dresses. Michel stressed consistency in his final product, and that was an important lesson to learn. Michel's daughter, Isabelle, and I also got along well. She lived in Paris and wanted me to work with her on some of her projects because she liked my energy.

I stayed the whole summer in a small, quaint bed-and-breakfast inn run by a wonderful three-generation French family who often invited me to their family table for meals. There were about a dozen rooms in the inn, with a common bathroom down the hall. When I first arrived, however, I didn't realize that their doors locked at six o'clock every night. I had gone to a movie and didn't return to the inn until about nine o'clock. I had forgotten my key, unfortunately, and ended up being stranded outside all night in the cold.

When I realized I was locked out, I grabbed two outdoor café chairs, put them together, and tried to lie down on them. Trying to stretch out on these chairs wasn't even remotely comfortable, and I was freezing. There was no way I could get any rest or sleep. The milkman finally arrived at 6:00 A.M. and, discovering this frozen American Popsicle, let me into the inn with his key. I didn't have the key to my room, so I stretched out stiffly on the lobby stairs until the owners showed up at 9:00 A.M. I was still suffering the effects of the deep evening chill.

The innkeepers were most concerned about my frozen condition. They helped me up to my room and into bed, where I stayed all the next day, fighting off a threatening case of pneumonia. After being called and told of my illness, Michel and Mr. French soon arrived to bring me chicken soup and wish me a speedy recovery from my ordeal.

After I recovered, I would walk to work from the inn while listening constantly to Barbra on my Walkman. Once I got to the factory, Mr. French was always there to greet me with more than open arms. That boy was a trip. I had to ward him off all the time. Luckily, I was seldom alone with him, so it wasn't that hard to put him off.

"It's so great to have you as a friend," I would tell him, while making sure he kept his roving hands to himself. While Mr. French was not my style, I was, however, really attracted to Michel. He was in his late forties and wore wire-rimmed glasses. I thought he was the coolest and wanted to get to know him better on a personal level. He was divorced, though he and his wife still worked together and were great friends. They shared his business and she also owned a kitchen accessories shop across town.

Michel and I did become great friends over the summer, and it was a magical time. He lived in a gorgeous château, a large country house facing a lake and surrounded by fields and countryside. Despite its size, Michel's home was warm and unpretentious, as if generations of his family had left their memories there. Horses and farm animals freely roamed the grounds. It was heaven.

Michel would invite me to his house for parties and dinners, and I also attended dinners at his friends' châteaus, which were often very froufrou and formal. We would gather in the drawing room for tea, dahling, then go into a formal dining room for dinner. The whole scene really blew my mind. Dreams really do come true. I was hob-nobbing, honey, with the elite, and I wasn't working in no kitchen, wearing no service outfit. I was in the drawing room, child, sipping tea with the best of them. Through Michel, I learned how the wealthy half lives.

His neighbors were like a who's who of the French aristocracy. I tell you, child, I've seen PLACES! I've been to paradise and I've seen it all! Fabulous castles that people can only dream about. Country estates. Dra-ma-tique, honey! Fa-bu! Vaison-la-Romaine is a beautifully quaint village, and chic, to say the least.

With Michel, I traveled to Spain and actually saw bull-fights that reminded me of my favorite opera, *Carmen*. While I didn't care for the actual bullfight, I loved the matador's costumes. Girlfriend, I dug those capes and I've since incorporated them into my fashion shows. They're always dramatic showstoppers.

Before I knew it, summer had stretched into fall. I explored the countryside, meeting some incredible local people and finally becoming intellectually in tune with the French. I was speaking French fluently by this time. The older local people shared with me their riveting firsthand memories of Josephine Baker, from the Resistance period; and of the famed African-American writer/activist James Baldwin. Many people there also knew New York entertainer Bobby Short personally, since he owns a house in that area. They love him there.

Toward the end of six months, heading into the Christmas season, I found myself getting a little homesick for the States as I watched the leaves change to gilded autumn colors. Vaison-la-Romaine was picturesque, but there wasn't much to do outside of work. Even then, I was married to my career, and although I enjoy many wonderful personal relationships, my hectic schedule has probably destined me to remain a "singular sensation."

At a local bistro that I frequented, Jean, the bartender, told me one night that two other Americans were there and he introduced us. They were teachers who had been living in Paris for a year and were as homesick as I was. It was just a blast being able to talk with other Americans. We closed the place down that night.

I couldn't wait to get home to Elizabeth for Christmas. Although I was home for the holidays only a short time, it was enough to relieve my homesickness. Before I knew it, it was time to go back to Paris to resume my work at YSL. I had hardly gotten back into my Parisian mode when Christophe Girard told me some tragic news—the loss of my cosmic twin, Patrick Kelly.

Patrick had died on New Year's Day, 1990, reportedly from complications stemming from a bone-marrow disease. Earlier, we had been surprised to hear that his latest collection had been canceled due to an illness he was fighting. It was hard to believe that he was seriously ill, though, because he always looked so healthy. I was devastated when I heard of his passing. I cried—really cried. I felt like I had lost a brother. We had all certainly lost a creative genius and friend. I was going to miss his whimsical spirit.

Losing the spiritual energy of Patrick seemed to sap my own and I knew I was going to have to make some important career decisions. Should I stay in Paris and keep on working for YSL or some other designer? Or should I go home to America and try my luck on Seventh Avenue?

After I had worked in almost every atelier at YSL, I felt as if I had done my tour. There were no clear avenues of advancement within the company, and I was anxious to go as high as the moon in fashion. I decided that I might have a better chance cutting my own path on American soil, in my own culture. My days at the House of Yves Saint Laurent were coming to an end.

"The party's over. . . ."
Once I had come to grips with my decision, I realized I was truly ready to go back home to America. I was tired and felt like everything was winding down for me in France. I wanted to prove to my own country that Anthony Mark Hankins had something to offer. I had completed my schooling and it was time for me to jump into the fashion pool with both feet. Even though I had loved working at the House of Yves Saint Laurent, I already envisioned someday having my own company.

Christophe suggested that I stay in Paris and work with other designers there, but I explained that I wanted to be my own person and do my own thing. He understood, and assured me that I had his help whenever I needed it. Joy was sad to see me go, too, and offered additional recommendations, which I really appreciated. A few days before I left, I briefly saw Yves Saint Laurent, along with his mother, who was so sweet. They both wished me well and told me how happy they were to have been able to help me.

I also wanted to thank Pierre Bergé for letting me be a part of the company. I called his secretary and asked her if I could see him for a few minutes. I had never really met him but had seen him often. He was probably in his fifties then, very handsome and distinguished-looking, reminding me of a doctor or a judge. I was surprised when I was granted some time with him. It meant a lot to me that he would see me.

Our meeting went great, and I loved his office, which was very elegant, filled with trophies, awards, and an antique desk. He seemed genuinely pleased that I had come to see him. We talked for about an hour and I described my ready-to-wear ideas and how excited I was about them. I had this idea to dress young-spirited, urban women, I told him, and I planned to go back to America and do a collection. I didn't know how I was going to do it, but I knew I was going to make it happen.

"Keep on going forward," he encouraged me. "Believe in yourself and be true to your work. Never sacrifice your craft."

Even in my business dealings today, I remember those words of advice.

Before I left the House of Yves Saint Laurent, my friends there threw a little party for me and Christophe took me to dinner, giving me a black YSL cashmere scarf as a bon-voyage present. I was going to miss all these wonderful people. They had given me the *tour d'horizon* there during my internship because they felt I should learn everything about the House of Yves Saint Laurent. They truly cared and I'll never forget them. Now, every time someone buys an Anthony Mark Hankins dress, they'll know just how much everyone at Yves Saint Laurent did for me.

I knew that it was time, though, to move on. In my pocket was an airline ticket back to the States—the flight that would carry me home. The day before, I had been handed my last paycheck from the House of Yves Saint Laurent, and when I walked out the doors of YSL, I didn't look back. I wasn't really sad, though. I was able to walk through those doors with no fear of the future. As I packed my trunks for the trip home, I anticipated that even greater adventures lay ahead.

18

Seventh Avenue

Flying home to the States, I thought something magical was going to happen with my career. I was on a natural high, having graduated from the prestigious École and completed an internship with the master himself, Yves Saint Laurent. Surely that meant that I would make a big splash in the fashion world when I returned to New York. Seventh Avenue wouldn't know what hit them when Hurricane Anthony blew back into town! It would be a quiet storm that would knock them off their feet. During the eight hours above the clouds and the Atlantic, I had to suppress my growing excitement. I was ready to tear up the fashion world and create my own label. Antonio Fierce had arrived!

My first dose of reality hit me when my plane landed and I realized with a thud that I was really just a cash-poor designer with no job. Even though I was thrilled to see my family, I was frustrated to find myself again living in my parents' house for lack of funds, just as if I had never left for Paris. The only difference was that now I had the experience. I just had to find a job.

I went to the New York offices of Yves Saint Laurent to apply for freelance work and met with Connie Uzzo there to discuss job possibilities. Although there were no immediate openings at YSL in New York, she encouraged me to go to Bidermann Industries, a manufacturer of designer-label men's dress shirts. I landed an entry-level job there, but the pay was practically nonexistent. I also thought the man who hired me suspected that I'd been sent from YSL in Paris to spy on him. He kept me busy doing grunt work like straightening up shelves in the sample room and moving sample boards from room to room. He was full of promises of advancement for me, but I felt I'd probably be stuck at the bottom of the ladder there for quite a long time.

I networked like crazy to try to find a better fashion-industry job in New York, calling my old New York contacts, like Judith Agisim and Christy Ferer. They advised me to go to Adrienne Vittadini, since they knew her and could put in a good word for me. Adrienne told them that I should meet with Odile Laugier at her company, and if Odile liked me, they would hire me. I was excited since Adrienne Vittadini is known for her sophisticated knitwear and I had experience with knitwear from my days working for Michel's company.

Odile, I found out, had also worked as an intern with YSL in Paris. She was about seven years older than me, but we really hit it off. She loved my portfolio, especially since I had a pink snow jacket in my portfolio that had faux fur around the collar with a pink stirrup pant that Odile exclaimed was just the type of thing they were currently working on.

She hired me as an assistant designer in knitwear and I was responsible for taking sweater concepts to full pattern form. These were paper prototypes. I would also research trim, come up with new ideas, and prepare storyboards that traced the line's direction, along with research showing different treatments of the sweater concepts.

In the sweater department at Adrienne Vittadini's, I worked with a woman who was brilliant at creating sweaters that sold so fast they practically flew right off the shelves. She liked me to work with her because I could proofread the cutesy little French sayings that were often added to the sweater fronts. Sometimes I'd catch wildly incorrect French on the sketches for these sweaters.

"Girl, they're going to boo you right out of Saint-Tropez with that bad French," I'd tease her, making her laugh. It always amazed me how fabulous her sweaters were because she herself preferred to wear clothes that were strictly fashion violations—dated old things from the 1970s.

Adrienne was always pleasant and courteous to me, and I worked in a room full of women who were wonderful, but after about four months I found myself again becoming restless. Even though the work I was doing had its importance, I was frustrated that I could never present all of my own ideas and designs.

I tried to figure out what my next step should be toward developing my own line and marketing it. As usual, I was impatient. Impatience is an unfortunate trait that I have had to work on constantly in my life. When I want something to happen, I want it to happen NOW.

I was also disenchanted with life on Seventh Avenue. It seemed like I was surrounded by people with *attitudes*. The designers on Seventh Avenue were a snobby, elitist group, and everything had to revolve around them. I may have my moods, girlfriend, but I can sit down and eat dinner with anybody, you know what I'm saying? To get by every day, I had to ignore all these attitudes. These haute couture snobs were just mere mortals, like the rest of us. I tried never to lose sight of who I was.

Still, it was hard for me not to be a little down. I was only making about $12,000 a year with this entry-level job— barely enough to survive on. It was really just scrapple money. I couldn't afford my own apartment and was feeling a definite need to fly out of the parental nest. It was time, but what was the next step?

Feeling a little down as I pondered this question, my "Aunt" Mildred Young, in Elizabeth, knew just what would lift my spirits. Her women's group was organizing a fund-raiser for our church's building fund. She decided it should be a fashion show and called me to get involved with it. I was thrilled. It was just the tonic I needed, and for this show, I was a designing dynamo.

Mrs. Young, bless her, helped me buy the materials I needed to create the fashions for the show, and to my surprise, the fashion editor of *Essence* magazine, Ionia Dunn-Lee, came to see it. She loved several of my dresses and asked me afterward if she could use them for the magazine. Child, those dresses were in her hands before she could finish getting the words out of her mouth! In December 1990, *Essence* featured one of the dress suits, a metallic brocade with a short wrapped skirt and a fitted jacket. Eddie Murphy's future wife, Nicole, was the model who wore it, and I was ecstatic to see my fashions in a national magazine, with full-page treatment.

Ionia was pleased with the response she received on Nicole's page in the magazine, so she featured one of my ethnic wedding dresses in the February 1991 issue called "Brides: Forget Me Not." My Afrocentric wedding dress was a short-sleeved, short white dress with wooden reeds and beads sewn all over the bodice and sleeves, duchess satin lining, a sheer neckline, and a raffia back with beads. From the back, a train of white taffeta flowed. I couldn't wait to buy this issue off the newsstands.

Other great things started happening, too. Gail Hamilton, the manager of the popular gospel/jazz group Take Six, saw my fashions in *Essence* and called me to ask if I was interested in designing some outfits for the group for a Carnegie Hall appearance scheduled for May 23 and 24, 1990. The group was on fire and had just won their third Grammy. I loved their music, which is a combination of gospel, jazz, pop, and blues. They're known for wearing an easy-elegance style. I was more than excited to create outfits for them and couldn't wait to get started.

For their Carnegie Hall appearance, I designed loose, baggy slacks with soft shirts, spiced with wide, colorful ties and boxy jackets. The concert also featured Stevie Wonder, Whitney Houston, Patti Austin, Branford Marsalis, and CeCe Winans, among others, all performing to raise funds for the Special Olympics in Africa.

It was exciting being backstage for this show, meeting all these music superstars. As Whitney Houston passed by me, she gave me this odd look like she knew me from somewhere but couldn't quite figure out where. I had no trouble remembering where I had seen her in person, though. She used to come sing in our church, Grace Temple, in Newark, all the time.

One of my first notices as a professional designer came out of this gig: I was briefly mentioned in a paragraph about Take Six in the *New York Carib News* for the city's Caribbean-

American community that week. Claudette Roper, a talent booker for *The Cosby Show,* also heard about me through the grapevine and asked if I would make some clothes for her to wear to an Emmy broadcast. Man, I was flying high.

I was anxious to learn even more about the fashion industry so I could apply that knowledge someday when I'd be running my own company. I knew I had an inner calling to do this kind of work, but I realized I had to find the right path to follow to make it happen. A friend suggested that I interview with Bob Mackie, the designing genius who has enjoyed an incredible career creating scene-stealing costumes for which he has won multiple Emmy awards.

During his eleven-year tenure with the weekly *Carol Burnett Show,* Mackie created over fifteen hundred costumes, including everything from stunning evening gowns to Carol Burnett's trademark charwoman rags. For *The Sonny and Cher Comedy Hour* and *The Sonny and Cher Show,* Mackie dressed Cher's exotic physique in bedazzling and revealing gowns that had the network censors working overtime each week to make sure their star was not revealing too much flesh.

I was in total awe of this man's immense talent. I nervously called his office in New York and asked for a job interview. To my relief, I was invited to come over and meet with Mr. Mackie's partner, Ray Aghayan. Mr. Aghayan reviewed my portfolio and liked it, and I was allowed to meet Mr. Mackie himself. I was delighted to find that he was one of the warmest, most phenomenal people I'd ever met in the industry. He looked at each and every one of my sketches and gave me positive comments on many of the sketches.

"You've got a good eye for gimmick," he told me. The ready-to-wear mass market was the way I should go, he advised, adding that learning the business from the ground up would make a great difference in my life. I knew he was right. When we were through with our meeting, he was gracious enough to walk with me to the elevator.

"Do mass product," he reassured me, "and you won't starve."

My meeting with Mr. Mackie left me wanting to learn everything about the fashion business. When I heard about a Quality Assurance job opening up with JCPenney in Los Angeles, I knew that it was meant for me. It was just the sort of job that Mr. Mackie had advised me to get. I had yet to see a full production run and this job would help me learn the business from the manufacturing end—crucial knowledge if I wanted to have my own design company someday.

As I wondered what direction to take, Tookie Smith, Willi Smith's sister, contacted me. She was putting together an event called Willi Smith Day which would honor her late brother and benefit Hale House, a home run by Clara "Mother" Hale to help drug-addicted babies. Tookie remembered that I had worked as an intern for her brother and was a student of Yves Saint Laurent. I was flattered when she called me and invited me to participate.

Singers Valerie Simpson and Nick Ashford also participated, along with actor/dancer Gregory Hines. They and other celebrities modeled the clothes for the fashion show, which ended with a retrospective of Willi Smith. Five of my creations were exhibited, and my name was listed in the program with all the other designers. It was a heady experience.

I was surprised and honored when Tookie invited me back to her apartment for an informal gathering after the show. I was so touched that she thought enough of me to invite me to her place. There, I met her boyfriend at the time, Robert De Niro—*Bobby* De Niro, honey—and found him to be extremely nice.

I interviewed for the JCPenney job soon after that with Tony Brogan, who ran the East Coast Quality Assurance team. I told him that I knew it was important for me to start at the ground level. He was very pleasant, and although I felt the meeting had gone fairly well, I left thinking that I probably hadn't gotten the job. I guess I was disappointed that he hadn't hired me right away.

A week later, though, I was surprised to get a call from JCPenney's personnel department, asking me to meet with Ted Krettecos, the head of all of Quality Assurance, for a second interview. I dressed my best for this meeting and tried my hardest to convince him that I would be a great addition to the JCPenney team. I talked my way into this job, girlfriend. My mouth has always gotten me everywhere I wanted to go. I just keep talking until I've convinced people that what I want is the right thing to do.

Ted offered me the job in Los Angeles at a salary over twice what I was making at Adrienne Vittadini's, and I could start the following week. I accepted his offer immediately. My friends thought I was crazy to leave a job with a top designer in order to go inspect factory work, but I knew it was the right direction for me. I was certainly relieved that my paycheck was going to be fatter. On the skinny salary I was earning in New York, I was still depending on my mother's fabulous cooking to keep me from being as thin as I had been in my lean Paris days.

I had definite plans for this job, too.

"I'm going to be a designer for this company, you watch and see," I vowed to a friend.

I was thrilled about my new position, but there was still one small and thorny fence to climb over: I had to have a car and a driver's license. While I had taken a driving course in high school, I had never driven much and didn't have my license. I had to take a driving course pronto! And, of course, I hadn't been able to afford a car. I was still bumming rides off my brothers.

Getting back to Elizabeth, I quickly enrolled in a driving school, and the owner himself took on the daunting task of teaching me to drive. Since I was more adept at riding subways than handling freeways, I'm sure I managed to scare a few years off his life.

After a week's instruction, I passed the written test with flying colors but made a mistake on the actual driving test by going past a stop sign that I didn't see in time. Horrified and with no time left to retake the test before leaving for Los Angeles, I begged and pleaded with the owner to bend the rules and pass me. He was sympathetic enough to my situation to pass me, thank God.

19

Inspector No. 12

I arrived in Los Angeles with nothing but two suitcases and a mother-whip determination to make it. My new boss, Ben Gray, an area inspection supervisor for the JCPenney Quality Assurance team, met me at the airport, along with his wife, Linda. I liked the Grays immediately; they were warm and very giving. On the way from the airport to my hotel, I told them about my plans to one day be a designer. I was thrilled to have this job in Quality Assurance, I said, because it was going to be a great learning experience. It was also a great stepping-stone toward my goal of designing—which I was determined to be doing in just a couple of years.

Ben confessed to me later that he had had reservations about me that first day because here I was, just twenty-one years old, telling the world I was going to be a designer and that my new job was just a short hop to that goal. Ben was a career JCPenney man who had worked his way up the corporate ladder over a period of more than twenty-five years—and there I was just gabbing my mouth off about my career plans. He wondered whether I would take my new job seriously and if we'd get along. As soon as we started working together, however, I proved my dedication to my new job. I was determined to work harder than anyone else and to show that I was good at any task they gave me.

Since I didn't have a car yet, Ben loaned me his own company car, a brand-new silver-gray Ford Taurus, for the first two weeks. I don't think he realized that I had just barely passed my driving test. I was nervous about driving such a new car that didn't belong to me, but I had no choice.

I managed to maneuver the L.A. freeways and relished the opportunity to meet the manufacturers and suppliers. For this job, I had to travel to tons of different factories from Anaheim to Simi Valley, but I got up every morning with a smile on my face. I was finally on my own, developing a wonderful network of friends and business contacts in this new job.

I couldn't wait to get my own transportation, however. I didn't want a fancy car, just one that would get me around. I prayed and prayed. Lord, I said, I don't want no Cadillac, Mercedes, or Rolls-Royce. I just want a c-a-r! All it had to have was four tires, an engine, and a steering wheel. My prayers were answered when my brother James' friend Michael loaned me $1,500 so that I could finally afford a used three-door hatchback Honda Civic.

That car never did give me any problems while I drove it around Los Angeles. Once, though, I did have a close call. After shopping one evening, I was starving, so I pulled into a Jack in the Box drive-through. As I was getting my order, I put the car in park, which is something I usually never do in a drive-through. Then, when I thought the car was in forward, I somehow put it into reverse and ended up ramming a Corvette behind me.

The Corvette was relatively undamaged, but I was distraught to see my baby Honda crunched. If you had heard me talking with the insurance people, you would have thought I had a relative in the hospital in critical condition. My baby recovered, though, from this accident, and I was greatly relieved.

In Quality Assurance, Carol Fischer, a field inspector who had been with JCPenney for over ten years, trained me, along with others, for our new positions. As field inspectors, we would arrive at the factories by appointment and pull random audits, learning from Carol how to do size and quality inspections. We would pull, say, twenty pieces out of a line at random. If we found only two pieces with a defect, the line was okay. If three were found to be defective, however, the line was not acceptable.

We had critical points to consider, which involved measuring the garments to our specifications and checking for visible or structural flaws. If the color came off the fabric onto our hands, for instance, that was definitely not acceptable. We also checked for stains or any fabric flaws that would keep a customer from buying the clothes. Holes and broken or skipped stitches were other negatives we looked for.

Laying the garments flat on a table, we measured the bust, waist, hip, sweep (the opening of the skirt), arm-hole circumference, sleeve length, shoulder length, and neck opening, among other parameters. We measured sizes 4–18, making sure, for instance, that the waist wasn't too small or the darts too big. The size listed on the label had to, of course, be correct, and the sleeves couldn't be too short. There were any number of a thousand things that could be wrong. We also had to make sure that the tag on the garment met with certain government requirements such as listing the care instructions, fabric content, and number codes that trace the garment back to the manufacturer.

People take quality control for granted and don't understand how important it is to the process. If a garment is made beautifully but doesn't fit, what good is it? If I found a problem with a manufacturer, though, I wouldn't just tell him that it had failed our inspection. I would go in and work with them to fix the problem. I always tried to be positive and upbeat about it.

I asked lots of questions, and the manufacturers appreciated my interest in what they did. I wanted to know how the owners got their businesses going and what I would need to get my own company off the ground. I also enjoyed sitting with the sewers, learning their techniques and showing them some of mine that I had learned in Paris. We had a great relationship.

JCPenney had a strict dress code which stated that you had to wear a suit and tie—dark, conservative suits with white shirts. I tried to meet that dress code, but I didn't have the money to buy several suits. I did the best I could, wearing slacks and sports coats, although sometimes they didn't quite match. It was very difficult for me to wear an outfit that wasn't creative. I hated that part of the job. Luckily, no one ever criticized me for not strictly following the dress code. I was a hard worker, so I guess they just let that part of the job slide.

After arriving in L.A., I stayed for a few weeks with Michael and his family in Torrance, just south of Los Angeles. Since I wasn't that familiar with Los Angeles, Michael helped me find a place to live. I screamed with excitement when I first saw Hollywood. And Beverly Hills was so grand. If I couldn't live in Beverly Hills, I wanted to live in Hollywood, where the action was.

I found a nice apartment at 1209 North Mansfield in a beautiful old Spanish-style building. I fixed it up in an eclectic decor that was a mix of Ralph Lauren and Laura Ashley—very comfy, very English, with trinkets decorating the bookshelves, roses in vases, and petit-point pillows. I dried my own flowers to create beautiful arrangements.

My new colleagues at JCPenney were very supportive, so I was surprised when a colleague warned me about trying to get to know Carol Fischer any better than we did, saying that Carol was a racist. I had never seen this tendency in Carol, so I went on with my natural self and approached all of our meetings with Carol with an open mind. Carol proved to be the wonderful person that I had always thought she was. I realized that my colleague had only been trying to keep me away from Carol so that she herself could keep the advantage. I couldn't believe that she would try to trip me up like that. This incident reminded me that you have to watch your back in the business world.

Carol didn't have anything to lose or gain by helping me, but she became a great friend and ally. She had two daughters and I became her adopted son. I called her my "California mom" and I enjoyed just being myself around her family. It was wonderful to have an adopted family in California. Carol and I would sometimes go to church together on Sundays.

I'd also call Carol up and we'd go shopping together. I especially loved stopping at garage sales, antique shops, and flea markets to look for pieces to add to my various collections. My doll collection was growing fast and included all kinds and nationalities. Nestled on an old chest in the corner, they were my babies.

Carnival glass and other collectible plates lined my walls; old lace and fabrics draped the chairs and couch. I would even brake the car for castoffs by the side of the road, and Carol once helped me haul an old leather club chair into my car which someone had thrown out. It went straight into my apartment, where it blended right in with my other flea-market treasures.

Carol and I would often visit with her elderly neighbor, Gwen Singh, who was in her eighties. A widow, this lady had traveled the world with her Indian husband and had wonderful collections from her travels. I loved to visit with her and listen to her stories. It's fascinating to me to know people of all ages and backgrounds. Hearing about their experiences can only enrich your own life, and often these people will surprisingly be the ones who will give you the secrets to a happier, even more exciting life.

One of my new friends, Robert, was a production manager in a factory that I often inspected. As we became good friends, he confessed that he had AIDS and described to me over the course of our many conversations how hideous the disease was. Sadly, I watched his slow decline, but during the Christmas season, he told me not to worry about him, that he'd be okay. He seemed peaceful, and I was glad he was coming to terms with his illness.

I called him after the holidays and was stunned to find out from his lover that he had passed on—by his own hand. I was shocked but not really surprised, as Robert was the type who had always wanted to live life to the fullest. Unwilling to suffer through a torturous disease any longer, Robert had ridden his dirt bike to Las Vegas and driven it off a cliff. I was sad that his life had to end that way, but I suppose this was the only way he could take back control over the disease.

In that same holiday season, I lost another friend, Bishop Saunders, who, my Mom told me, had died peacefully in his sleep of heart failure. Bishop Saunders had always been there for me while I was growing up, and I hoped I could live up to his expectations for me. Losing such friends made me more concerned about the people I cared about, and I felt so miserable about these losses that I threw myself even harder into my work.

I always tried to show Ben that I could work above and beyond my job description. As a training exercise for inspectors, we were asked to prepare a fabric presentation once a month. When it was my turn, Ben, along with everyone else, was stunned when I went so far as to make miniature fashions with the fabrics and display them on knockoff Barbie dolls.

Each person at that presentation was given a little Anthony Mark Hankins creation in doll-size miniatures. The dolls were displayed on little stands in front of every-one's place at the conference table. A friend and I even made a video in which the Barbies "performed" in their own fashion show, wearing the fabrics we were discussing at the meeting. The presentation was a hit with everybody.

Walking through a JCPenney store one afternoon, I made mental notes of how I would merchandise the sale items and advertise them. The next day, I presented my ideas to Ben and he encouraged me to send my suggestions to our corporate offices in Dallas. Ben was a wonderful man to work for. Instead of shooting my ideas down because I was an underling, he was always very willing to give me a shot at trying new things.

Ben was an enthusiastic supporter of my dream and encouraged me to take my design concepts up the ranks at JCPenney. He had heard about me trying to get attention for my fashion line with magazine articles, such as the one in *Essence* magazine. I was doing a lot of wedding designs at that time. We met for lunch one day so that we could discuss my goals, and afterward Ben recommended me to the senior executives in Dallas and even made appointments for me to meet with them.

One day, I received a call from a Miss Vera Hope Walston, who worked on *The Home Show,* which was hosted by Gary Collins. Miss Vera was contacting me because she was putting together a segment for the show on ethnic wedding dresses and *Essence* editors had referred her to me. She had also heard about me through a friend.

I agreed to meet Miss Vera at her home in Compton on Sunday after church to show her some of my wedding fashions. She arrived at her house slightly after I did, and I was delighted to meet this small lady who had delightfully warm, chocolate Betty Boop eyes. Holding a pocketbook on her arm, she was wearing a designer suit and a big old church hat. She was also wearing a huge smile that was all love.

"Come on in, baby," Miss Vera said. "Let me see what you got for Miss Vera."

I unwrapped my most ethnic wedding dress for her, the short white dress with the African beadwork that had appeared in *Essence.*

"Oh, baby, this is beautiful," she cried. "We've got to have this for *The Home Show*."

She asked me if I could meet her there on Monday morning so that the dress could be okayed by her executive producer. Of course, I told her, my excitement soaring. That piece of business settled, Miss Vera invited me to stay for lunch, which included fabulous down-home cooking and a delicious chess pie for dessert.

I was nervous, though, about whether the producers would accept my dress.

"Don't worry, Anthony," Miss Vera reassured me. "Baby, with your energy there on Monday morning, ain't no way they're going to tell you no."

I arrived at *The Home Show* production offices bright and early Monday morning and met Miss Vera there. The producers were limiting the number of dresses to five, and the last selection came down to choosing between mine and another designer's. Miss Vera put in a quick word for me to try to sway the selection committee.

"What about this young man's creation?" she asked.

"Let's see it on the model," the producer suggested. When the model came back in the room with my wedding dress on, the producer's eyes lit up. "Yes!" she said. "That's it!"

"You see, baby, you did it," Miss Vera cried, giving me a hug.

I was so excited, I couldn't wait to tell Carol. I called her as soon as I got home.

"Carol!" I yelled at her through the phone lines.

"What, Anthony?"

"Carol!" I said again, trying to catch my breath.

"What!" she said.

"Carol!" I gasped.

"Anthony, will you please tell me what's going on?"

"My dress is going to be on *The Home Show*!" I blurted out to her before hyperventilation got the best of me. Carol was thrilled and helped me spread the news around the office on Monday morning. When the show aired, we were all in front of a television set, cheering as my dress was being broadcast across America.

In Los Angeles, I had a very active social life and enjoyed meeting people from all professions. One friend invited me to her house for a pool party, and the hostess introduced me to a ladies' evening wear designer who was based in Los Angeles—Tadashi Shoji.

Tadashi was a dignified and handsome Japanese man in his thirties, with a gentle, wise spirit. He wore a retro pajama print to the party which he had made into walking shorts and a camp shirt print-on-print with a leather belt. He had on tortoiseshell sunglasses. I was eager to get to know Tadashi since he was an experienced designer.

With our common interest in fashion, he and I soon became great friends, often hanging out together. Tadashi proved to be a great mentor, taking the time to listen and help me with my career. He was more relaxed and patient than I was. Patience, he said, was important for me to learn since he thought I was trying to rush my career too fast.

Tadashi didn't give me the standard pep talks, though. His support was more subtle. I felt that I was worthy in his eyes because he would invite me to join him for dinner or to just hang out with him and his friends. Tadashi let me enjoy the taste of sweet success with him by taking me along to fabulous restaurants before I could afford them. He was about sixteen years older than me, so I'm sure I was just a kid to his crowd, but it was a tremendous boost to my self-esteem that they included me. I was still feeling insecure, in spite of my Paris experience.

Tadashi would introduce me to influential people, saying, "This is the young man who studied with Yves Saint Laurent." He told me he wanted people to know that I had been to the top. He was so wonderful to give me that endorsement.

I was obsessed with fashion, but Tadashi made sure I knew there was more to life than obsessing about work. He never brought his work home with him. Tadashi often invited me to his home, which was a fabulous Japanese-style house in Pasadena. He collected many things, including African art with its kuba cloth and primitive statues. He also had a phenomenal library in his home with everything on fashion you could think of. I was in heaven in his library, reading his books, magazines, and industry-forecasting materials.

I would ask Tadashi his opinion on things and he would always give it to me straight, even though it may not have been the answer I wanted to hear.

"If you don't want my opinion, then don't ask me for it," he'd say, if I complained that his answer wasn't quite what I had expected. He was a wise old soul. Very caring. He always gave me the feeling that I could accomplish my goals, that nothing could stand in my way.

One thing that really inspired me about Tadashi was that he had come from Japan with nothing. In a relatively short period of time, however, he had managed to build a multimillion-dollar business. He worked hard and persevered until he had accomplished his goals—a truly self-made man. I figured that if he could come all the way from Japan and make it, so could I.

I used this period to quietly make plans for my own line of urban contemporary clothing tailored for the minority woman, who I felt was underserved in fashionable clothing. I spent a lot of my free time at the library doing fashion research, realizing long ago that knowledge is power. I read everything I could get my hands on, listened to motivational tapes, watched the fashion trends, read the trade magazines, and talked to everyone in the business. I even read biographies of accomplished people so that I could figure out their formulas for success.

20

Climbing the Corporate Mountain

Ted Krettecos had told me that "all roads lead to Dallas" at JCPenney, since their corporate headquarters were located there. I was determined to be a designer for the company, even though they had never had an in-house designer before. When the vice president of product development, Don Scaccia, was scheduled to be in Los Angeles on business, I made arrangements to meet with him.

Don stood me up, however, without so much as a phone call, and I was very disappointed. I found out later that, rather than meeting with me, he had just been killing time, shooting the breeze with friends at another company. He didn't know that a friend of mine worked at that company and that this information would get back to me. When I finally presented my ideas to him over the phone, he told me that JCPenney was simply not interested in them.

I still pursued it, however. I managed to present my concepts later to the head of the women's division, where the answer was again negative. I ran my ideas up the chain of command, and the answer didn't seem to be changing. No one seemed interested in my ideas.

Disappointed, I asked Ted Krettecos what I should do. He recommended that I call Bruce Ackerman, who was then manager of minority supplier development for JCPenney in Dallas. I called Bruce up and described to him my line and what the situation was. As fate would have it, my designs for an urban contemporary clothing line happened to be just what Bruce had been looking for, since the company had recently begun trying to attract the African-American customer. Bruce was a member of the task force in charge of addressing this marketing issue.

For this project, he was already gathering up samples of beautiful handcrafted products from Africa which covered everything from clothing and accessories, jewelry, wood carvings, and tie-dyed kaftans. While the buyers loved these items, top management was cool toward them. JCPenney managers had always dealt with large manufacturers and weren't accustomed to dealing with cottage-industry craftsmen.

Bruce was searching, however, for a mass-manufactured line of urban contemporary clothes that would be of interest to the African-American woman. JCPenney's catalog division was also coming out with a new specialty catalog aimed at the African-American customer, and Bruce had been asked to be a part of the team that would create the catalog—although the team was mainly composed of African-American employees from the company's merchandising and catalog divisions.

Bruce was excited about my ideas and seemed more than happy to help me set up a series of meetings with executives in Dallas. Technically, he wasn't in a position to work with me since I wasn't a supplier, but he thought that maybe my ideas could help him explain to management what he had been pushing for in connection with this new area of merchandise. Bruce suggested that I come to Dallas to meet with whomever I wanted at corporate headquarters, and he offered to make the appointments for me.

With that invitation in hand, I left no stone unturned. The next day, before Bruce knew what hit him, I faxed him a list of twenty-two people in the Dallas corporate offices whom I wanted to meet with! I wanted to meet with everyone from the buyers, to the merchandising managers, to the vice presidents.

Bruce, true to his word, set a whole week aside for me and arranged all twenty-two meetings for me. We had back-to-back meetings lined up! Bruce had even recommended that the buyers invite their staffs to the meetings. I flew to Dallas from Los Angeles in early May 1992. Tony Haake, a vice president and director of Quality Assurance, paid my way out of his own budget and was very supportive.

Our first meeting was scheduled for Monday at noon, and arriving with nervous butterflies fluttering around my stomach, I was stunned to learn from Bruce's secretary that Bruce wasn't even in Dallas. He wasn't there for the meeting. Reeling for a moment, I thought he had stood me up, just like Don Scaccia had. His secretary assured me, however, that Bruce was just returning late to Dallas because of a delayed flight from New York. With Bruce's assistant's help, I started my presentation at noon, as scheduled. Bruce arrived as quickly as he could and joined us by one o'clock.

For this momentous day, I was wearing a chartreuse jacket with an ascot—definitely not considered corporate attire at JCPenney. Later, I found out that Bruce's boss had pointedly asked him, "Why don't you tell Anthony to wear a suit to these meetings?"

"He's a designer," Bruce had replied. "Why would I tell him what to wear?"

The JCPenney corporate headquarters were located at Lincoln Center in Dallas at that time, with three main buildings. As we went from building to building and from meeting to meeting, the lower ranks at JCPenney were hearing about this new and different line being presented. We were stopped repeatedly in the halls and asked if we were coming to their areas for our presentation. The groundswell of interest was growing, and everyone wanted to take a look at this new line.

After we met with the women's fashion coordinator, Bruce was surprised when she later commented to him, "He has a lot of nice things here, but he really needs to be groomed. He needs to learn the JCPenney way."

For my meeting with Gale Duff-Bloom, then a vice president in the merchandising area and the top woman at JCPenney, I made sure I wore a suit—a circa-1932 suit I had found at a retro fashion store called American Rag in Los Angeles. She complimented me on it, though.

We received all kinds of responses from the brass about our proposal that JCPenney launch the new Anthony Mark Hankins signature line in-house. Launching something in-house seemed to be a foreign concept to these executives. One puzzled manager said to me, "This is really interesting stuff, Anthony, but we're in this box and you're in that box over there. How are we going to get from here to there?"

Another asked me if I had shown my line to the Flori Roberts company, which specialized in fragrances and makeup for African-American women. Now, why would I want to show apparel to a fragrance company? Still another very high-ranking executive asked me if I'd leave the room for a moment after we'd presented the line to her so she could discuss it privately with Bruce. She shocked Bruce by announcing, "Either Anthony's a genius or he's a con artist."

I don't think they could see past the fact that I was only twenty-three. Bruce reminded this woman that I had been preparing for this career since I was seven years old. He knew that a lot of these executives had children older than myself who were not yet through school or who were working in entry-level jobs, still trying to find themselves. So how could I have accomplished so much in such a short period of time?

Bruce and I could tell that our efforts were finally meeting with some success, however. The groundswell of interest from the troops was forcing top management to take a closer look. I may have been only twenty-three, but I was prepared for their professional scrutiny. I had my sketches, themes, fabrics, samples, and everything else ready and waiting for them.

Just as I began to believe that JCPenney was interested in my design work, though, I heard through my former employers at the Elizabeth courthouse and other friends that they had been receiving calls from someone at JCPenney asking about my background. I guess JCPenney wanted to find out if I was a con artist after all. I was very stressed out about this investigation and felt like my privacy was really being invaded. Was I a criminal or a designer? I thanked God that I had never really had a wild period in my life. I had been too busy working for that.

Luckily, too, I have always saved and documented everything I've done, since reading about Thomas Edison's extensive and thorough record-keeping. If someone questioned my schooling in France, for instance, I could present all the necessary documents and even drop Paris subway tokens onto the table. We found out later that Bruce's boss had begun this investigation on me. I couldn't understand the reason for these calls, since I was already an employee of JCPenney.

The JCPenney brass wanted to know everything about me before they made a decision, though, so they put a black personnel employee in charge of interrogating me. When I met with her, I was prepared. I brought with me my diplomas, grades, and other documents, along with three huge leather portfolios of my work. I knew this was their final attempt to find out anything negative about me.

Once I had passed that test, it was decided that I should put on a fashion show for top management. I was sent back to Los Angeles to develop a line that would be presented to the corporate "suits" in the form of a fashion show. They didn't give me a deadline, but I wanted to get back to them quickly, before the fire we had started had a chance to cool down.

With a lot of help, I managed to pull off the impossible— a three-hundred-piece fashion show from absolute scratch in a matter of a few weeks. Tony Haake had provided me with a modest budget, and Carol went with me to the manufacturers to make sure they understood what we were requesting from them. Lower management, vendors, manufacturers, models, and even secretaries were interested in my line, and they all pitched in to help me make it happen.

From my job in Quality Assurance, I knew all the manufacturers' designers who created the patterns and executed the designs; they respected my QA abilities, as well as considered me a friend. The manufacturers and vendors, sensing that something exciting was happening, all wanted to be a part of it and volunteered to make the samples of dresses and sportswear for the show for free.

The manufacturers donated the samples, absorbing the costs of making them, because they considered this a great opportunity for themselves, too. Samples are expensive to produce because each one is done completely by hand, from the creation of the pattern to the sewing of the garment. Everything is created from scratch. One sample could easily cost fifty dollars and straight up from there. The fact that all these manufacturers were willing to take a chance on my line meant a lot to me.

There were eight to ten manufacturers in L.A. involved with this fashion show. We also received the support of an African-American manufacturer in New York, Kermith Morgan, who supplied boys' suits to JCPenney through Bruce's minority supplier development program. He agreed to produce the men's suits in the fashion show. Another African-American supplier from Bruce's program, Randy Clark, who had a T-shirt screening company in Dallas, offered to make the T-shirts for the casual part of the program. All of the manufacturers were doing their specialty, whether it was T-shirts, blouses, skirts, dresses, or pants.

Carol attended meetings with me to act as my straight man since I was so excited I was having a hard time reining my boisterous self in. We were a great team, working fast and furiously to coordinate all our plans with the manufacturers. Since I was developing a large line involving so many manufacturers, Carol helped me devise forms and organizational tools to keep it all straight.

Three weeks after returning to Los Angeles to prepare, I called Bruce and told him that we were ready to roll with the fashion show. Bruce was stunned that we had gotten everything together in so short a time. I was prepared to return to Dallas with my samples so that we could accessorize them.

At Lincoln Center, Bruce and I went to the company's shoe buyer to find just the right shoes for the show. She didn't seem to have anything, though, that I wanted to use. I described to the buyer what I was looking for, and she said, "Wait right here." She went to the back storeroom of her department and returned with boxes of fabulous shoes—sample shoes that had been rejected. This scene was repeated with just about every buyer. We found the right shoes, the right hats, the right jewelry—all among samples that had been rejected for the stores.

Toni Turner, an assistant to the fashion coordinator in the women's division of JCPenney, helped me put the show together. She coordinated the professional models, who were age-wise and ethnically diverse, and worked out the choreography with them. As a young African-American, she understood exactly what I was trying to do, so she and I hit it off immediately. I also asked the audiovisual department to help create the staging and backdrop. The background was all white with white cutout palm trees—a very cool backdrop for summer sportswear and business wear.

I presented the fashion show at Lincoln Center on June 26, 1992. Top management was invited to the fashion show by formal invitation, along with key managers from every department. Everyone working on the show was really proud of it because it was different from anything JCPenney had done before. JCPenney fashions, to me, had felt so conservative and traditional before this.

I sat silently on a stool in the corner of the set, dressed in white summer casuals, as the models swept past me to the soulful, sensual, and playful music soundtrack we had put together, letting the clothes speak for themselves. This fashion show was movin' *forward*, girlfriend, and the models reflected this excitement in their exuberant performances. I presented four scenes depicting women's and men's casual wear, business wear, and sportswear, along with children's casual wear.

The JCPenney brass watched the show in stony silence, however, many with their mouths hanging slightly open, their poker faces revealing little of what they must have been thinking about this brash young designer who was single-handedly trying to bring a new look and spirit to their company.

After the show, I remained on my stool for a question-and-answer session. I tried to maintain a cool composure while they grilled me. So many of these conservatively dressed "suits" seemed utterly stunned by my un-corporate-like demeanor and youthful enthusiasm. The highest-ranking black executive at JCPenney wanted to know, given the demand that must be out there for my kind of talent, why I was choosing JCPenney for an in-house design job.

I wanted to answer him, "Why *not* JCPenney?" but I explained in depth.

"My mom is a frequent shopper of JCPenney," I said, "and I really feel that it's been a part of the American dream. JCPenney's been around so long, and it's a real comfortable place to be—a family atmosphere. I feel really confident being with this company."

They wanted to hear about my background again, and I told them everything I had done so far, beginning with the suit that I had made for my mother at the age of seven.

"My mother and I are very close," I told them, "and she wore the dress I made to a big wedding. If that's not confidence in someone, I don't know what is. She still has the suit."

I described my experiences in France and then in New York. From there, I told them, I had met Ted Krettecos. He, along with the others in the Quality Assurance program, had embraced me and allowed me to go to Los Angeles, to roll up my sleeves and learn the mechanics of the industry.

I sat on the stool, answering their questions as coolly as I could, talking to top executives as if I did that sort of thing every day of my life. I hoped they didn't see my hands shaking as I held the microphone. I wanted to design fashionable clothing that my mother could afford to buy, I told them. The line would hopefully appeal to every woman who wanted to wear very stylish fashions but couldn't afford to buy them at Fifth Avenue prices.

After the questioning, the executives were quiet, subdued. A meeting was later called to discuss what to do about me. A bigwig told Bruce that he noticed I often talked about my mother and wondered if I had AIDS—a not-so-subtle stab at my possible sexual orientation. Bruce didn't tell me about this remark for a long time because he didn't want it to affect my feelings for the company.

"What should we do with Anthony?" the executives asked.

"Make him a designer," Tony Haake replied.

"But we've never had a designer before," they argued.

"Yes, you have," Bruce argued. "He already works for the company, and he's a designer."

It was suggested, then, that maybe I could work on the Jacqueline Ferrar line, an in-house brand. Bruce was incredulous. Why should Anthony work on this line when he had already created his own new and exciting line? Finally, it was agreed that a job description could be written up for Anthony in the role of in-house designer, with my salary doubled from what I was currently making in Quality Assurance.

While I believe some of the executives still harbored a few reservations, the groundswell of interest in this new line persuaded them to give me a shot, and I was ultimately hired as JCPenney's first in-house designer in its over-ninety-year history.

21

✂ -

Maverick

From Day One, however, I don't think the corporate moguls at JCPenney knew what to do with me because I didn't fit the corporate mold. I was a little stunned to realize that my new boss was to be Don Scaccia, of all people—the man who had originally turned down my ideas. I shouldn't have been surprised at this because Don was in charge of product development, but I still wondered if I was in for a hard time. I had heard from others in the company that he could be a difficult person.

When I first arrived in Dallas, I was given a large sample room for an office which was close to Tony Haake's office. It was a great space for me to work in, with worktables, racks, grids on the walls, good lighting, and a storage room. The company was in the process of moving its offices from Lincoln Center in Dallas to their newly built world head-quarters in Plano, just twenty miles north of Dallas, so my new office was just a temporary space.

Surfing through my E-mail messages soon after I set up my new office, I was stunned to discover that six or seven disgruntled African-American employees from JCPenney offices in different cities had written to me, wishing me good luck in my new position but wondering if my new title represented a positive change from their perceived ill treatment of blacks within the corporate structure of JCPenney. One person angrily wondered, "Are you the remedy for this illness?" I never will forget that.

These employees had even signed their real names, and I felt that they wanted me to respond to them with solutions for their problems. I was new to the company, however, and wasn't there to be their savior. The African-Americans in our corporate headquarters all gravitated toward my office and seemed to be looking to me for answers that I didn't have. I didn't want to be their Malcolm X or Martin Luther King. Although I was certainly sympathetic to their problems, I just wanted to do the best job I could for the company.

This incident with the E-mail messages made me nervous about how the whites and blacks at the corporate office perceived me. Every time my black friends came by my office to chat, I always had the feeling that management was eyeing me suspiciously, as if I might be trying to rally the troops against the white folks at JCPenney. Management probably thought we were all talking about them, but we weren't.

For the first few days, a buyer had not yet been assigned to my line, so Bruce, Toni Turner, and I planned the assortment of items that we thought would sell well in each store. Management had picked their top ethnic stores in each of four regions, which amounted to about sixty-two stores. Our large assortment was pared down to a manageable level a few days later, when a label buyer for JCPenney, Sharon English, and her assistant, Pam Washington, a young African-American woman, arrived to help us until a permanent buyer could be assigned.

I used my real signature on the logo for the "Anthony Mark Hankins" signature line and realized that the subject of trademarking had to be addressed with the company. When the JCPenney executives expressed zero interest in trademarking my line, I was surprised. I suppose they thought my line wouldn't take off, so there'd be no need to invest any money in trademarking.

Their decision gave me the opportunity, though, to trademark it myself and retain the rights to the name. Bruce and I sought out a patent attorney for legal counseling on the process of trademarking. Then we gathered the funds we'd need for all the legal fees, which came to about $2,000.

I was thrilled that my line was going to be introduced in the new *Fashion Influences* catalog. During a meeting about the catalog, however, I noticed that management never got around to saying how they planned to promote it. I asked them what their plan was—if they were going to place ads in such appropriate magazines as *Ebony* or *Essence,* among other avenues—and was shocked when they told me there was no marketing plan. There would be no promotion! The catalog would simply be available in the stores, as well as sent out to the names on a mailing list.

I may have been the new kid on the block, but I felt instinctively that the catalog was getting the short end of the stick because it was aimed at African-Americans. During the meeting, I kept pressing the president of the catalog division about promotion opportunities for *Fashion Influences.* He was, of course, perturbed that I wouldn't let him off the hook in front of everyone. Maybe I was naïve about corporate protocol, but I wasn't going to let go of the issue just like that. As soon as the meeting officially adjourned, however, the president suddenly grabbed me by the arm and hauled me outside in full view of everyone.

"You ruined this meeting!" he berated me.

I was really upset that I had been scolded like a disobedient child in front of my coworkers, and felt that the president's rough treatment of me inhibited anyone else from speaking up as well. Later, I talked to Tony Haake about it and he tried to calm me down. While I did cool off after a while, the incident definitely left a lingering bitter taste in my mouth.

My line made its store debut in November 1992, and the first *Fashion Influences* catalog featured my fashions on the cover, with the first eight pages devoted to my line. I could hardly contain my excitement. My expectations were high, and sure enough, the catalog made money on its first issue—an unusual achievement for most catalogs.

Fashion Influences was mailed to about 100,000 households and received a very positive response from customers. Although it made a profit on its first issue, this incredible feat was not broadcast by the brass at JCPenney. Bruce and I heard about the positive sales results through a black executive in the catalog division who had access to the statistics.

The first few issues of *Fashion Influences* prominently featured my new line, and the catalog sales remained very successful. Suddenly, however, management removed the largely African-American team that had created the catalog and replaced it with a "mainstream" team, thus knocking the wind out of its successful rise in popularity with customers. The catalog lost its focus after the original team was dismantled. Although the company had received mostly positive responses from customers on the catalog, the only response officially acknowledged by management was one negative response by a single white customer who mailed in his cut-up JCPenney credit card to protest the catalog's publication.

Since I was told that JCPenney liked to test its products first before promoting them, Don and other executives informed me that there wouldn't be any advertising for my line either. I was not supposed to even talk to the press about it. The company was more accustomed to dealing with national brands that have their own independent promotional campaigns behind them already. I was competing against these lines in the stores, and I knew I had to get some promotion for my line out there some-how. I had to find a way to make posters and hang tags myself.

Through my own budget, I ordered two thousand pho-tos of myself to hand out during trunk shows at JCPenney stores, and I used five hundred of them for homemade press kits that I had put together to send to fashion editors around the country. My secretary helped me by typing up the mailing labels. Then we boxed up the five hundred press kits, put the boxes on a cart, and took them all down to friends in the mail room, who made sure the press kits somehow went out.

When I was invited to do a trunk show that November in Atlanta at the South DeKalb Mall store, Bruce called an Atlanta journalist, tipping her off to a good article possibil-ity. She wrote the first major newspaper piece on the line, and, back home in Dallas a few days later, Bruce and I couldn't wait to get to a newsstand that sold out-of-town papers. We bought a dozen copies of the Atlanta newspaper and high-fived each other—the word about the line was getting out in spite of it all.

We sent management copies of the article, hoping they would see that the line was being favorably written about. We received no comment from them, however, except for James Hailey, the president of the women's division, who sent me a nice note saying, "Keep up the good work." I imagine the rest of the JCPenney brass were probably asking their PR department how in the hell the journalist in Atlanta even knew about Anthony Mark Hankins.

When the corporate offices moved from Lincoln Center in Dallas to their new headquarters in Plano, just outside of Dallas, I discovered that I had not been allotted an office or even furniture. I realized it wasn't a personal slight, however. I just hadn't been written into their five-year plan. For the first year there, employees were being shuffled all over the complex in an effort to fit everyone in.

For an office, I was initially given a long, narrow storage closet with a support column in the middle of it. I had to fit my desk, filing cabinets, samples, designs, and everything else into this space, which was as narrow as a hallway. Management tried to insist that I use a cubicle as an office, but cubicles provided no privacy for my design work and no way to lock up sketches at the end of the day.

I was finally given another storage closet for locking up designs, but I ended up using it for my office. I was also assigned a double-size cubicle that I used to house my personal accouterments, decking out my bookshelves with brightly colored toys and a whimsical collection of dolls from around the world. My coworkers and I would occasionally play loud and spirited games of paper "volleyball" over the cubicle walls, which I'm sure raised a few corporate eyebrows.

Although I took my new job very seriously, I still couldn't bring myself to dress corporate. It just wasn't me. I sometimes even wore jeans, flannel shirts, and baseball caps to work. Don seemed to hate the fact that I was never in a suit and tie; he couldn't stand it that I dared to wear what I wanted. One day, I came to work in an Errol Flynn–inspired "pirate" shirt and Don said to me, "Where'd you get that shirt—in some women's blouse shop?"

I just didn't think it was important that I didn't dress "corporate" as long as I worked hard and brought in excellent results for the company. Since I was working very long, late hours, I felt it was more important to be dressed comfortably.

One night, at about eleven o'clock, I happened to be leaving work at the same time as the highest-ranking female executive in the company. It was late, so we didn't engage in any conversation, but I thought to myself, We both have to work long hours, don't we? We've got that much in common. She got into her Jaguar and I got into my little brown Honda, and we both went home.

A friend of mine who was a stewardess once told me about a guy who'd sat in her coach section. The man smelled like a hamburger joint and his clothes were covered with flour and grease. She was courteous to him during the flight, however, and when the plane landed in New York, the man thanked her and handed her his business card, as well as coupons for free meals at a major hamburger chain of which he was the CEO! A CEO flying coach and smelling like fried hamburgers. Just proves that you can't always judge a man by his appearance.

* * *

JCPenney had an active mentor-protégé program. Bruce had been designated as a mentor but had never been assigned a protégé. When he asked about it, the officials told him that a protégé wasn't available. Bruce, however, told them he knew of one—me. At first, they balked, saying that we were in the same department and they encouraged mentors and protégés to be from different departments within the company. We may have been in the same department, Bruce argued, but we were doing totally different jobs.

Management reluctantly allowed Bruce to become my "interim" mentor until I was officially assigned one. Months later, they did assign a mentor to me—the highest-ranking African-American in the credit department. I didn't have anything against this guy, but I felt that management had assigned him to me simply because we were both black.

I admit I had a bad attitude about the whole thing, since I was obviously learning so much about the business from Bruce. He was a natural fit as a mentor for me, whereas this other guy was assigned to me simply because of race. I never really met with him. Management later tried again to assign me to another black executive mentor, and I ignored this assignment as well for the same reason. I had to laugh when management soon made a rule that mentors and protégés could not be of the same race or sex. Now, where's the practical logic in that?

I wanted to prove to JCPenney that I was worth the chance they had taken in hiring me as their first in-house designer. I worked night and day putting the line together, sketching and creating the new styles, marketing and promoting the line as best I could, given the company's restrictions on me. Bruce and I carpooled to work every day, and he worked with me on the line constantly.

I wanted to put on a fashion show for the InfoMart Visions Conference, a large women's conference being held in Dallas in the fall of '93. I had to present this show without any support from management. No help on the coordination, the stage background, nothing. Luckily, friends who worked in the corporate offices volunteered to help us set up and take down the staging. An artist friend, Brad, did the backdrop for me, which was a Spanish village scene. Another friend of mine, who was visiting from London, offered to do the makeup and hair for the show.

To steady myself from stress stemming from management's lack of support, I had to think again of Barbra and her struggles. When she was a fresh young singer, she signed her first recording contract with Columbia Records. It seemed they had no faith in her commercial potential. They just couldn't get past the funky way she dressed and were convinced her singing was limited to nightclubs and stage performances. She was too much of a free spirit for their corporate sensibilities. Columbia pressed a minimal number of copies of her first album with little or no promotion.

When her fans flocked to the stores to buy this album after finally hearing her fabulous voice, there often weren't any copies available because the record company hadn't printed nearly enough. Barbra, of course, managed to become a recording sensation despite the lack of marketing support from Columbia. When she proved to them that she could knock the socks off everybody, the suits at Columbia were probably the first to claim they'd known all along she was going to be a big star.

Getting back to the Visions Conference in Dallas, though, most of the JCPenney executives were not planning on attending the programs until noon. My fashion show was being presented at 11:00 A.M., however, so only Gale Duff-Bloom and a few other executives from the company were there.

I made sure the music was sizzling and the fashions even hotter, including models of all races, ages, and sizes. They looked fabulous as they strutted saucily toward the audience to the rhythm of a spirited Cuban salsa beat in flowing, classic dress ensembles that were spicy with a retro forties feel. Closed fans in hand, they'd reach the end of the stage, flip open the fan with a quick coquettish wave of the hand, bat their eyelashes seductively for a brief moment, then turn jauntily on their heels, leaving the men in the audience panting and the women desiring to look like them.

These models looked HOT in my clothes, and they knew it. They were turning everyone's heads, girlfriend. Picture Madonna striking the pose as Evita Perón in *all* of Evita's dazzling fashions. These were classic looks, designed to stop traffic and accessorized to the nines with scarves and hats. I even featured a turban, usually worn by women undergoing chemotherapy, and proved that even this item could be an asset to a woman's wardrobe.

After the last model vamped off the stage, Gale gave me a hug and praised the show. We were also ecstatic when people in the audience commented that it was like watching a Neiman Marcus fashion show, rather than conservative and staid old JCPenney. Pushing my exhaustion to the back of my subconscious, I felt triumphant that day.

Buyers for JCPenney show their product lines via a live, closed-circuit direct broadcast from corporate headquarters to the stores. The direct broadcasts were fun but challenging, incorporating lots of detail work. I had to merchandise the clothes, get them all accessorized for the models, write copy, and then "host" this mini fashion show in front of a video camera once a month. I was really nervous about it at first, but I received positive responses from store managers across the country, who commented that they liked my genuine and straightforward presentations. They also liked my fashions because they quickly flew off the sales racks.

One afternoon, just when I was knee-deep in the hectic chaos of preparation minutes before a direct broadcast, W. R. Howell, then the chairman and CEO of JCPenney, came through my area on a show-and-tell tour of the complex with twelve members of the board of directors. He came up to me and introduced himself.

"Hello, I'm W. R. Howell," he said congenially, shaking my hand.

I didn't know what else to say except, "Hello, I'm Anthony Mark Hankins." I was taken aback at meeting such a top VIP at that particular moment, since I was harriedly trying to get ready for the tightly scheduled broadcast and not looking my best. It was an honor, though, to meet him.

I think Don was surprised that my line was actually succeeding and he never seemed to understand why the store managers were excited about the line. He also never complimented my efforts and seemed to find fault with every little thing I did—from my sketches, to the way I dressed, to the toys on my desk, to the fact that I followed my own vision instead of his. I was really getting fed up, but I was too busy designing and presenting the line to the stores to worry too much about Don.

Kay Baker, the head of JCPenney publicity, was always very nice to me and asked for my help one day with a special project. The company was sponsoring Lyn St. James, the 1992 Indianapolis 500 Rookie of the Year and one of the few female race-car drivers at the time. She had driven in her first Indianapolis 500 in 1992, placing eleventh, and was the first woman ever to be named Rookie of the Year in this classic race. Lyn was getting married soon, Kay explained, and needed a bridal outfit for the ceremony. Kay asked me if I would design her wedding ensemble, and, of course, I was flattered and enthusiastic about the project.

Kay brought Lyn by my office the following week, and she and I clicked immediately. Lyn loved my colorful, playful office decor. Her fiancé, Roger Lessman, managed ski resort properties, and Lyn needed an unusual wedding outfit since she and her new husband planned to go snowmobiling immediately after the ceremony.

Working with Lyn, I designed for her a beautiful white jumpsuit with crisscross latticework in the back. The creation included a bolero, with a beaded jacket and a veiled hood. Gale Duff-Bloom was very appreciative that I was taking time out of my stressful schedule to create the dress for Lyn, and she personally came down to my office to thank me for doing it.

While Don and other number crunchers argued about who was going to absorb the cost of Lyn's wedding ensemble, I just concentrated on designing it and getting it ready for the big event. Lyn lived in Daytona Beach, Florida, so we sent the sketches and later the actual garment-in-process back and forth. The suit fit her like a glove after only a few fittings.

When everything was completed, we packaged it very beautifully with flowers and ribbons and sent it to her. Gale attended the wedding, which was held in Idaho, and reported back to me that Lyn had looked lovely in the jumpsuit. *USA Today* also published a notice of her wedding, describing her bridal ensemble and noting that Lyn "didn't have to shop for a dress, because JCPenney, sponsor of her first Indy ride, introduced her to one of its young designers, Anthony."

I read the short article again. Where was the rest of my name? I was pleased that I had been mentioned, but wished the article had included more identification than just "Anthony." Lyn later sent me pictures of the ceremony, which I really appreciated. She also called and wrote me a beautiful letter thanking me for helping to make the big event special for her. Lyn let Gale know, too, how pleased she was with my work.

After the wedding, however, Don came into my office, complaining that we had spent $700 on this affair and that JCPenney was not in the business of making couture dresses for people. Don was also upset that I had worked on the dress without getting his permission first; never mind that I had been asked by Kay to do it, with Gale's full knowledge and approval. In that case, Don argued, why hadn't he been included in the project? Don *had* known about the project, so I ignored him. There was just no winning with this guy.

Wedding couture was a big thing for me that year, though. Harriette Cole, an editor with *Essence* magazine, soon featured two of my ethnic wedding ensembles in an African-American wedding planner book called *Jumping the Broom*, which was published in 1993. The dresses included an angora sweater trimmed in rhinestones with a "poor boy's quilt" skirt, and a silk charmeuse coat and skirt with a veiled hat.

The title of her book refers to the African slave tradition of the bride and groom jumping over a broom during the wedding ceremony to symbolize the beginning of the couple's domestic life together. Slaves were not allowed to be married by clergy, so this ritual formalized the couple's marriage. This practice has been revived in the African-American community today, thanks to Alex Haley's dramatization of the ritual in his epic saga *Roots*. Harriette Cole's book has been very popular with people planning African-American–inspired weddings, and I was proud to be a part of it.

22

Designer in a Box

Although my line was popular in the stores, I was continually frustrated that it was not being formally promoted by JCPenney. Store managers were constantly calling me asking for promotional packages, and I felt hobbled by the company's no-promotion policy. I was still not allowed to do interviews or prepare any advertising to advance my line. Store managers, however, were requesting that I do more and more trunk shows in their stores. They also wanted display materials for my line, and I knew I somehow had to accomplish this.

My efforts to get the company to back me in a promotional endeavor met with deaf ears. I had permission, though, to design my line's hang tags, which included my photo along with a brief bio and statement about the line. These informative hang tags attracted the media's attention, as did the posters that I managed to create for the stores.

I wasn't given any money to mass-produce these posters, so I made some myself and sent them up to senior management to ask for support in producing more of them. Possibly because I had gone over my boss's head, my assistant was taken away soon after that and assigned elsewhere. I had to work without an assistant for months after that, which made my already impossible schedule even more hellish.

Finally, I was allowed to share a secretary with someone else, providing me with some relief. Lillian was very organized, and she used a color-coded filing system that worked quite well, along with a detailed logbook that contained all the letters and memos of the most recent thirty days. After thirty days, documents would go into a permanent file.

Her immaculate filing system ultimately saved me when certain documents seemed to be disappearing out of my office. Lillian told me that a higher-up sometimes called my office to see if I was in and, if I wasn't, she'd see him go into my office. He would also try to get information about me out of her. I was furious to realize that I had to really watch my back. Since some people seemed determined to nail me for any indiscretion, I made a special effort to save every memo, in addition to Lillian's copies.

Meanwhile, Don seemed cold and impatient with me, and it was getting harder to deal with him. He put my designs down all the time. It was hard not to feel completely deflated. After a while, I noticed that he actually avoided talking to me and became more aloof every day. It was a challenge to endure the increasing pressure I felt.

I was becoming completely stressed out trying to design lines of clothing for every season, as well as presenting the lines for the company's direct broadcasts to their stores, in addition to fashion shows for JCPenney stores and women's conferences all over the country—all without any support from Don. This nonstop work schedule was taking its toll.

In my second year at JCPenney, my schedule became even more demanding. I had to compete against myself to beat last year's numbers, and the company was expecting more from me as well. Sometimes the strain would so deplete my body's batteries that I would be too wound down even to talk. Of course, this unusual quietness from me would spark rumors that I was upset about something or was simply copping an attitude. It never seemed to occur to anyone that I could just be exhausted and stressed to the max. I never seemed to have any downtime.

I felt I was being stereotyped as a black designer for black women, even though sales were jumping all over the place. White, black, yellow, green, and purple people were buying my line. Although my creations were now only in 244 out of a total of 1,200 stores, they were selling off the racks quickly, no matter what neighborhood the stores were located in.

I felt stymied by what I thought was JCPenney's tunnel vision—their belief that only black people would buy my fashions. Every time I tried to encourage the company to try something new, I was essentially told, "You're a little tugboat and we're a great big ship—it takes a long time for us to turn around."

I was an anomaly that they just didn't know what to do with.

"We're in this box and you're in that box over there," they had told me.

It was becoming clear to me that with my line, JCPenney was being asked to be the maker and promoter, as well as the distributor. I think most of the people at JCPenney meant well but just weren't equipped to handle all those roles. They didn't know how to promote the label because they weren't promoters. Even though successful promotions can be done on a shoestring budget, it still takes the know-how to accomplish it.

Don refused to budge as I argued with him once again about the lack of promotional materials for my line. Lillian and I were still sending out my illicit homemade press kits, which included a black and white glossy of me with a bio, a description of the line's concept, and contact numbers for publicity. I told Don that I wasn't the only person asking for promotional materials. The store managers were also behind my requests.

Don replied he didn't care what they wanted. He had to go by the budgets that corporate gave us. If corporate said I didn't have the money in my budget for press kits, then I didn't have it. JCPenney was a big company, and if I didn't like it, he challenged me, why didn't I just resign?

"Not on your life," I told him. "I'm not going to resign. I'll just work with what I have, and hopefully the store managers will understand. But when they call asking for these things, I'll just tell them to call you."

"Fine," he retorted.

Soon after this confrontation, a friend of mine at JCPenney, who was a young black woman, warned me that plans were being made to take my ideas forward without me. She told me about a memo that had been written that discussed preparing for my departure and replacing my line. They were apparently already planning to fill the budget that I would leave behind.

I felt completely demoralized and shattered after hearing about the memo. I told an immediate supervisor, Ron, that

I had seen this memo after it had been slipped under my door anonymously. Ron's response was that he would look into the matter.

The next day, however, I was stunned to learn that my friend had been fired for something nebulous like not following company policy. Although they couldn't prove it, I'm sure they immediately suspected her of slipping the memo to me because she was black and a friend of mine. We were both very upset about this turn of events, but luckily she landed quickly on her feet with another job.

As Bruce and I were driving home together from work after this particularly stressful week, he finally told me, "You know, Anthony, someday you'll have to make the decision to leave the company."

I knew Bruce was right; the time for that decision was getting closer. Even though I sent messages to the higher-ups about my difficulties getting support for my work, their silence about the matter just let the situation with my boss slide further downhill. Don didn't want to back down, and neither did I. I think he became more and more frustrated that he couldn't control me, and things quickly went from bad to worse.

I coped by concentrating on the end results I wanted to achieve, reminding myself that this job was simply a stepping-stone in a hopefully long career. I tried to just do my job, but everything about it was a hassle, right down to ordering paper clips. Every dime had to be discussed and accounted for.

Over the next several months, while I managed to increase the number of stores carrying my line to almost three hundred, the company still cast me as a Black Designer for Black Women. I hated that—I mean, is Donna Karan considered just a designer for Jewish women? I fought hard to shed this image, pointing out to my bosses that sales results indicated that more than just African-American women were buying my designs. Case in point: one JCPenney store in Houston was what management called "the Country Club Store." No blacks lived near it, and yet this was one of my best stores with the highest sell-throughs.

Yes, black women loved my line because it was designed with them in mind, and they supported it because they were proud that a young brother was making it. But there was no definite black or white to my fashions. Every ethnic group has a love of great design and color, and I saw my designs as the new flavor of America. Rather than a melting pot, we Americans are more like a tossed salad.

I knew that my clothes appealed to women of all backgrounds, and I was disappointed by the lack of excitement from the corporate "suits" at JCPenney. No one seemed interested in my sales figures, even though they were strong. The first year for the line had grossed over $10 million in retail sales for JCPenney; the second year, it was up to about $17 million. That's a lot of *schmattes,* as inexpensive dresses are called in Yiddish.

Despite corporate's lack of enthusiasm, the store managers were excited and applauded my efforts, ordering more and more of the Anthony Mark Hankins signature line. The fashion press was also reviewing my line with very positive comments, and I was contacted by Black Entertainment Television, which wanted to film me on the job for a story on a young, black fashion designer. Since I was soon leaving on a business trip to New York and several other cities, I invited the BET camera crew to go along with me to the fabric houses.

As part of this trip, I took an Amtrak train from New York City to Rochester, New York. I had always been a good team player in high school and felt as if JCPenney was not really accepting me as a part of their team. I needed something positive to lift my sagging spirits.

As fate would have it, I picked up a magazine on the train and was inspired by a story in which Connie Chung related her difficulties breaking into broadcasting, the hardships she faced and the prejudice she encountered as a Chinese-American journalist. Her story illustrated to me that being a team player doesn't always erase the rules of bigotry. The glass ceiling often remains cold, hard, and seamless.

The story that BET did on me managed to bring even more attention from the fashion press, and management was shocked at how interested the newspaper and magazine editors were in my line. The increasing media interest only seemed to exacerbate my growing rift with corporate, however.

I was suddenly summoned home by my boss before my trip was complete and even had to cancel a trunk show at a JCPenney store in Farmington, Connecticut, to head back to Texas. When I returned to Dallas, I was reprimanded for talking to the press without first routing it through public relations. JCPenney had put me through their media classes so I would know how to talk to reporters, and I had thought I could handle it. Looking back, of course, I should have followed their protocol.

Upon my return, I discovered that someone had alerted management that my whole trip had been unauthorized. Knowing this was a false accusation, I reached into my desk to pull out my copy of the authorization memo, only to discover that it had mysteriously disappeared. Lillian saved the day, however, with her detailed filing, and I was able to prove to my bosses that the report about my indiscretions had been false.

To me, though, the handwriting was on the wall. Increasingly unhappy about the confining corporate structure and lack of support, I discussed the idea of forming my own company with Bruce, who agreed to join me in the new venture. For advice on how to proceed with a business plan, Bruce called a friend, Joyce Foreman, a very influential minority business owner in Dallas, who suggested we contact Cheryl Wattley, a dynamic young black attorney in Dallas, to guide us.

When we first met with Cheryl, I told her how restricted I felt at JCPenney and asked her to give me some advice on what I should do. As I related my history at JCPenney to her, she couldn't believe the amount of success I had achieved in such a short time. After hearing of my continuing battles, however, Cheryl encouraged me to stop fighting my frustration and just move on.

Bruce and I met with Cheryl every night for the next several months, hammering out a business plan for our new company. There was no turning back for me now. Because of our respective schedules, we would sometimes get together at 10:00 P.M. and not end our meeting until one or two o'clock in the morning. Cheryl invested so much time and dedication in helping us design our business plan that we asked her to become a partner in the company.

The prospect of starting my own company gave me a feeling of freedom. Mom, however, voiced her concern that I wouldn't be getting a paycheck if I resigned, and she tried to encourage me to first secure another job before leaving JCPenney. Bruce and I convinced her, though, that it had to be done this way. I knew that I had maxed out at JCPenney. Part of being in business is knowing when to let go and move on.

First, however, I had to let management know that I was planning on resigning. I sent a letter of resignation to James Hailey and asked for a formal meeting with management so that I could further explain my reasons for resigning. In preparation for this meeting, Cheryl and I worked all night putting the finishing touches on our presentation, and even on the way to the meeting, we were frantically perfecting it in the car. We were organized, though, with all my papers color-coded and triple-filed.

At the meeting, Cheryl and I explained that I was ready to move on to something new and was therefore resigning from my current position with the company. The corporate environment just wasn't right for me, but I thanked them for the opportunity they had given me. I hoped to start my own company and do business with them as a vendor in the future, I told them.

Cheryl and I then whipped out the business plan for Anthony Mark Hankins, Inc., which listed Bruce as the CEO and president. We asked for a one-year guarantee of purchases from JCPenney, in return for exclusivity of the label, which would provide us with an income to start the business.

Cheryl and I left the executives with our business plan, which described in detail our goals for the first several years of the business. They promised they'd discuss the offer and get back to us. In a few days, to our relief, they came back to us with a contract that agreed to our requests.

While I don't think the JCPenney brass were surprised that I was anxious to break out of the corporate box and create my own company, I'm sure they had been stunned to read within the business plan that Bruce Ackerman was listed as the CEO. He had joined Anthony's camp after thirty-seven years with JCPenney. After they realized this, Bruce's longtime colleagues gave him the cold shoulder.

As president and CEO of our new company, Bruce would be responsible for implementing our marketing plan, for staffing, and for overseeing the overall business operations. He was also going to be responsible for keeping a tight rein on our expenses, and for monitoring the margins and cost of items.

I would be responsible, as the chief designer and vice president of the company, for overseeing all design operations, as well as product development. This included selecting the vendors, fabrics, sample approvals, and fitting sessions. I would also, of course, be responsible for quality control.

Our new parent company was listed as well—which I had named after my father. It certainly wasn't done to honor him, because he hadn't been there for me as a father. But I had always fantasized about who Ramone Moya really was—in my mind, he was a mysterious, handsome man whom women found irresistible, like Rudolph Valentino, the legendary Latin lover. The sound of my father's name had the right charisma, since my clothing lines were dedicated to making women feel good about themselves.

23

Antonio Fierce Arrives

June 1, 1994, was Day One for Ramone Moya Ltd., the limited partnership created between myself, Bruce, and Cheryl. It served as the umbrella company under which would be the AMH Group and Anthony Mark Hankins, Inc. I felt like a soaring bird flying away from the nest for the first time. I couldn't wait to spread my wings like Jonathan Livingston Seagull.

Bruce and I worked out of Cheryl's office for the first couple of weeks, while we looked for a studio/office space of our own. We had fun visualizing our new design headquarters, while buying antiques and fashionable furniture for it. Soon, though, we had all the furniture but no studio to put it in. We had to find a place quickly, and locating the right space proved to be difficult. We searched for days.

Finally, Bruce and I visited another real-estate agency and described what we were looking for. The following day, we were shown a modern studio/town house at 3913 Prescott Avenue in the tony residential area called Oak Lawn. As we walked through the two-story space, I knew we had found the right place to house our company. This two-story, modern town house was exactly what I had envisioned: plenty of open space for our design work, but with a homey atmosphere that included a kitchen, a fireplace, and even a neighborhood dog park right across the street. It was really perfect for our needs.

"Bruce, this is wonderful!" I exclaimed. "Get the checkbook out!"

This was certainly not the best thing to blurt out right before you're going to negotiate with a real-estate agent, but I was too excited to hide my enthusiasm.

We saw the space on a Saturday and moved in the following Tuesday, in the middle of June. All the furniture we had gathered for the office, along with my extensive doll and toy collections, immediately filled our new studio with a bright, playful attitude. We mixed antique pine worktables with modern Italian pieces—along with tables, chairs, and cabinets hand painted by a Romanian artist who had been an opera-set designer.

After all of our planning, everything was finally falling into place. Fashion is all about image, and even our furniture had to be cutting-edge to create the right impression. Finally, I had the atelier I had always dreamed about. I had to pinch myself to make sure it was real.

The first article about our company appeared on July 2, 1994, in the *Dallas Morning News.* Headlined BREAKING OUT OF THE PATTERN, the article chronicled my departure from JCPenney, along with the debut of our new company. The writer, Maria Halkias, reported in the piece that I was wearing a backward baseball cap and wide-laced Jack Purcell tennis shoes for the interview. Thank God, I thought, I could finally wear what I wanted to work without a Don Scaccia glaring me down.

We framed the article and proudly hung it on the wall of our new headquarters. I finally had my own *schmatte* shop and was free to be my own kind of fashion designer. There would be no black or white to my fashions, girlfriend. My customer is the contemporary urban woman—period.

When it came to fashion, I wanted Anthony Mark Hankins to be considered "everybody's boyfriend." I've always wanted to design clothes that appealed to every woman—whether they were full-size, petite, white, black, yellow, or green. My clothes have always been designed for real women with real lives, and to be sure my fashions will work on all different body types, I've always used at least eight different fit models.

My goal is to empower women with my clothing. All women are superstars, and I don't think they hear it enough. Every woman is victorious because she's a missionary to so many people. She's a mother, a sister, an aunt, a caretaker, a teacher. . . . My clothing lines celebrate all women and their need for work, travel, and casual attire. It's dress-up, dress-down, go-anywhere fashion.

When I worked in New York, I received some valuable advice from the designer Willi Smith, who said, in essence, "Don't have an attitude, because you're only as good as your last collection." Designing for "a woman with an attitude," however, is another story. My clothes are for the woman who feels she can conquer the world.

Now that Bruce and I were settled into our new offices, we had to let people know we were there. We planned a launch party/fashion show for August which would introduce our company, as well as benefit the African-American Museum in Dallas and the United Negro College Fund. We sent out over seven hundred invitations that included two donation envelopes—one for each charity. We asked that the invitees return the envelopes of their choice, with a donation included, as their "ticket" to the event.

We chose to have the affair at the impressive Hall of State Building in Dallas' Fair Park. Built in 1926, it is a marvelous Art Deco building, with a rotunda in front and a gold statue of Mercury, the god of commerce, outside the building. Inside the building, which is curved like a half-moon, is a large museum-style space, along with a great hall. The ambience is totally elegant, with black marble floors and fifty-foot-high ceilings.

A red carpet, three hundred feet long, greeted our guests. At the entrance to the rotunda, ten mannequins were on display, each one wearing something I had created at a pivotal point in my life, with storyboards next to the mannequins explaining the history of each one. High-tech lights illuminated the forty-foot runway for the fashion show and a huge video-monitor wall with sixteen video screens formed the backdrop for the stage.

We used mainly minority vendors and entertainment for this charity event, many of whom donated their services. The models, about twenty of them, were all professionals I had known from JCPenney. Normally paid $150 an hour, these lovely ladies generously donated their time for the benefit. As usual, we had complete diversity of models—Asian, Hispanic, black, white, over-fifty, full-size, everything.

Angie, too, participated as a model on the runway, turning heads as usual. She had completed her four years with the Air Force and was now an honors student at the

Stevens Institute of Technology, in Hoboken, New Jersey, studying electrical engineering, with her future goals set on law school.

Almost everyone who participated or attended knew how much this celebration meant to us. The show was filled with a natural exuberance, matched by the spirited music we had chosen for the fashion show. The models outdid themselves on the runway, especially the over-fifty model, who, wearing a sports outfit, did a spontaneous cartwheel on the runway. The crowd went wild.

I was sure I had made the right decision to leave JCPenney, especially when I looked out into the audience of friends and colleagues and saw my mom, stepfather, sister Angie, and Angie's boyfriend, Richard, all beaming with pride. I knew I had finally arrived.

Once the launch party was a fait accompli, we settled down into an exhilarating but grueling schedule. Bruce handled the business end of the company, and I was in charge of the designing, product development, and marketing. I kept a war board in the studio which was constantly updated to reflect our daily and future goals. I also maintained the presentation boards, which were the blueprints for each line.

One thing I like about what I do is that I get to set the image. I guide the direction for my company and decide what it should represent. My design staff doesn't move on something without my stamp of approval on it. The most challenging part of the job is taking the concept from the sketch and following it through production, making sure that every aspect of the process comes off without a hitch. You have to make sure that the piece-goods people send the right fabric, that you receive the trim and other details, that you ship the garments on time, and that your product retails.

We do separate product programs for each store, so it's an exhausting schedule, involving the creation of five to six sportswear groupings a month, as well as up to thirty dresses. From these, we'll decide on three top groups to fully develop. Then we'll send the manufacturers the specifications and fabric samples.

I have to be a diplomat to troubleshoot all the problems that can arise, like the time we created beautiful Christmas sweaters that were supposed to be shipped to the stores around Thanksgiving. Unfortunately, the stores erroneously received them in September, and store managers suddenly realized that they had five thousand sweaters on their hands which weren't selling. Now, who's going to buy Christmas sweaters in September? You can have the best product, but somebody else's mistake can still mess it up.

I also deal directly with the buyers, even though our company has a full sales force. I go to New York often to meet with the buyers to make sure they're comfortable with our product. We're frank with one another, and our relationship goes beyond meetings. We know one another on a personal level, as well. With business, I think it's important to enjoy the journey and build solid professional relationships.

It's important to stand for something positive; you've got to stay focused and honest with your customers. I'm very careful about the manufacturers that I choose, and I've walked away from possibly very lucrative deals because I didn't like their direction, quality, or business practices. I wouldn't feel right making a huge profit by using third-world sweatshops to produce my clothing. You have to follow your inner voice.

* * *

During our first summer as a design entity, we were contacted by Lyn Berman, a Dallas businesswoman who volunteered at the Cape Center, a program that took women off the welfare rolls and increased their self-esteem by teaching them skills and showing them how to project a professional image. The center provided just about anything these women needed to get back on track. If a woman needed her teeth fixed, for instance, they would somehow find a way to arrange that, too. Lyn had read about me in the newspaper and called to ask if I would talk to her students at the Cape Center.

There were about twenty young women in Lyn's program. I talked to them about my job and how I wanted to empower women by making them feel good about themselves with my clothing line. It was the first time I had spoken to a group of people about my life, and I was inspired by the way my own story seemed to build a fire of determination in these people.

We donated our dress samples to the Cape Center so that women there could have access to nice clothes for their jobs. After the Cape Center folded, Lyn started a similar non-profit program called "Attitudes and Attire," which we also supported with donations. Lyn is really an inspiration. She gets such satisfaction helping women overcome obstacles.

Talking to the people in Lyn's program was so emotionally rewarding that I decided I wanted to speak to students, as well. While in Washington, D.C., to give a trunk show for JCPenney, Bruce and I contacted Cozette Carter, a very tall and impressive woman who was the retired superintendent of schools in the area. She arranged for me to give a motivational talk to students at Bell Multi-Cultural High

School. Mrs. Carter also arranged for students from four or five other schools to come to the big auditorium at Bell for my presentation.

In addition to the talk, we put on a fashion show for the kids, with students and teachers modeling our clothes. This event was covered by Cathy Horyn, a journalist then with the *Washington Post.* Cathy coined my motivational talk "The Fabric of Dreams" in the headline of her article, and it has been called that ever since.

I love working with young kids because they tell it to you straight and aren't afraid to ask direct questions, like why I left Yves Saint Laurent. Nothing grows under a big tree, I explained to them, and Yves Saint Laurent is a huge tree.

I told them my story, how I had my mother's support and encouragement to draw and sew—even though these activities might have brought me ridicule. I went after what I wanted on faith and with a lot of determination. I didn't let anybody tell me it couldn't be done. I just didn't take no for an answer where my dreams were concerned. You have to start living your own dream, I encouraged them. You've got to walk the walk, live the life.

I've since given this talk over a hundred times to kids of all ages, from elementary to college students, and it is so gratifying to see the spark of hope shine through their eyes when they realize that their own dreams are possible. When my talk is finished, they often crowd around me, enthusiastically declaring their own goals for the future. They want to be doctors, lawyers, singers. . . . It never fails to thrill me to see young people voicing their own dreams.

In December of that year, Bruce and I traveled to Miami to prepare our summer-collection press kit and to enjoy a few days of vacation there. I had stayed at the Cardozo Hotel in South Beach while doing a trunk show for JCPenney and had loved its Art Deco decor and friendly staff. It's a jazzy hotel with oceanfront views, built in 1939 and now beautifully restored by its current owner, singer Gloria Estefan.

My earlier stays in Miami and my visits to the Caribbean islands nearby had inspired me to create the new summer line utilizing the bright, spicy colors of Brazil, Cuba, and Latin carnivals. I loved exploring the Latin side of my ancestral culture.

When we arrived at the Cardozo, we looked up some models I had worked with in the past for our photo shoot. We utilized the natural assets of Miami's South Beach for the backdrops. All we had to do to reach our "set" for the photo session was to walk across the street from the hotel to the beach. Since the early sun casts a beautiful illumination on everything, we were up early—fishermen's hours.

For the photo shoot, we stayed within our tight budget any way we could and still had a great time. The models did their own makeup, and when some of the photos called for fresh flowers, I simply "borrowed" the orchids from the hotel lobby and returned them ten minutes later, when the shots were completed. It was so early in the morning that nobody noticed the empty flower vases. The local photographer we hired was fabulously efficient and had the photos back to us by that evening.

Finally, work completed, we lazily sipped fine Cuban coffee at a sidewalk café and enjoyed the steady stream of beautiful people gliding by flaunting their best "I'm too sexy for you" haughtiness. South Beach is sizzlin', girlfriend. It's the American Riviera—the East Coast version of Hollywood, where it's common to see film crews or celebrities at any given moment. I've read that Madonna herself is the co-owner of the hot and happening Blue Door Restaurant at the Delano Hotel in South Beach. You just never know who you're going to bump into there. It's a nonstop party that moves to a salsa beat, and my half-Cuban self just can't stop dancin' to the conga rhythms all night long, child.

With the holiday season in full swing, our high spirits were dampened one evening when Bruce and I went Christmas shopping at a high-end mall in the greater Dallas area. After hours of shopping, we decided to grab a bite to eat in the mall's food court. Bruce held a table for us while I stood in line for sandwiches.

I was chatting with a white woman and her son when a black security guard came up to me. A white security guard stood close by.

"Would you take that rag off your head?" the black security guard asked me, his tone definitely not cordial.

"Excuse me?" I asked him, flabbergasted by the request. I was wearing a blue bandana on my head, along with Arizona jeans and a jean jacket. Okay, maybe it wasn't the height of fashion for the day, but I hardly thought it was worth being hassled about.

"Take that rag off your head," he repeated.

"I'm not taking this off my head," I responded, stunned. "Last time I looked, I was in America."

The security guard said nothing and walked away.

"Can you believe that guy?" I asked the white woman and her son, both of whom seemed just as incredulous as I was. I took our soft drinks to the table and went back to get the sandwiches. Suddenly, it seemed like seven cops had surrounded me!

"Did he just tell you to take that rag off your head?" a white cop asked me, referring to the security guard who had initially approached me.

"Yes," I told him.

"Well, are you going to?"

"No!" I was getting angry now.

Bruce stepped in quickly to try to calm me down.

"Let's go to Foley's to eat," Bruce told me. "*They* didn't seem to have any trouble with us being in there."

Bruce stood up with our packages to encourage me to leave when the cop shoved me while actually saying to me, "Stop shoving me."

Now I was furious. What did this cop think he was pulling?

Bruce held his hand up to me and warned, "Hold it, Anthony, don't do anything."

The cop then picked up my sandwich and threw it on the floor, some of it landing on my shoes. I wanted to slug him, but Bruce stopped me. I was incredulous when the cops whipped handcuffs out. Everyone in the food court was watching as I was handcuffed and escorted to the mall's security office. Bruce hurried to the car to grab the mobile phone so he could call Cheryl for legal counsel.

The cops kept asking me why I wouldn't take off my bandana. When Bruce returned, he asked them if they realized that I was certainly not a gang member. By this time, senior security officers had arrived. Two years before, we found out, there had been a gang shooting in the food court at the mall, and one innocent bystander had been killed. Since then, mall security discouraged the wearing of gang attire in the mall.

Why they thought I was a gang member just because I was wearing a blue bandana on my head is beyond me. My behavior that evening in the food court certainly didn't fit any gang profile. What kind of gang did they think I was in? I was with an older, sophisticated-looking white gentleman, surrounded by Christmas packages and chatting amiably with a white woman and her son. Did that constitute threatening behavior?

And if there were signs prohibiting gang attire, they certainly weren't very visible. Later, we discovered there was a small sign at the left of a mall door that stated in tiny print that mall patrons should wear "appropriate dress." It didn't describe in any way what they considered to be gang-related apparel. It certainly didn't mention anything about wearing scarves or bandanas.

This incident only underscores the fact that I don't believe people should be judged solely by the way they dress. Yes, clothes definitely do send a message about who you are, but it's not the whole picture. No matter how people are dressed, they should be treated courteously, unless their behavior warrants otherwise.

That spring, I learned that Marian Wright Edelman, the president and founder of the Children's Defense Fund, would be coming to Dallas to accept the prestigious Juanita Kreps Award, which is annually sponsored and presented by JCPenney. The award's namesake, Dr. Juanita Kreps, had been President Carter's Secretary of Commerce, and had gone on to become a James B. Duke Professor of Economics at Duke University and a trustee of the Duke Endowment, as well as a board member of JCPenney. The awards were established in 1993 by W. R. Howell to honor "the spirit of the American woman."

Marian Wright Edelman was to receive the award that year. Since her Children's Defense Fund helped pay for the camp I attended as a child, I have always appreciated her dedication to working with inner-city kids. Mrs. Edelman is one of my heroes, and I was looking forward to meeting her and attending the ceremony. Cheryl Wattley had already received her invitation and asked if I had received mine yet. I hadn't, so I called JCPenney's PR department and was pointedly told that I was not invited to the event.

The explanation was that they were primarily inviting African-American women who were influential in the business community. Next on their list were African-Americans who were influential in the community at large. The PR representative reiterated her stance that I would not be getting an invitation. Her decision didn't change even after I mentioned why I wanted to meet Mrs. Edelman.

Undeterred, I pondered how I could change this situation. Bruce reminded me that our friend in Washington, D.C., Cozette Carter, knew Mrs. Edelman's sister. This connection made, I explained to Mrs. Edelman's sister who I was and that I'd like to send flowers to Mrs. Edelman to introduce myself to her. Her sister was kind enough to give us Mrs. Edelman's home address and to let us know that she was especially partial to gladiolas.

Thanking her sister for this tip, we ordered several dozen gladiolas and sent these, along with a press kit and an Anthony Mark Hankins dress in her size, directly to her house the night before the event in Dallas. As you can guess, I was determined to meet this incredible woman when she arrived in Dallas—invitation or no invitation to the awards banquet.

Sure enough, I heard that when Mrs. Edelman got off the plane in Dallas, she looked around and the first thing she said to the waiting JCPenney representatives was, "Where's Anthony Mark Hankins?"

The day of the event, however, I still lacked an invitation. Joyce Foreman, our good friend who is also on the board of directors of Texas Commerce Bank, offered me her ticket, but I wanted to get my own. It was the principle of the thing. Jill Louis, another friend and an attorney, got on the phone with JCPenney's community affairs department that day to ask them why I wasn't on the guest list. Possibly to avoid answering the question, they finally granted me an invitation and I was delighted.

The ink on my name tag may have still been wet, but I made it to the awards luncheon and had my chance to meet this remarkable lady. During the event, someone from W. R. Howell's table walked over to me and announced, "Mrs. Edelman would like to speak with you."

I felt that everyone's eyes at W. R. Howell's table were following my movements closely as I made my way to Mrs. Edelman's seat. Did they think I was going to create an embarrassing scene? When I approached her, she jumped up, hugged me, and said, "I'm so glad to meet you."

It was a warm, fuzzy moment to be with this woman I had long admired. This meeting, and a subsequent one later that year at the Trumpet Awards in Atlanta, have resulted in a continuing correspondence between us. She is truly a remarkable woman.

I have tried to follow the example set by Mrs. Edelman by also becoming involved with the community. I am on the advisory board of Easter Seals, as well as on the board of the Dallas SPCA, among other civic activities. Believe me, it's true that what you choose to give comes back to you tenfold. Not only does it do your soul good, but it's also a wonderful way to meet people and develop a network, along with a brotherhood/sisterhood. I've gotten to know people from all over Dallas and from every walk of life.

Though my line was exclusive to JCPenney for this first year, Bruce and I were busy preparing for the day we could offer our fashions to other companies. Contractually, we were already allowed to create patterns for Butterick's catalog. Mary Fotherby, a vice president of Butterick, had called me because she had read in an article that I had used a Butterick See & Sew pattern for that first dress I had made for my mother. She thought an association with Butterick would be a natural fit, and so did we. I created a line of patterns for women, as well as a new line of children's clothing, for Butterick.

We also approached the Mercantile Group, which included such stores as Gayfers, J. B. White, and Castner Knotts; the Federated group, which included Rich's, Burdines, Macy's, the Broadway, and Bloomingdale's; as well as Dayton Hudson, Target, Kmart, and Sears, among others. The merchandise manager of JCPenney once commented to us that he hoped we'd never ship to Sears after our exclusivity to JCPenney ran out because Sears was such a direct competitor of theirs. We, of course, would have welcomed the opportunity.

Our line for Target, which we called Authentics, was ready to ship as of June 1, 1995, when our exclusivity with JCPenney expired and we were free to market our lines everywhere. While we still retained JCPenney as one of our major accounts, we now also had an account with Target, as well as a line for Kmart which we called Anjalise. Once we were no longer restricted to JCPenney, our sales zoomed to the $40 million level.

We were soon also selling our lines to the worldwide PX stores of the Army and Air Force Exchange Service, or AAFES. We were surprised to find out that AAFES is one of the top ten retailers in the world. They have huge stores that carry every item that a major retail store would have. Our account with them required me to travel to PX stores throughout Europe, the United States, and the Pacific, to present trunk shows. These trips also enabled me to give "Fabric of Dreams" talks to the children of our armed-services personnel in various parts of the world, including Okinawa, Japan; England; and Germany.

Our pattern line for Butterick was officially launched in July 1995, and Butterick sponsored an Anthony Mark Hankins Day in Elizabeth, New Jersey, to celebrate the occasion. For this event, I gave a "Fabric of Dreams" talk at my alma mater, Elizabeth High School, for about five hundred summer students there. Then we put on a trunk show in downtown Elizabeth at Mr. Wolper's fabric store, now called Sunset Fabrics and owned by Ali Batuman, who had decorated the store with banners and signs welcoming us. It was a heady experience to sign patterns and programs for hometown friends, including the mayor of Elizabeth.

Even with all this wonderful attention, I knew that one of the keys to continued success was getting the word out about our new company. I remembered a quote from Ted Turner when he had been asked why he thought his Turner Broadcasting System had succeeded against the odds. He answered with three simple words: "Marketing, marketing, marketing."

Heeding that advice, I aggressively pursued a marketing strategy for our new company, which included getting as much publicity as possible through newspaper and magazine articles. Through her expert public relations efforts, our friend Judith Agisim kept our company's accomplishments in the news, and we eagerly rode the rising wave of press coverage. In our first year of operation, there were over three hundred articles and news features written about our lines.

During our second year, we kept that momentum going by hiring an on-staff public relations person. Our product is great, but it's another job to keep your name out there. No matter what your product is, it's the name recognition and marketing that really gets the orders. We frequently send our buyers promotional items that are mostly fun and personable stuff that gets my face in front of them. In our mailers, I am usually pictured in whimsical poses, like fishing in a trout stream, riding a bicycle, dancing in a tux with a model, spinning a Hula-Hoop, or dressed as a gospel preacher. Anything to get their attention.

Buyers can feel the energy of our company through these campaigns, and they want to get to know this playful jester they see on our mailers. The media, too, seems to appreciate our sense of fun. In the press, I've often been called "the Bill Cosby of fashion" and "the Calvin Klein of the coupon-clipping set."

I also believe in leaving buyers a little something to remember us by, like maybe a small care package or a calling card with antique buttons on it. I've always tried to turn my uniqueness into an asset. If you're from Texas and doing business in New York, for instance, I don't think you should try to be something you're not. The fact that you're from Texas is what's going to set you apart from the pack and help them remember you.

If fashion magazines hesitated to write articles about me and our new company, I would plop myself down in their New York offices and persuade them to write one. I also began to appear on local radio and television shows in Dallas like *Good Morning, Texas; 5 Talk Street;* and *Insights,* a show aimed at the African-American and Hispanic communities; as well as on nationally seen talk shows such as *Mike & Maty* and *Crook & Chase.*

I felt unstoppable until I witnessed a relatively small incident in Jackson, Mississippi. There for a trunk show at Gayfers, I was pleased to see that two little old white ladies had taken my dresses to the counter to buy them. Then I saw them notice my picture on the hang tags. They were shocked to see my black face peering up at them from the tag.

"We don't want this," they quickly agreed, and left the dresses sitting on the counter.

I was stunned, especially since this scene closely followed a call that Bruce had recently received from the manager of one of our accounts, asking us to remove my picture from the hang tags so that customers would not perceive my line as being solely for African-Americans. I called Bruce immediately and, still feeling the sting of the two women's rejection of my line at Gayfers, told him I thought all the hang tags should be without a picture from here on out.

Bruce thought this was a mistake, but I insisted they be removed. We took the pictures off, but soon our customers, across all racial lines, were asking us why we had removed them. They liked seeing who the designer was and didn't care that I was African-American. Customer feedback has since consistently shown us that most people like the picture on the tags; in fact, many people save them, as they would baseball cards, since our hang tags are changed or updated periodically.

We pride ourselves on having a close relationship with our customers. We do a lot of surveys and talk to customers every day on customer service lines. I enjoy doing the trunk shows all over the country because I love to talk directly to our customers.

One of our office assistants, Elfrieda, often wears selections from our lines. As a full-figured woman, Elfrieda loves the comfort as well as the uptown look that the dresses give her. She can dress them down or dress them up to fit any occasion. One week, she had to serve on jury duty and showed up in an Anthony Mark Hankins black tunic ensemble with an accent scarf. When the other ladies on the jury complimented her outfit, Elfrieda told them all about my fashions, how affordable and comfortable they are.

She was surprised to find out the next day that three of the women had gone shopping that very night and had bought their own Anthony Mark Hankins dresses! I was thrilled when Elfrieda relayed this to me. One of the ladies, however, couldn't find the corresponding scarf to her new outfit and asked Elfrieda for help in locating one. I was more than happy to send the woman, one of our newest customers, the scarf and matching earrings to go with her purchase.

Mom, too, has an active role in our company. We send her just about every piece produced for our lines, and Mom enjoys "wear-testing" our fashions. Her job is to tell me the honest truth about how the garment fits and wears, as well as what others comment about them. Even though she's my mother, you'd be surprised how frank and honest she is with me. I really rely on her and her friends' comments on the lines.

Although our sales were strong, the powers that be at JCPenney still insisted on pigeonholing me as a black designer for black women, with my line mainly being offered to those stores with a heavy concentration of African-American customers. Our other accounts were progressive enough to see past the skin color of the designer to acknowledge that the clothes he created would appeal to every woman. Somehow, I wanted to get across to the managers at JCPenney that I was offering them much more than just an ethnic product.

I got my chance to express my views at the JCPenney stockholders' meeting, which was held in Dallas that summer. As a stockholder, I am entitled to get up and speak after the general meeting has adjourned. I worked and worked on my speech, which was a tricky one to write because I wanted to get my points across without being confrontational about it. Although I will always be grateful to JCPenney for the opportunity they gave me, I felt there was certainly room for growth within our business relationship.

I addressed the board members as a stockholder, as a former associate, and now as a supplier to the women's division. My goal, I told them, was to speak on behalf of all minority business owners who did not want to be looked upon as merely fulfilling some sort of minority quota system. We had the talent to become major players but needed their support in order to reach our full potential.

I explained that I planned to graduate to a new level as the creator of a major apparel line. I may be a minority vendor, I told them, but I designed for all women and wanted to bring to JCPenney the concept of a designer label on the level of Liz Claiborne or Carole Little.

I wanted JCPenney to recognize me as a universal designer, just as other companies did. JCPenney had given this young African-American a chance when they had appointed him as their first in-house designer, I reminded them, and I looked forward to furthering our relationship.

Although I received no official response to my speech in front of the board, I hoped they had taken my message to heart.

I set aside these adult concerns to have fun that summer with my seven-year-old nephew, Johnathan Pantoja, Katie's son, who came to stay with me for two months. He was already a budding photographer who loved to document our trips to Six Flags Over Texas, the giant amusement park in nearby Arlington, and our other fun adventures. He came with me to trunk shows that summer and took wonderful photographs of these events.

Whenever I'm in New York on my frequent business trips, I like to help Johnathan with his homework while Katie is at work, thus taking on the role of surrogate parent for a few hours. I love to be with all my nieces and nephews whenever possible. It helps keep the child in me alive. Johnathan helped me that summer to realize what is really important in life. I had so much fun with him that I often forgot the pressures of my design work.

Toward the end of the summer, Rolonda Watts and I also had a wonderful reunion of sorts. I was invited to appear as a fashion consultant on her nationally syndicated talk show, *Rolonda,* which is taped in New York. The segment was about a group of young schoolkids who had all successfully lost weight over the summer at camp, and they were to model a new school wardrobe on the show. Before the taping of this segment, I had a blast taking these kids all over New York, finding them great outfits.

Rolonda and I, too, enjoyed seeing each other and catching up on our recent endeavors and accomplishments. Our lives had intersected at the beginning of our professional careers, and we were proud to see how far we both had come.

24

✂ ‒

Hitting the Airwaves

In our first year of operation, Bruce and I were approached by the QVC home-shopping channel to present our product on their network. They already had a segment that featured Afrocentric-inspired merchandise. Michael Crowley, QVC's director of merchandising, was trying to further develop this area and was interested in me doing a segment called *Anthony's Places & Spaces,* which would center around collectibles that I designed, along with apparel. Each segment was to feature dolls, pillows, and other accessories—all based on a particular theme, like cows or spring flowers. Michael agreed to meet with us at our studio in Dallas to discuss our ideas for these segments.

Enthusiastically, I worked with our staff to design product for *Anthony's Places & Spaces,* and we quickly blocked out themes for twelve segments, putting together a professional book for each one. When we were ready for a presentation, Michael and his team from QVC arrived in Dallas. We had gone all out for them, hanging "Welcome, QVC" banners and balloons across the outside of the studio.

Michael and his colleagues loved our presentation, and our negotiations progressed further. I flew up to the QVC headquarters in West Chester, Pennsylvania, outside Philadelphia, to develop the details of the segments with them. Their buyer also came to Dallas several times to work with us there.

Just as we were really getting things rolling, though, the QVC buyer we had been working with left the company and another buyer was sent to Dallas to catch up on the details of our plans. This was the first glitch in our fledgling association with QVC. Then, knocking the wind out of everyone's sails, Michael Crowley suddenly left QVC for an opportunity at Saks Fifth Avenue, and we had to start all over again. The momentum was lost from that point on. Michael was such a visionary that his leaving took the support right out from under our project.

One thing that bothered us about the QVC negotiations was that they wanted us to do more than just apparel. We were expected to also create home accessories, including linens, pillows, and decorative kitsch. While we were interested in creating it all, how were we supposed to get this much product off the ground so quickly?

Bruce and I also weren't happy with the standard QVC contract we were expected to sign, and the QVC executives seemed unwilling to negotiate with us. They asked me, however, to fly up again to meet with the buyer and the vice president of merchandising. In West Chester, though, I realized that since Michael had left, I hadn't felt the same enthusiasm from QVC. The vibes just didn't seem right somehow. The energy I had felt before simply wasn't there.

Returning to Dallas from my disappointing trip to QVC, I needed to hear an encouraging word. Miraculously, I received a call from Gwen Jenkins, the buyer for Black Entertainment Television's *BET Shop,* a home-shopping program that was then a division of the Home Shopping Network. The executives of *BET Shop,* Gwen told me, were very interested in meeting with me.

I was ecstatic about this new turn of affairs, and as soon as Bruce and I could arrange it, we flew to New York to meet with Gwen and her associates from *BET Shop.* We met with them over dinner at Chez Josephine, a fabulous restaurant owned by Jean-Claude Baker, one of Josephine Baker's adopted sons. It's one of my favorite places to dine in New York. I could tell the vibes were already cooking with *BET Shop.*

I felt a lot of great energy from Gwen, who was a jazzy, classy young black lady with a straight Cleopatra haircut. For this evening, she was wearing a stunning black Armani suit with black suede evening shoes. I loved her look and her personality. I also clicked with her BET associates, who had joined us for dinner.

Gwen told me that if I did well on *BET Shop,* they could easily get me on the Home Shopping Network. Bruce and I were more than excited by this news. Here were two major avenues opening up for us.

"Let's do it!" I told them.

For years, I had watched the Home Shopping Network and was a fan of their show hosts, like Terry Lewis Mason and Tina Berry. Tina specialized in selling dolls, and I had ordered many items in my extensive collection through the Home Shopping Network. Since I'm the doll king, with my dialing finger poised by the phone to order my next acquisition from the Home Shopping Network, I had spent hours studying their hosting techniques and admiring their work. I often imagined myself hawking my own products on a home-shopping show.

The next time we received a call from a QVC representative, Bruce and I told them that we were going with *BET Shop* and the Home Shopping Network. We were then informed that if we went with BET, we could never go back to QVC. Bruce and I were confident, however, that we had made the right decision. Within a few months, I was making my first appearance as a "guest" on *BET Shop*, which is broadcast live from Tampa, Florida. I couldn't believe that my fantasy of being on a home-shopping channel was coming true. I thanked God that Gwen had come into my life.

I was nervous as I prepared to go before the cameras, but Gwen and the segment's host, Tina Berry, were right there to assure me that I'd do fine. Before we went on the air, my mother called from Elizabeth and asked Tina to please be good to her son and let him talk on the show. Tina, though, soon found out she didn't have to help me carry the segment. Once the camera lights went on, child, I started talking and never stopped! Tina couldn't shut me up, and it's been that way ever since.

"Always see yourself as a star," I told the home-shopping viewers. "You're someone special. Think, I KNOW I look good! Have that aura around you. Make everyone smile when you enter a room. Wear professional, beautiful clothes, because if you don't look good, you're not going to get that job or that promotion. . . ."

Selling on a home-shopping show is my medium, honey. I loved the lights, the camera, the people. Tina Berry called me "Mr. Sparkle." Put me in front of a camera, she said, and I just ignite. The gratification is immediate since telephone operators are working the phone banks on one side of the stage, taking orders as you're showing your merchandise. The sales results are instantly tallied on the screen and, bam, you know immediately whether you have a good product or not. There's nothing like it. It's a life-altering experience for me every time. It's better than any talk show, fashion show, or trunk show.

Not only do you get immediate sales results as you broadcast live, but your audience phones in and gives you immediate feedback as well. The audience especially enjoyed it when Mom called in, enjoying the chance to chat with her son on national television. She signed off with a "God bless" for everyone, and the viewing audience loved her.

During the first segment I did for *BET Shop,* our sales blew out the doors! We sold everything in fifteen minutes, even though we were scheduled to be on the air for an hour. After that successful debut, Gwen told me our sales results had been phenomenal and that I would definitely be invited back. Girlfriend, I was on cloud nine.

I did six more *BET Shop* segments over the next few months. The audiences loved the apparel, although privately Tina did point out one fashion faux pas in one of our lineups—a dress with bright horizontal stripes of Caribbean-inspired hues. Tina took one look at the dress in the upper sizes and burst out laughing.

"Anthony, what were you thinking with these horizontal stripes on a size 18?" she asked. "This is one time you should have gone with a solid fabric."

"Dahling, wearing that dress is a matter of attitude," I retorted, before reluctantly admitting that she did have a point in this case. On second glance, that dress, in the larger sizes, did look like a test pattern for a drive-in picture show.

With the success of my appearances on *BET Shop*, Gwen, true to her word, got me an audience with all the big guys at the Home Shopping Network. They quickly made a deal with me to appear on the Home Shopping Network on March 31, 1996, with the assumption that I would make more appearances if my product sold well.

The HSN executives were straight-to-the-point about their requirements, and I respected them for that. They tell all of their guests how much they're expected to sell if they want to be invited back. The same is true if your merchandise has a high return rate. If you don't make the numbers, no matter who you are, you will not be invited back.

Before my first segment aired on the Home Shopping Network, I taped some promo spots for the show and was surprised to receive calls from long-lost friends and relatives who had recognized me on HSN! It was a kick already. I was having a blast.

I loved the set they had created for me on the Home Shopping Network, with my name in big letters amid giant clothes hangers and pin cushions. My first cohost was a beautiful woman named Bobbi Ray, who is phenomenal. She really made it happen! She wore one of my outfits and looked stunning, which helped our sales start buzzing. We were supposed to be on for an hour, but we sold out in only forty minutes! Mom called in and we enjoyed chatting via the airwaves. Our conversation was followed by a woman who called in and said, "Any man who loves his mother like that—I love him, too."

The callers just embraced me, and that felt wonderful. I knew I had taken a major step that day. By this time, I knew all the show lingo and had the people at *BET Shop* to thank for teaching me to look so natural. From all my trunk shows with JCPenney, too, I had developed an easy rapport with the audience.

"Now, this look is hot," I exclaimed as a model burst onto the stage in an explosion of tropical color. Grabbing a fan from a table full of accessories, I fanned the model furiously, setting the loose folds of her tunic and skirt fluttering. The audience responded with a flood of phone calls. I rhapsodized about the outfit—the lively mix of prints, the flowing lines, the machine-washable fabric, the touch of elastic that offered "room for expansion" at the waist, the fact that each piece could be teamed with a solid-colored top, skirt, or pant to create several additional outfits.

"And both pieces for only sixty-eight dollars, ladies," I cried. "Can you believe your luck? Dress up, dress down, throw your gorgeous self around! Bold, bright, easy-fitting, freewheeling, going-to-church, Brazilian-carnivalesque party time."

The phones next to the stage started ringing off the wall.

The second time I appeared on HSN, I was scheduled for the morning of Palm Sunday. Everyone at HSN sympathized that Palm Sunday was one of the toughest times to be on—but we did it, girlfriend. We sold out again well before the allotted hour was up.

Selling on a home-shopping show becomes more than just hawking apparel. It's entertainment for the viewers who want to learn more about you. As I appeared on more segments, the audience and I got to know each other. Through television, which is such an intimate medium, they feel like they're a part of your life and that they know you. They know that Anthony Mark Hankins really cares about them. My label is more than just a brand name; it's a feeling, a spirit, a lifestyle—like Martha Stewart.

One young woman called in to say that her mother had seen my segments on HSN and loved them, then had phoned her daughter to tell her that she had ordered a dress as a gift for her—our limited-edition "Ladies Who Lunch" dress, which came with my limited-edition, signed sketch of the dress. This short-sleeved, scoop-neck dress had a simple black bodice with a very colorful scene, of women sitting in a Paris café enjoying their afternoon together, around the flowing base of the skirt.

The daughter was calling to say how much she loved the dress and that, poignantly, her mother had died right before the dress had arrived. The dress meant all the more to her since it was one of the last things she and her mother had chatted about. That was such a moving call, and it made me realize just how much of a connection we have with our viewers.

When I was doing my first show for HSN, we heard that Barry Diller had gone from heading QVC to the top position at HSN. I was thrilled to hear this since I was sure he'd run a sound ship. The next pleasant surprise was to hear that Michael Crowley was leaving Saks Fifth Avenue to come to HSN as vice president of merchandising. All this time, I had thought that Michael Crowley and I might never have the chance to work together.

Michael was happy to see that I was with HSN, and I was likewise thrilled to see him. He called me once he had arrived to take his new post and told me, "We're going to make this show fun, Anthony. We're going to make it happen and I'm glad we're working together."

I felt a surge of electricity go through me. Michael and I were finally going to accomplish what we had originally planned to do! Michael came to my next segment and stayed until the end. He didn't have to do that, but he cared enough to and that meant a lot. He stayed until the last dress was sold.

HSN executives were thrilled with the sales figures and the low rate of returns for my segments. They began to schedule more and more appearances for me. I was soon flying monthly to Tampa, where I loved staying at this huge old, classic Spanish-style hotel called the Vinoy. Staying there is like coming home since I'm there every month and have gotten to know a lot of the hotel personnel.

While the calls and letters I receive on HSN have been overwhelmingly positive, there's been at least one hate letter among them. A woman wrote me a seven-page letter saying that she didn't like anything about me—not my looks, my clothes, the way I talked, my jewelry, my glasses, nothing. What I couldn't figure out was, if she didn't like anything about me, then why was she watching? At least she cared enough to write, and in very neat penmanship, too.

Being on television and receiving all kinds of audience responses makes you realize that you're very visible and that the opportunity to be on television carries with it a great burden of responsibility. You realize that you have to be a responsible person in your daily life because your customers might not want to buy from a socially reckless designer.

That fall, HSN hosted a Personality Day featuring their most popular "personalities" who sell products on their network. We enjoyed an informal reception that Saturday, and then, on Sunday, we were interviewed on the air by Bobbi Ray, now known as Bobbi Ray-Carter, on a talk show–type set so that the audiences could get to know more about us. It was a celebrity-driven event, including such HSN personalities as singer Olivia Newton-John;

Ivana Trump, who'd been selling apparel and fashion jewelry on HSN for over five years; and the beautiful cosmetic maven Adrien Arpel, whom I adore.

I couldn't believe that I was included with all these people I recognized from television! I was a bit nervous about the reception since I had to rush over to it straight from working on *BET Shop* without a chance to change, but John Pinocci, the vice president of special events at HSN, made me feel so welcome, meeting me at the door and saying warmly, "Anthony, come on in. We're waiting for you."

I was in a heavenly daze as Ivana hugged me hello and we chatted about our families. Yep, just like next-door neighbors talking over the back fence. Can you believe it? Adrien and I are often scheduled back-to-back on HSN, and I love to watch her work—such a professional. I was shocked at the luncheon when Olivia Newton-John actually introduced herself to *me!* Fred Hayman, the cofounder of Giorgio Beverly Hills and now the proprietor of Fred Hayman Beverly Hills on North Rodeo Drive, was also very friendly and complimented my line.

Michael Crowley, as usual, made me feel wanted and needed. He always greets me with, "How's my star?" Michael is that rare person who is real and sincerely cares. He loves the retailers, the customers, and the fashion designers. He knows how to work with personalities, and that's one of the keys to his success.

I am now appearing on HSN roughly once a month and working with a great buyer there, Jenny O'Malley. Most newcomers, I am told, are lucky to be on about six times a year, so I'm thankful for all the support that the HSN team has given me. They're a joy to work with.

25

✂ –

Following the Dream

One woman who has made a marked difference in my life has been Xernona Clayton, a charming and dynamic civic leader in Atlanta who is also the assistant corporate vice president of urban affairs with the Turner Broadcasting System. She and her first husband, the late Ed Clayton, who was the executive editor of *Jet* magazine, were good friends with Dr. Martin Luther King, Jr., and his family. Although she grew up in a segregated America, she never let it stop her from achieving all her goals.

Mrs. Clayton has always worked tirelessly to end discrimination practices and bring racial harmony to our nation. Her gentle powers of persuasion once even moved a Ku Klux Klan leader to change his racist views and leave the Klan. In 1968, she became the first black person to host a nationally syndicated television show in the South which enjoyed a black *and* a white audience.

Mrs. Clayton had joined Ted Turner's Superstation in 1979 as a part-time producer of documentary specials and later began hosting and producing *Open Up*, the station's weekly one-hour talk and public affairs show. In her current position at TBS, she serves as the station's liaison to various civic groups in Atlanta and across the country.

After reading her autobiography, *I've Been Marching All the Time*, I was blown away by the dignity and strength of this beautiful and gracious lady. Despite her petite stature, she had moved mountains in terms of social and political change. To meet her, I thought, would be such an honor. Mrs. Clayton is a famous American in the area of civil rights, just like Rosa Parks.

On my next trip to Atlanta, my official business was to put on a fashion show there, but unofficially, my goal was to meet this incredible woman. I called her office at the CNN Center in Atlanta and arranged to meet with her there for a one o'clock appointment.

I arrived at the center around 11:00 A.M. because of my flight schedule and decided to try to catch up on some paperwork before my meeting with Mrs. Clayton. As luck would have it, however, Mrs. Clayton and her assistant happened to walk by me in the lobby. She recognized me from the promotional material I had sent her and, giving me a warm hug hello, invited me to join them for lunch.

"You're a twin, aren't you, Anthony? I'm a twin, too!" Mrs. Clayton exclaimed, after we'd been seated in the restaurant. She quickly put me at ease and we had a delightful lunch, filled with laughter as if we were old friends. I found Mrs. Clayton to be a wonderful listener. After lunch, she gave me the royal tour of the center, and I felt as if I had known her forever.

Since 1993, Mrs. Clayton has been the executive producer of the prestigious Trumpet Awards, which she created under the auspices of the Turner Broadcasting System
to salute the outstanding achievements of African-American
men and women who have distinguished themselves in
the fields of medicine, education, literature, politics, sports,
business, and entertainment.

During our visit, Mrs. Clayton encouraged me to become
involved behind-the-scenes with the Trumpet Awards and
suggested that I create a couture item to be given to a lucky
recipient at the 1995 Trumpet Awards, whose honorees
included Marian Wright Edelman, Hank Aaron, Diahann
Carroll, Phylicia Rashad, and Billy Dee Williams.

I was honored that Mrs. Clayton had asked me to con-
tribute to the awards and I appreciated the chance to get
my name out there with all those distinguished people. For
this event, I designed a black velvet cape of African colors
with pearls, stones, and gems on the back, as well as a
matching jacket and hat. We sent it to the Trumpet Awards
planners, beautifully packaged with exquisite paper and
fresh roses.

The following year, I also created several haute couture
jackets for recipients of the 1996 Trumpet Awards in
Atlanta. I was proud when Mrs. Myrlie Evers-Williams,
civil rights activist and then NAACP board president, and
Mrs. Nat King Cole each received one of the jackets. Mrs.
Cole was accepting an award in honor of her late husband.
Other recipients that year included the famed international
opera star Kathleen Battle; defense attorney Johnnie
Cochran; country western singer Charley Pride; entertainer
and activist Harry Belafonte; and Tiger Woods, the young
golf phenomenon—then the U.S. amateur champion.

In attending several of the awards ceremonies, Bruce and I have realized that everything Mrs. Clayton does is first-class and is accomplished with very careful planning. Even the seating arrangements at the ceremony are designed to provide everyone with the best networking advantages. One year, Bruce and I had a delightful time visiting with our tablemates, Tom Burrell, the owner of Burrell Communications, and his lovely wife Joli. We have enjoyed a wonderful friendship and business relationship with the Burrells ever since, and I'm sure Mrs. Clayton planned it that way.

My involvement with the Trumpet Awards has already been a godsend to me. In March 1996, I was in New York on business when Bruce called saying that Faith Morris, a vice president with Burrell Communications, had recently met with Sears executives who were trying to develop ethnic lines to attract minority customers. Faith had immediately thought of me. The Sears executives were interested in talking to me, so Faith wasted no time in contacting us in Dallas.

Bruce and I soon found ourselves flying to the Sears headquarters in Hoffman Estates, Illinois, outside Chicago, to present a fashion show for the Sears executives. I was determined to prove to them that Anthony Mark Hankins could be a premier designer. My theme for the show, I schemed, would be "seasons." I would give them the look, the energy, the pulse of a whole year of seasons.

I pictured models strutting to "Jump" by the Pointer Sisters, wearing hats, coats, capes, fur. . . . I'd give them Kwanzaa with bugle beads, metallics, and silver. . . . For spring, everything would be fresh and new. Then I wanted them to literally feel the hot city pavement under their feet for the summer line. It was going to be a sizzling show, and I wanted the audience to scream with excitement.

I worked like a fast-spreading fever on this new project. I even accessorized the garments myself, making sure each ensemble was perfect, from the tip of the hat to the heels of the shoes. I felt like an old racehorse getting the chance to hit the starting gate again. It was the same excitement I had felt when I first started designing for JCPenney.

In my head, I kept hearing Natalie Cole singing "Starting Over Again," and it was an appropriate theme for me during my mad rush to meet this opportunity with Sears head-on. I ended up sending over twenty-five garment cartons to Chicago, which cost over $1,000 to accomplish, but this new venture was worth every penny. Something deep in my soul was telling me to take the chance.

In the O'Hare Airport for our visit to Sears, Bruce and I ran into some former associates from JCPenney, who were surprised to see us there. I was standing at the gate with a uniformed driver who had been sent by Sears for our arrival. As I waited for my staff to disembark from the plane, I reassured myself that I looked good that day, wearing my Foster Grant shades and my all-black, casual-but-sleek apparel. After our hellos, the JCPenney executives, of course, wanted to know what I was doing in Chicago.

"I'm putting on a fashion show for Sears," was my cool and oh-so-casual reply.

I noticed as we were waiting for our luggage to appear on the carousel that these former associates had already rushed to the phones to spread the news about my possible involvement with their nemesis, Sears. I relished the thought that their eyes must have bugged out when they saw us leave in the limo Sears had sent for us.

The Sears people were wonderful, providing us with a phenomenal stage and fabulous models. There were easily three hundred people gathered for our presentation, and it was standing room only. This blow-out attendance demonstrated to me how much the corporate leadership valued the importance of attracting the minority consumer to their store and their willingness to take a young designer seriously.

The fashion show went off flawlessly, thank God, and we received enthusiastic applause for almost every outfit, as well as a standing ovation at the end from the Sears executives assembled there—quite a different response from the stony silence that had greeted me at the end of my very first fashion show for JCPenney.

Again, though, there was a question-and-answer session following our presentation. I was nervous but knew something magical was happening when the first response to the show was from a key store manager who stood up and said, "All I want to know is—how soon can I get this line into my store?"

Getting back to our hotel after the fashion show for Sears, Bruce and I were stunned to hear about the tragic crash of TWA's Flight 800. Katie and Johnathan had been visiting us in Dallas and had just left to go back to Elizabeth when I dreamed they were sitting in a plane in the sky, smiling and waving from the window. In my dream, I was in Elizabeth, watching them waving from the plane as it descended in the night, coming into Newark airport. To my horror, I suddenly saw the plane explode, pieces of it falling into the water. I could clearly see "TWA" on the tail wing.

Rattled by this nightmare, I had been relieved that the dream hadn't been a premonition of their flight or ours. We had all arrived safely at our destinations. A week later, however, TWA's Flight 800 exploded in midair not more than fifty miles from Elizabeth. I became almost physically ill when I heard this tragic news.

Soon after our triumphant fashion show for Sears, I also participated in a vendor fair in Chicago. While most people only rent one booth space and don't decorate it at all, I took two booths and created a virtual stage set in our large space with a black-and-white-checkered floor, Mondrian curtains, cream-colored drapes with gold trim and large tassels to hold them back, white gladiolas and calla lilies in vases, bright-jeweled picture frames, clothes hanging on top-of-the-line hangers, and an "Anthony Mark Hankins" sign floating on the wall. Our space even had sofas, chairs, and tables. Man, it blew everybody out.

An African-American woman came by my booth, and I was pleased to see that she was wearing one of my dresses. The CEO of Sears, Arthur Martinez, happened to come by just as this woman was rhapsodizing about how she loved my lines and owned about thirty of my dresses.

"Where did you get them?" Mr. Martinez asked her.

"At JCPenney," she sheepishly replied. Martinez just smiled and nodded with a look that said, "Well, we can do something about that."

Sure enough, Sears buyers soon invited us back to Chicago to meet with them and discuss merchandising possibilities. Since then, we have agreed that I'll do more than apparel for Sears. My signature collection for Sears will initially include women's sportswear, hats, and coats, as well as coordinated bed and bath linens. Other lines are also in the pipeline at Sears.

Good news, as well as bad news, often comes in threes, and that fall I was blessed with a series of good news. Not only had the Sears deal become a reality, but I was very honored to be chosen as an awardee at the twenty-sixth annual gala awards dinner of the Black Retail Action Group (BRAG), which was held at the Grand Hyatt Hotel in New York City on October 11, 1996.

BRAG is a nonprofit organization dedicated to promoting the total acceptance and inclusion of African-Americans and other minorities at all levels of retail and related industries. Proceeds from this event benefit many self-help projects for minority retail executives and for the minority community.

Awardees are those who have distinguished themselves through individual achievements as well as serving to further the progress of minorities in business, industry, and the minority community. The gala kicked off a weekend of activities, and I was also asked to present a fashion show during the Saturday luncheon, which was a total pleasure to do.

A month after I received this award, as Bruce and I worked hard and enthusiastically to meet the exciting new challenges that Sears was offering us, I was blown away to learn that I was also going to be the recipient of the Young Star award at the 1997 Trumpet Awards, scheduled for January 13 in Atlanta. The previous year's winner had been Tiger Woods. This was my third piece of fantastic news.

I was speechless. It didn't seem possible, even when a video crew arrived in Dallas from CNN to film me at work for the introduction segment of the award. I learned that I had been chosen, by a committee, from a list of several nominees, all of whom were very high-profile young African-Americans.

Throughout the days leading up to the awards ceremony, I couldn't concentrate on what to say in my acceptance speech. Every time I tried to start writing one, my mind would just spaz out and butterflies would flutter all around my stomach. I hardly ever get butterflies, but this event was beyond the realm of my imagination.

I was used to working *behind* the scenes on the Trumpet Awards, and while I did enjoy being in front of television cameras, it had always been in the context of marketing my lines. I was out there simply being a pitchman for my product. This time, though, the attention would be concentrated more on me and not on my apparel. I hoped I wouldn't make a fool out of myself with my family in the audience.

Filled with nervous energy, I threw myself even further into my work. Over dinner one evening in November at the Fog City Diner in Dallas, Helen Giddings, one of our state representatives and a friend whom I have gotten to know through our mutual participation in civic events, confessed to me that she didn't know what to wear to an upcoming charity function that Saturday night. Helen is a magnificent person, and I was inspired to design a gown for her right there on the spot.

"Let me show you what you're going to be wearing," I told her, excited by the challenge of creating a gown on such a short deadline. In five minutes, I had sketched out her dress on the small notepad I always carry with me. Helen had her first fitting on Wednesday, her second on Friday, and it was ready for her on Saturday in time for the gala.

I enjoyed this accomplishment, and as the holiday season approached, I also made an effort to get back to my roots by making Christmas gifts for friends by hand—such as fabric dolls like my Grandmother Toy used to make, only a little more elaborately detailed.

At Christmastime, too, I had a blast playing Santa Claus for the Easter Seals kids, who suffer from various handicaps. When you're Santa Claus, the kids hug you all over and you realize that there are more important things in life than work and yourself. When I think of my nephews and nieces, I realize that you can't replace children with anything.

After surviving the busy Christmas season and New Year's celebrations, the time finally came to travel to Atlanta for the Trumpet Awards. The actual awards ceremony is preceded by several days of cocktail parties, luncheons, dinners, and seminars, including a book-signing party featuring seven nationally acclaimed authors. Each event is presented in first-class fashion, and the honorees are treated as top VIPs during their stay in Atlanta.

When we arrived for the beginning of the festivities, a limo had been dispatched to pick us up at the airport. Angie, who had been working with us in Dallas as a model for our '97 spring press kit, flew to Atlanta with us. My mother and stepfather, along with my brother Jeffrey and his wife, Barbara, were also treated to limo service when they arrived from Elizabeth.

This magical weekend was a whirlwind of events: from a wonderfully warm get-together Saturday night for the honorees at the mansion of George Winslow, a senior executive with Turner Broadcasting, and his wife, Sandy; to a "Coffee with the Authors" gathering on Sunday which included Steve Allen and his wife Jayne Meadows, Jonathan Kozol, Kwiesi Mfume, Sharon Robinson, Susan Taylor, and Andrew Young. A VIP reception followed.

For the reception on Sunday, held at Atlanta's Planet Hollywood, our limo took us to the restaurant, where we found ourselves in a sea of limos lined up along the curb, slowly pulling up to the front entrance one by one.

"We'll just get out here," I told the driver as he pulled up alongside the curb a few limo lengths away from the entrance.

"Oh, I think you'd prefer to get out at the front door," answered the driver with a wink.

I wasn't sure what he meant until we had made it to the front of the line. As we stepped out of the limo, child, paparazzi cameras were flashing all around us! With all the hoopla, you would have thought Sylvester Stallone had just stepped out of the limo for a film premiere. It was a trip. Every arriving honoree was formally introduced to the crowd and given the same celebrity treatment. The awards' presenters were also treated royally.

The place was packed, and we found ourselves literally rubbing elbows with famous people like the incomparable singer Gladys Knight and her husband, motivational speaker Les Brown; legendary blues singer B. B. King; acclaimed actor Louis Gossett, Jr.; Olympic medalist Florence Griffith Joyner; CNN news anchor Bernard Shaw; Dallas mayor Ron Kirk; singers Charley Pride and Dionne Warwick; actress Jane Fonda, who is now Mrs. Ted Turner; and Congresswoman Maxine Waters, among many others. I suddenly felt like Dorothy again, landing in Oz. It was definitely a surreal and dizzying experience.

At the briefing dinner Sunday night, I was seated with Gladys Knight and Les Brown; Dionne Warwick, who was a presenter; and Clarence O. Smith, the president of *Essence* magazine, and his wife. Heady company, indeed, but all very friendly and down-to-earth. I was surprised to discover that these celebrities are just real people like everyone else. Still, I worried about how I was going to get up and speak in front of all these famous faces tomorrow! I still hadn't even written a speech.

"Just speak from your heart," Bruce advised me.

Monday evening was really a blur, from the rehearsal to the real thing. Limos lined up around the CNN Center for miles, and elegant couples emerged wearing their black-tie finest. There were enough sequins and gems on these beautiful ladies' gowns to light up Times Square. Mom looked very regal in the gown I had made for her of black velvet with a royal blue satin floor-length duster, and Angie looked like an elegant model herself in her sleek black gown and shawl.

Waiting in the green room for my announced entrance to the stage, I found myself sitting with another honoree, Bernard Shaw, the renowned CNN news anchor. I had admired him for years. The butterflies in my stomach were working overtime now. He could tell that I was beyond nervous, so he was kind enough to talk with me and calm me down. We listened as the video segment for my award began. My breath was coming in short, shallow gasps as I stood up, preparing to be called onto the stage.

"There's freedom in sewing because you can make any-thing you want," I could hear myself saying in this introductory video. I went on to say, "You can't sit on the sidelines. . . . You've got to stand up and use your assets. . . ." After a few moments, the videotape ended. This was it. My body felt frozen and it was suddenly hard to breathe.

"You're going to be just fine," Mr. Shaw reassured me as I was summoned to the stage.

A young white girl in the control booth blew me kisses and gave me two enthusiastic thumbs-up as I made my way to the stage, and singer Nancy Wilson, a presenter, quickly gave me a hug. These wonderful people all gave me the strength I needed to walk into those glaring lights.

A beautiful woman met me halfway across the stage and led me to the podium. I was eloquently introduced by Jerry D. Florence, a vice president of Nissan, and the R&B vocalist Monica.

The first person I saw in the audience was Mom, sitting up front and beaming proudly, and suddenly I knew what I was going to say. As I began my speech, I struggled against hyperventilating; focusing on Mom, however, I found my breath and my voice after a few moments.

"Wow . . ." I managed to say shakily. "This is so incredible. . . . One thing that comes to mind as I receive this award is growing up in Roselle, New Jersey, and being a twin, the youngest of seven children. I remember my mom worked so hard, three jobs, and she'd come home smelling like doughnuts. . . . I wanted to pray with my mom, who had confectioners' sugar all over her apron, to thank God for having her. My mother's been my inspiration all these years. And now, as I go into 1997, I'm really happy because I've been embraced by the oldest retailer, Sears, to do a line for them. And with Mom being the fit model and looking at quality control, there's no way we can lose. Thank you and God bless you."

As I left the stage, my mom led a standing ovation. It was a heady experience.

After the awards ceremony, Mrs. Clayton hugged me and whispered, "I love you and I'm so proud of you, Anthony." I love her dearly, too, and she's responsible for some of the most memorable moments of my life. Mrs. Clayton is one of those soft-spoken angels on earth who accomplishes miracles with her gentle, kind, and determined spirit.

I hoped that my speech at the Trumpet Awards ceremony sent out a message to other young people that limitations are only what you make them out to be. I reached for the sky and made it with the help of all the wonderful mentors in my life, from my mother to Mrs. Clayton, Bruce, Tadashi, Christophe, Mrs. Papetti, Mrs. Mayner, Homer Layne, and many, many others. Seeking out their collective wisdom has been one of the reasons I've been able to achieve my dream. I believe that everyone should find their role models and not hesitate to ask them for advice and assistance.

I was fortunate, too, that I came from a united family, with a parent who cared enough to instill a strong sense of values and pride in her children, as well as a strong belief in God. My mother is still a constant source of strength and inspiration for me. My frequent business trips to New York enable me to visit my parents in Elizabeth often and I enjoy staying with them in their comfortable two-story Dutch Colonial home. Pete is retired now, but Mom still works for the city of Elizabeth's Parking Authority.

To Mom's credit, we're still a close family, and I know she is proud of all her children. At this writing, Katie has recently moved to Dallas from Elizabeth with her son, Johnathan. Jeffrey is retired from the armed services, James is a New Jersey state trooper, Kevin is a carpenter and also works for the city of Elizabeth, Raymond is a technical sergeant in the Air Force, and Angie is finishing up law school at the University of Virginia in Charlottesville.

Mom's success with her children is a perfect example of the powerful combination of determination and faith. She has always been an integral part of my success. There are so many times when faith is the only thing that keeps you going, especially when everyone else is declaring your dream impossible.

I was determined, even as a child, to be a fashion designer, and I've achieved that goal beyond my wildest dreams. Success is not just a matter of luck, I've come to realize. It takes a lot of perseverance. People need to know their dreams are possible to achieve if they'll just believe in themselves. Look at me, for instance. My dreams seem to make no sense when you consider my background. I was a black kid from New Jersey who was determined to study fashion in Paris and work in the House of Yves Saint Laurent! People thought I was crazy when I voiced my goals.

Child, I was determined to go even further than that in my career plans. I *knew* that I was going to be a designer, with my own clothing labels in stores all around the world. When it came to my dreams, honey, I wouldn't take no for an answer. You shouldn't, either. While it's true that a certain amount of luck is helpful, luck is really a matter of preparation meeting opportunity. Whatever your own dream is, visualize yourself achieving it and dedicate yourself to whatever it takes to make it happen. Then network, network, network to create the opportunity.

I'm still driven to reach seemingly impossible goals. I'd like to fill every department store in America with my lines, and as this book is being written, our company is in negotiations with several major department store chains that will also hopefully carry our apparel in the near future. This past year, in addition to Sears, our clothing lines were introduced into Nordstrom and Carson Pirie Scott department stores, among others. Liz Claiborne—look out, girl! Whatever happens next, I know that I'll give it my best shot.

Only time will tell if all of my goals will come true. Meanwhile, I'm enjoying the journey. That's the important thing. While I have found my own passion in fashion, each one of us has a unique destiny that's within our grasp—if only we believe in our ability to make it happen. After all, that really is the fabric of dreams.

bonsoir